ASP.NET 2.0
Web Parts in Action

ASP.NET 2.0
Web Parts in Action

Building Dynamic Web Portals

DARREN NEIMKE

MANNING

Greenwich
(74° w. long.)

Manning Publications Co.
Cherokee Station   Copyeditor: Sharon Mullins
PO Box 20386   Typesetter: Gordan Salinovic
New York, NY 10021   Cover designer: Leslie Haimes

ISBN 1-932394-77-X

Printed in the United States of America
1 2 3 4 5 6 7 8 9 10 – VHG – 10 09 08 07 06

To Bill Wilkinson, for teaching me to program

brief contents

contents

foreword

I never realized how satisfying it would be to read the final version of Darren's book. Let me start with a little background to explain why that is.

The Web Parts team began working on the ASP.NET project almost four years ago. The vision was to provide a set of controls that allow end users to assemble a Web User Interface using the browser. The user would put the content he wanted in a web page by adding and removing "Web Parts." He would have the ability to adjust the web UI using drag and drop.

You might think that once the Web Parts technology was released with ASP.NET 2.0, the job was done. However, our job won't really be done until the Web Parts model is widely used and deployed. Thanks to our customers and to authors like Darren, we are moving ever closer to that goal. *ASP.NET 2.0 Web Parts in Action* is a fundamental tool for any ASP.NET developer who wants to leverage Web Parts to its fullest potential.

As we developed the Web Parts technology, an outstanding team of engineers routinely engaged in passionate discussions on how to build the features. One area to which we devoted a lot of time was making sure that Web Parts was extensible and would fit every need. *ASP.NET Web Parts in Action* brings out those points of extensibility, allowing you to exploit Web Parts in the best possible ways.

Web Parts in ASP.NET has created an inflection point in control development. In this model, individual controls themselves are the heart of the web application. As I look to the next four years, I can safely say that we have only scratched the surface of what can and will be done with Web Parts. As you jump on the Web Parts train—and read *ASP.NET Web Parts in Action*—you will be preparing yourself to take advantage of many new innovations in the years to come.

ANDRES SANABRIA
Lead Program Manager
ASP.NET and Server Application Frameworks

preface

I had often thought about writing a book on the topic of development, a book whose focus would be on the role of the lead developer. I started saving my thoughts, even creating snippets that I hoped would eventually find their way into that book. I was edging my way slowly to committing to the project, knowing that the topic was timeless and that I could take my time to get things right and to do the book justice.

When Manning approached me about writing a book on web portals and web parts using ASP.NET 2.0, I knew that with this topic timing would play a large part in determining when the book would need to be delivered. There would be no taking it slow with this one! A new and exciting technology such as this results in a huge hunger for information about how to create solutions using the new bits and pieces. Regardless of the timing, I needed to convince myself that I could write a book that would share with others the lessons gathered in my years of solutions development experience and that would not simply focus on the new stuff. With the book now behind me, I believe that I have managed to achieve this goal.

This book showcases three of my passions: ASP.NET, web portals, and custom solution delivery. I was challenged during my writing to present each of these passions in a real and dynamic environment and in a way that underlines the extensibility of the ASP.NET portal framework. It is my hope that you will be equally challenged as you work through the book and as this framework reveals itself to you, inspiring you to build great things!

acknowledgments

First and foremost, I'd like to thank Anne for bending the lifestyle and events of an entire household to fit this book into our lives. Hopefully one day Harrison and Charles will see "Dad's silly book with the picture of a pirate on the cover" and they will be reminded of the pirates of their youth.

Thanks to my editors, Mike Stephens and Mitch Denny, for coming along for the ride and staying with it the whole way through—a journey with lots of memories for us all, I'm sure. Thanks also to my very special development editor on this project. When Betsey Henckels was first assigned to help me, I asked, "What exactly does a development editor do?" By the time we finished I sure knew—they do a lot! Thanks, Betsey.

To the highly respected bunch of guys who reviewed this manuscript during development, thank you! You helped make this a more solid product. I feel confident and proud in knowing that the book has your stamp of approval. Thanks to James Curran, Stuart Caborn, Doug Warren, Berndt Hamboeck, Aleksey Nudelman, Joe Litton, Robbe Morris, Dennis Gorelik, Dave Corun, Benjamin Gorlick, Bernard Farrell, Paul Wilson, Arul Kumaravel, Sergey Koshcheyev, Dan Hounshell, Richard Xin, and Andrew Deren. Special thanks to Anand Narayanaswamy for his technical proofread of the manuscript, just before it went to press.

Finally, a big thank-you must be extended to Marjan Bace and his great staff at Manning Publications. It was an absolute pleasure working with all of you.

about this book

Over the past few years you will have likely noticed the rise and rise of web portals and seen the impact that they are having on the way that we use the Web. Portals such as Sharepoint, Live.com, Google, and DotNetNuke have transformed the way that we consume our daily information. Regardless of whether or not you are new to portals or an old hand with them, this book will provide you with all that you need to know to start building them.

This book is unlike many other popular ASP.NET books in that it focuses solely on teaching you how to use the web parts and portal framework features of ASP.NET 2.0 to build portal applications. By removing unnecessary details of other parts of ASP.NET and reducing the amount of information that there is to consume we can view portal creation in a very clear and concise manner.

Road map

This book is divided into two parts and is designed to guide you from the very first moment that you start using the portal framework right up to the point where you need to design and build a portal for an enterprise scenario.

The first part of the book spans chapters 1 through 6 where, after an introduction to ASP.NET 2.0, you will learn about the core APIs of the portal framework. In these chapters we will be rolling up our sleeves and pulling these APIs apart as we learn how to customize, extend, and secure our portal through code and configuration settings. It's here that you will learn about the very nature of each of the parts in the portal framework.

Chapter 1 serves as a high level introduction to ASP.NET 2.0 and offers a glimpse into some of the terminology of portals. In this chapter we will also learn about the fictional Adventure Works business which will serve as the example business for which we will be building a portal throughout the remainder of the book.

In chapter 2 we will look at web parts—the useful little units that allow us to add content to a portal. It is in this chapter that we will build our very first basic portal. By the end of the chapter we will be up and running and will familiar with the APIs surrounding web parts and also learn about web part internals when we use interfaces within the portal framework to customize the behaviour of our web parts.

In the third chapter of the book we will delve into the world of web part connections and learn how to connect web parts using transformers and connections to increase the value of data and empower users to use data to suit their own unique needs.

Chapter 4 is possibly the most important chapter in the book as this is where we learn about the web part manager. Here I'll show you what role the web part manager plays in orchestrating the runtime behaviour of the portal. Again, we'll be diving in under the covers so that we can learn how to customize this control to provide just the behaviour that we need. For example, we will see how to write code in our very own custom web part manager that checks each web part on every page to check whether the user has permission to view each part.

After learning about the web part manager, we'll turn to chapter 5 where we learn about the important topic of zones. On the surface, zones appear as inanimate objects in the world of portals, but by the time we've pulled them apart, you'll see that zones play an important role in how web parts are rendered and provide us with the perfect way to customize the look and feel of all web parts in our portal, as well as create a unique and engaging place for visitors to our site.

If chapter 4 was the most important chapter, then chapter 6 is certainly the second most important one because this is where we get our hands dirty playing with personalization. Given that users place such high importance on the ability to customize and personalize their portals to create their own unique spaces, personalization is a very important topic indeed. In this chapter we will learn about the key extensibility points of the personalization system that we must use to give our portals that special edge!

The second part of the book begins with chapter 7. By now you've learned about the core APIs in the framework. Prior to this chapter, we've read a lot of the theory of portals and put it into practice with small prototypes, but now it's time to learn the special art of portals. You'll master how to mix each of the things that you've learned thus far into a recipe that will help you to produce portals that are not only highly customized but portals that users also enjoy using. We'll do this by looking at some of the common customizations that are applied to modern portals and seeing how to apply them to our own portal. Some of these customizations include the collapsible/expandable editor that we create in chapter 7, as well as the feature we will implement in chapter 8 that is similar to the data versioning that comes as a standard feature in Sharepoint 2007. You'll also learn how to mix server-side and client-side code in chapter 8 when we create a cool pop-up catalog zone dialog.

By chapter 9 our portal is nearing feature completeness and the only thing that remains is to deploy what we have created so that our users can start using it. I won't bore you with information about configuring web servers and copying files. Instead we'll take a different approach to deployment, learning how to instrument code and more about health monitoring. Learning these important lessons will give us visibility over the health of our portal when it is no longer under our direct control.

In the last chapter we take a look back at what we've learned; and then we turn around to view the possible future of our little portal. By looking at Atlas technology we will gain an understanding of how XML and JavaScript can combine to improve the responsiveness of web applications across the board.

Finally, the appendix shows how to create an ASP.NET web project in Visual Studio 2005. This web project forms the basis for the web portal that we will be building throughout the book.

I fully expect that the little journey I have planned for you in this book will be both insightful and engaging. After reading this book you will be well on your way to having full control over the design and behaviour of your portals and you will be confident that users of your portals will have a great place to start their daily web activities!

Source code

All source code in listings or in text is in a `fixed-width font like this` to separate it from ordinary text. In some cases, the original source code has been reformatted: we've added line breaks and reworked indentation to accommodate the available page space in the book. In rare cases even this was not enough, and listings include line-continuation markers. Code annotations accompany many of the listings, highlighting important concepts. Bolding in code listings is used for emphasis as well.

The source code for all of the examples in this book as well as for the web project can be downloaded from the publisher's website at www.manning.com/neimke.

Author Online

Your purchase of *ASP.NET 2.0 in Action* includes free access to a private web forum run by Manning Publications, where you can make comments about the book, ask technical questions, and receive help from the author and from other users. To access the forum and subscribe to it, point your web browser to www.manning.com/neimke. This page provides information on how to get on the forum once you are registered, what kind of help is available, and the rules of conduct on the forum.

Manning's commitment to our readers is to provide a venue where a meaningful dialogue among individual readers and between readers and the author can take place. It is not a commitment to any specific amount of participation on the part of the author, whose contribution to the AO remains voluntary (and unpaid). We suggest you try asking the author some challenging questions, lest his interest stray! The Author Online forum and the archives of previous discussions will be accessible from the publisher's website as long as the book is in print.

about the title

By combining introductions, overviews, and how-to examples, the *In Action* books are designed to help learning and remembering. According to research in cognitive science, the things people remember are things they discover during self-motivated exploration.

Although no one at Manning is a cognitive scientist, we are convinced that for learning to become permanent it must pass through stages of exploration, play, and, interestingly, retelling of what is being learned. People understand and remember new things, which is to say they master them, only after actively exploring them. Humans learn in action. An essential part of an *In Action* guide is that it is example-driven. It encourages the reader to try things out, to play with new code, and explore new ideas.

There is another, more mundane, reason for the title of this book: our readers are busy. They use books to do a job or to solve a problem. They need books that allow them to jump in and jump out easily and learn just what they want just when they want it. They need books that aid them *in action*. The books in this series are designed for such readers.

about the cover illustration

The figure on the cover of *ASP.NET 2.0 in Action* is a "Tatar," a Turkic-speaking inhabitant of Russia. The name "Tatars" was originally used for the people that overran parts of Asia and Europe under Mongol leadership in the 13th century. It was later extended to include almost any Asian nomadic invaders, whether from Mongolia or the fringes of Western Asia. The illustration is taken from a collection of costumes of the Ottoman Empire published on January 1, 1802, by William Miller of Old Bond Street, London. The title page is missing from the collection and we have been unable to track it down to date. The book's table of contents identifies the figures in both English and French, and each illustration bears the names of two artists who worked on it, both of whom would no doubt be surprised to find their art gracing the front cover of a computer programming book...two hundred years later.

The collection was purchased by a Manning editor at an antiquarian flea market in the "Garage" on West 26th Street in Manhattan. The seller was an American based in Ankara, Turkey, and the transaction took place just as he was packing up his stand for the day. The Manning editor did not have on his person the substantial amount of cash that was required for the purchase and a credit card and check were both politely turned down. With the seller flying back to Ankara that evening the situation was getting hopeless. What was the solution? It turned out to be nothing more than an old-fashioned verbal agreement sealed with a handshake. The seller simply proposed that the money be transferred to him by wire and the editor walked out with the bank information on a piece of paper and the portfolio of images under his arm. Needless to say, we transferred the funds the next day, and we remain grateful and impressed by this unknown person's trust in one of us. It recalls something that might have happened a long time ago.

The pictures from the Ottoman collection, like the other illustrations that appear on our covers, bring to life the richness and variety of dress customs of two centuries ago. They recall the sense of isolation and distance of that period-and of every other historic period except our own hyperkinetic present. Dress codes have changed since then and the diversity by region, so rich at the time, has faded away. It is now often hard to tell the inhabitant of one continent from another. Perhaps, trying to view it optimistically, we have traded a cultural and visual diversity for a more varied personal life. Or a more varied and interesting intellectual and technical life.

We at Manning celebrate the inventiveness, the initiative, and, yes, the fun of the computer business with book covers based on the rich diversity of regional life of two centuries ago, brought back to life by the pictures from this collection.

Portals and web parts

In chapters 1 through 6 you will be introduced to ASP.NET 2.0 and you will learn about the core APIs of the portal framework. You will also be introduced to Adventure Works, the fictional business for which we will be building a portal in the later chapters of this book. You will be asked to roll up your sleeves and pull these APIs apart as you learn how to customize, extend, and secure our portal through code and configuration settings. In these six chapters you will learn about the very nature of each of the parts in the portal framework.

C H A P T E R   1

Introducing portals and web parts

1.1   INTRODUCTION

ASP.NET 2.0 introduces many exciting and important features for web developers. One of the most powerful is the portal framework. You can use the portal framework's new Web Parts technology to build dynamic web portals. Sounds great, but there's a catch. Depending on whom you ask, a *portal* may be anything from a generic home page to a complex information dashboard. In this book, we'll take a close look at how to build portals using the ASP.NET 2.0 Web Parts. Along the way, you'll get a better picture of what goes into a true portal and see practical examples of useful ASP-driven portal design.

By the time the ASP.NET 1.0 framework burst onto the scene in January 2001, its users had built up high expectations. ASP.NET is a web framework that was built from the ground up with a vision of providing the most advanced platform for creating dynamic, modern web applications. Using the framework freed developers from many of the time-consuming and most error-prone operations in existing frameworks, and set them free to focus on meeting application requirements. Newly eliminated operations included common coding tasks as well as more complicated coding for security, web services, and deployment.

At this time, the expectations placed upon web frameworks were becoming increasingly demanding, as businesses were now embracing the web as an application platform in ever-increasing numbers. This was due in part to the success of the web-based business models of companies such as Amazon, Yahoo, and E-Bay. ASP.NET 1.0 had arrived with all the answers to solve the new problems of the day, and it was just in time to take advantage of all this demand. The rest is history. Growth of the platform was stellar as developers and businesses streamed into this new platform in droves. Much of this growth was due to the migration from the earlier ASP platform to .NET. At the time of writing, some statistics that highlight this growth are

- Compilers have been developed for over 30 languages that target the .NET Framework.

- Over a hundred books have been written specifically on the topic of ASP.NET and related topics—such as web services.

- There are approximately 1,000 registered .NET user groups worldwide.

- There are more than a million users of Visual Studio, the premier tool for developing .NET applications.

Today, ASP.NET is the fastest growing web development platform in the world! For the architects of ASP.NET 1.0, the success of that release marked the beginning of planning for the next evolution: ASP.NET 2.0. ASP.NET 1.0 established a common page model as a standard for programming and provided a sleek new runtime environment for processing requests. The 1.0 release also simplified how we work with web services and made them much easier to build and deploy. Finally, the 1.0 release gave us server controls. Server controls are pre-packaged components that encapsulate common tasks; these include controls such as a calendar for displaying calendar information and data grids for displaying data in a tabular manner. Server controls provide a consistent programming model—a standard that developers follow to write code.

The vision for ASP.NET 2.0 was that it would become a sexier second generation of the platform that would address not just the common controls, but also common application functions such as Navigation, Authorization, and Membership. All of this planning culminated with the release of .NET Framework version 2.0 in November 2005. ASP.NET 2.0 has achieved the vision by delivering a set of components that are common to most web applications. Now it's time to take advantage of the ASP.NET 2.0 components and see how they are used to build the next generation of web applications. Throughout this book we will use one of the new features of ASP.NET 2.0—the *portal framework*—as we learn how to create web portals.

As we'll see throughout this book, the portal framework is a set of controls and services that specifically target the growing demand for web portals creation. This book explains the portal framework and shows how to put it to work. The first half of the book is written to provide a deep understanding of all the controls and services that make up the portal framework. The second half of the book goes in under the covers and explains how to customize each aspect of the portal framework to suit our own requirements.

Given that web portals are all about presenting and working with data, this book supplies practical business examples of creating portal solutions in the context of the Adventure Works database. This database was created by Microsoft and is packaged with SQL Server 2005 as an example of how to create a real-world database using SQL Server. This database includes an extensive set of tables and provides data that is reflective of a real business. Using this database allows the book to show a wide variety of scenarios.

Section 1.2 begins our exploration by delving into the term "portal" so that we can establish an understanding of what it means. We'll also acquaint ourselves with some other terminology that is used to describe individual pieces of a portal, such as web parts, personalization, connections, and more. By the section 1.2, we will have introduced most of the common sub-elements of portals.

> **NOTE** Because this chapter is introductory, some of you might best jump in at chapter 2 instead of starting here. This chapter may appear to be old hat for those of you who have solid experience with ASP.NET, or a general understanding of the concepts necessary to build web applications.

1.2 WHAT IS A PORTAL?

Like so many of the terms that we encounter in our industry, the word portal has come to mean nearly anything; in fact, it is probably the most overused term on the web today. But what does it mean? What do you do when your boss comes to you and says he wants you to build a portal? Most people will tell you that a portal is some kind of entry page that represents a larger section of content. Wikipedia, for example, defines it as follows:

> *A web portal is a website that provides a starting point or gateway to other resources on the Internet or an intranet.*

So, given a definition as loose as that, what isn't a portal? Each of the following examples would fit the definition of a portal quite nicely:

- *http://Google.com*—as a search engine, it could easily be considered as the starting point for the entire Internet.
- *The front page of your company's intranet*—it has links that lead to all of your company's content.
- *Any page on the Internet that contains hyperlinks*—these would pretty much satisfy those definitions.

Given such a simple definition, each of the three listed items must be a portal because each provides a place from which to start an excursion on the Internet. However, when the term portal is used to describe websites, it implicitly refers to other, more specific characteristics beyond simply being a page with hyperlinks on it. So we'll need to come up with a definition of our own which better describes the type of websites that we think of when we refer to portals.

1.2.1 Anatomy of a portal

Before we can embark on a mission to come up with our own useful definition of a web portal, we should first look at components that are common to portals and are generally expected in today's modern portal web applications. The first stop on our tour is the web part control.

Web parts

Suppose that we want to create a page that allows users to easily add information about topics that interest them. Some users might add information about the latest news updates from Reuters, whereas others would add the latest Dilbert comics and updates to recent sporting results. If you've ever used SharePoint or other modern Internet portal applications such as http://www.live.com and http://Google.com/ig, you've seen that applications already exist that allow these types of additions by users. The different informational components that are added to the pages, such as news updates or Dilbert comics, are known as web parts.

> **NOTE** SharePoint is a Microsoft portal product for managing team participation in projects. For example, a publisher could use a portal such as SharePoint as a central location for writers, editors, and reviewers around the world to share and review chapters for a book like the one you are holding in your hands. Chapters could be posted on the portal to be marked up by reviewers and editors. The SharePoint portal could be used to track the progress of documents, share information, pass responsibility from one member to another, and a number of other document management functions. This book on web parts is designed to give you the skills to develop a portal just as sophisticated and useful as SharePoint.

Web parts are considered the building blocks of portal applications because of the way that users can add them to the web pages to customize those pages to meet their needs. Users typically browse a catalog of web parts to select the particular one they want to add to a page. There is no limit to the number of web parts that the catalog for a portal can contain. In fact, the more web parts a portal can offer via its catalog, the happier the users are with the possibilities available for customizing their pages.

Personalization

Modern portals offer a dazzling array of customization options. Users can customize portals to display a wide range of information and they can choose how this information appears on a web page. For example, a user could display the weather information for whatever city he chooses and could then arrange how and where the weather appears on the page. These customizations are made possible by a portal service known as *personalization.* If web parts are the building blocks of a portal, personalization is almost certainly the glue that holds the entire solution together.

Personalization acts as a medium for storing and retrieving user customizations. When a user adds a web part to a page, it is personalization that remembers to put it there the next time the user visits that page. When the user configures a weather information web part to display the weather for his city, it is personalization that remembers which city the user chose, and also whether that user chose to have the temperature displayed in Celsius or Fahrenheit. When the user specifies that a particular web part should be displayed on the right-hand side of the page instead of the left, personalization remembers this preference. What's more, personalization saves and remembers these changes on a per-user basis. This means that the same page can appear totally different, depending on who the user is and how he or she has chosen to customize the page. For one user the weather web part might appear on the right hand side of the page, whereas for another, it might appear on the left hand side, or not at all!

When using web parts in ASP.NET 2.0, personalization comes as an automatic feature. This means that the developer doesn't need to write any code to "remember" personalization changes that have been made by the user.

Zones

When I suggested that the weather web part could appear on either the left or right side of the page, I was really referring to another component of portal applications called *zones.* Pages in portal applications tend to be drawn up into zones that can each contain web parts.

On a web page in a portal application, users are allowed to move web parts freely from one zone to another. These zones ensure that the web parts are constrained to regions of the screen that conform to the overall format of the page. Personalization ensures that once a user has moved a part from one zone to another, that part will appear in the same zone whenever that user visits the page—although it might appear in a completely different zone for another user, depending on where he positions it.

The relationship between web parts and zones is shown in figure 1.1. It shows a typical web page for a portal application. The page shown contains two zones and each zone contains different web parts. As we can see, the zone on the left contains the "News" and "Financial" web parts, while the zone on the right contains web parts for "Stocks" and "Weather." A user visiting this page could use his mouse to drag any of these individual web parts into the other zone. For example, the user could choose to drag the Weather web part across to the left zone.

Developing a concise definition

Now that we've seen some of the common components of a portal—the web part, personalization, and zone—I'd like to supply a simple, concise definition of the term

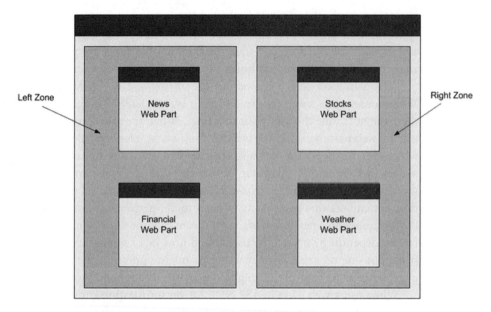

Left Zone

Right Zone

News
Web Part

Stocks
Web Part

Financial
Web Part

Weather
Web Part

**Figure 1.1   This image shows a web page that contains two zones. The left zone
contains the News and Financial web parts, whereas the right zone contains the
Stocks and Weather web parts.**

portal so that throughout this book I can use the term and you will know exactly
what I mean.

> *A portal is a web application which consists of pages that can display many
> different types of information based on user selection. A portal also allows the
> user to perform a variety of customizations on those pages that are remembered
> between viewing sessions.*

This definition will serve as a useful device as we progress through the book by ensuring that we have a common way to describe the subject matter. Now that we've
defined what a portal is, let's get started with an example exercise that provides us a
chance to work with a portal as we've defined it. In the example exercise we'll take the
basic building blocks we've seen so far, such as web parts and zones, and use them to
create a simple portal.

1.2.2   A portal example

The portal example we are about to create will consist of a single web page that has
two zones: a zone on the left side of the page and another on the right side. Each zone
will contain a single web part. The page will also have a button which enables the user
to switch the page into a mode that allows the web parts to be moved between the
two zones. When web parts are in this mode, properties, such as their titles, can be
edited at runtime. Figure 1.2 shows what our example page will look like when it is
complete, and highlights some of the key points.

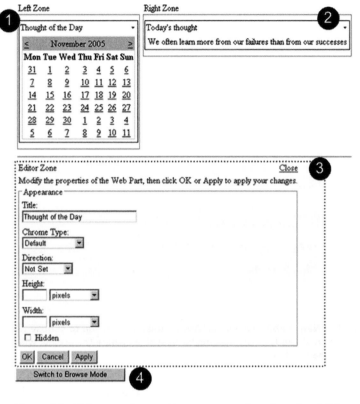

Figure 1.2 This example portal has two zones (numbers 1 and 2) between which you can drag web parts. There is also an editor that allows users to customize the properties of the web parts.

Figure 1.2 contains the following zones:

1. The left zone contains a calendar web part. This web part is titled "Thought of the Day."

2. The right zone contains a label and is titled "Today's thought."

3. An editor zone allows the user to customize the properties of the web parts. In this figure, the editor has the properties for the web part in the left zone displayed.

4. A button allows the user to place the page in a state that allows customizations to take place.

To get things started, open Visual Studio 2005 and create a new ASP.NET WebSite project named `MinimumDefinition`. Save the project to a convenient location in your file system. Figure 1.3 shows a dialog being displayed within Visual Studio and a web project being created in a folder location named C:\WebPartApplications\Chapter1.

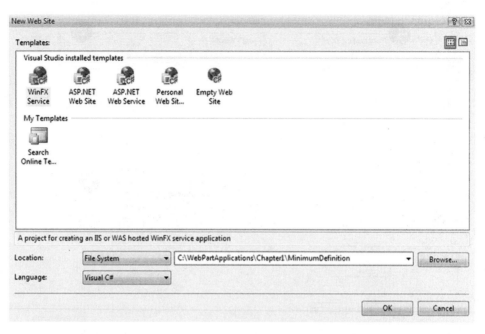

Figure 1.3 The New WebSite dialog in Visual Studio allows you to choose what type of project type to create and specify options for it, such as where the project will be saved to and what language will be used.

Open the website project that was just created and, if it is not already present, add a file named `Default.aspx`. We can now add some markup to the page to create the format for our page and specify the layout for the two zones that will ultimately contain the web parts. Listing 1.1 displays the wayour HTML looks at this stage.

Listing 1.1   Basic Html layout for the Default.aspx page

```
<%@ Page Language="C#" %>
<html>
        <head id="Head1" runat="server">
                <title>Minimum Definition Web Parts Page</title>
        </head>
<body>
<form id="form2" runat="server">

<div id="container" style="width: 400px">
    <div id="rightpanel" style="float: right">          Placeholder for
                                                        right zone
    </div>

    <div id="leftpanel">          Placeholder for left
                                  zone
    </div>
</div>
```

```
</form>
</body>
</html>
```

Adding zones to the web part page

While in design mode, expand the Visual Studio Toolbox and open its Web Parts category. It's from here that we can start adding web part controls to our page. Figure 1.4 shows the Web Parts category of the Toolbox displayed.

In ASP.NET every web parts page must contain one and only one `WebPartManager` control. Furthermore, in a web parts page, the `WebPartManager` must be the first web part control in the control hierarchy. We'll discuss this control and these constraints in much more detail in chapter 4; but for now just understand that, as its name suggests, it is the manager part and therefore responsible for many of the operations and events that occur within a portal application. Drag the `WebPart-Manager` control from your Toolbox and add it to the top of your page.

Next, drag a `WebPartZone` control from the Toolbox into each of the HTML DIV elements that we added previously; that is, add one `WebPartZone` to the leftmost DIV and add another one to the DIV on the right. These two zones will contain the web parts. When we've completed the page, you will be able to drag web parts between the two zones and have the personalization mechanism automatically keep track of which zone each web part belongs to.

Right-click on the left zone (`WebPartZone1`) and choose "Properties" from the context menu. This will display the Visual Studio Properties window and allow us to change the properties of the `WebPartZone` control. In the properties window, locate the `HeaderText` property and set its value to `Left Zone`. Do the same for the middle zone but set its title to `Middle Zone`. From within Visual Studio your page should now look similar to figure 1.5.

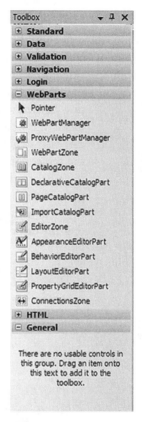

Figure 1.4   The controls for creating portal applications are contained in the Web Parts category within the Visual Studio 2005 Toolbox.

Adding web parts to the page

Now that the page has zones, we can add the web parts to it. Open the Standard category panel of the Toolbox and drag a calendar onto the left zone and drag a label

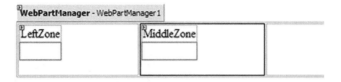

Figure 1.5 Viewing the page in design mode within Visual Studio provides an approximation of how it will appear when viewed in a browser.

web control onto the middle zone. Notice that when those controls are added to the zones, additional user interface (UI) elements are wrapped around them—namely, a title and a little down arrow. These UI elements are not related in any way to the underlying calendar or label controls but instead are specific to web parts. It should now be clear that these controls are no longer ordinary server controls when they live inside the web part zones, but they have in fact become web parts. To demonstrate this fact, switch the page into source code view and add a `Title` attribute to each of the server controls. Title the calendar server control "Thought of the day," and give the label a title of "Today's thought." Listing 1.2 shows how the markup for the web parts should appear when viewing the page in source code view, while figure 1.6 shows how the page should appear when viewed in the Visual Studio designer. Notice that the titles we added are displayed above each of those controls.

Listing 1.2 The calendar and Label server controls appear within the WebPartZones with their titles set.

Calendar control
```
<asp:WebPartZone ID="WebPartZone1" runat="server" HeaderText="Left Zone">
      <ZoneTemplate>
            <asp:Calendar ID="Calendar1"
                  runat="server"
                  Title="Thought of the Day"    ◁─────  A title attribute
                  />                                     has been applied
      </ZoneTemplate>                                    to each control
</asp:WebPartZone>
```

Label control
```
<asp:WebPartZone ID="WebPartZone2" runat="server" HeaderText="Middle Zone">
      <ZoneTemplate>
            <asp:Label ID="Label1"
                  runat="server"
                  Title="Today's thought"   ◁─────  A title attribute
                  Text="We often learn more from our failures than
            from our successes"                        has been applied
                  />                                    to each control
      </ZoneTemplate>
</asp:WebPartZone>
```

The title for each control
appears just above it.

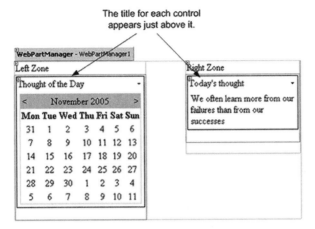

Figure 1.6
When displayed in the designer, the title of each control is displayed just above the control.

Right-click on the `Default.aspx` file and choose "View in Browser" to run the page in a browser.

Allowing a user to customize controls

Now that the page has web parts, we'll add an `EditorZone` that allows us to personalize the page at runtime. Switch the page into design mode within Visual Studio and then drag an `EditorZone` control from the Toolbox and place it beneath the two zones. Then drag an `AppearanceEditorPart` control from the Toolbox onto the `EditorZone`.

You probably noticed that, in addition to the `AppearanceEditorPart`, there are other controls in the Toolbox for editing web parts, such as the `BehaviorEditorPart`, the `LayoutEditorPart`, and the `PropertyGridEditorPart`. Each of these editor controls allows the user to customize different features of a web part. The appearance editor will allow users to edit things such as the Title of a web part and its Height and Width. The other editor controls allow customizations to be made to other attributes of web parts such as what zone they appear in, or whether the title is displayed as a clickable hyperlink. I'll walk through each of the editor parts in much more detail in chapter 5, but for this simple example the `AppearanceEditorPart` is all we need for now. The code for the `EditorZone` control should now look like the following snippet:

```
<asp:EditorZone ID="EditorZone2" runat="server">
        <ZoneTemplate>
                <asp:AppearanceEditorPart
                  ID="AppearanceEditorPart1"
                  runat="server" />
        </ZoneTemplate>
</asp:EditorZone>
```

Now that we have a web part page and an editor, all that remains is to provide a way to switch the page into edit mode at runtime so that we can edit the web control properties and change their layout. By default, web pages will appear in browse mode, so we'll need to add a button to allow us to switch into edit mode. Drag a button from the Toolbox onto the page, and set its text to "Switch to Edit Mode." Next, add some code to handle the Click event of the button for switching between display modes. At this time the markup for the button should appear as it does in the following snippet:

```
<asp:Button ID="Button1"
       runat="server"
       OnClick="Button1_Click"
Text="Switch to Edit Mode" />
```

The code simply needs to allow us to switch the mode of the page between "browse" and "edit" modes. To do this we set the DisplayMode on the WebPartManager instance for the page. The following snippet shows the simple logic for switching between Edit and Display modes when the button is clicked.

```
protected void Button1_Click(object sender, EventArgs e) {

        if (Button1.Text.Contains("Edit")) {
                WebPartManager1.DisplayMode =
                WebPartManager.EditDisplayMode;
                Button1.Text = "Switch to Browse Mode";
        } else {
                WebPartManager1.DisplayMode =
                WebPartManager.BrowseDisplayMode;
                Button1.Text = "Switch to Edit Mode";
        }
}
```

Right-click on the Default.aspx file and choose View in Browser to run the page. When the page is first displayed it will be in its default state—browse mode. Press the button a few times to toggle between browse mode and display mode. Notice that when you are in edit mode the name of the zone appears above each zone.

With the page in edit mode, drag both web parts into the middle zone. Close the browser and then start the application up again. Notice that the web parts page "remembered" which zone the web parts were in. This is the result of the personalization saving the customization changes and reapplying them for us.

One feature that we haven't seen on this page so far is the AppearanceEditor-Part. To view this control, we must first switch the page into edit mode. When the page is in edit mode, each web part will have a verb—such as Minimize, Close, and Edit associated with it—that allows a user to perform additional operations on the web part. Figure 1.7 shows these verbs being displayed for the Calendar web part.

Clicking on the Edit verb for a web part will make the EditorZone visible. We then use the editor to manage the properties and layout for that particular part. Let's try this. Select the Calendar, and then select its Edit verb. The EditorZone should now be visible as it is in figure 1.8 allowing you to change the Title to "My Calendar" and press OK or Apply to have that change saved.

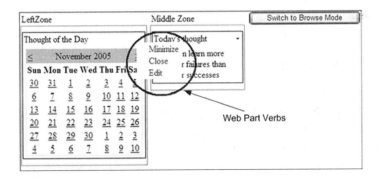

Figure 1.7
Verbs associated with a web part

Once the change has been saved, close the browser and then start the application up again. Notice that the title change was remembered between sessions. This, again, is due to the personalization feature.

You've built a portal!

That's it for this example. As promised, you've now built an information portal that meets our minimum definition of a portal, and here's the definition again, just so you can verify that your portal meets the requirements:

> *A portal is a web application which consists of pages that can display many different types of information based on user selection. A portal also allows the user to perform a variety of customizations on those pages that are remembered between viewing sessions.*

We also saw the three common ingredients of modern portals in action; that is, web parts, zones, and personalization. Of course there is still much to learn, but it's instructive to pause and reflect on just how much has been achieved with less than a dozen lines of C# code.

To summarize, we dragged seven web controls from the Toolbox onto a web page and wrote less than a dozen lines of code. By the end of that we had a page that exposed some very advanced functionality and was capable of remembering page customizations on a per-user basis. The mere fact that we can drag an `AppearanceEditor` from the Toolbox and have it automatically create the one hundred or so HTML controls and the thousands of lines of application code needed to present a working editor control is quite amazing. Building atop this sort of tested application logic means that we can now start to build more advanced applications with fewer bugs than we could previously.

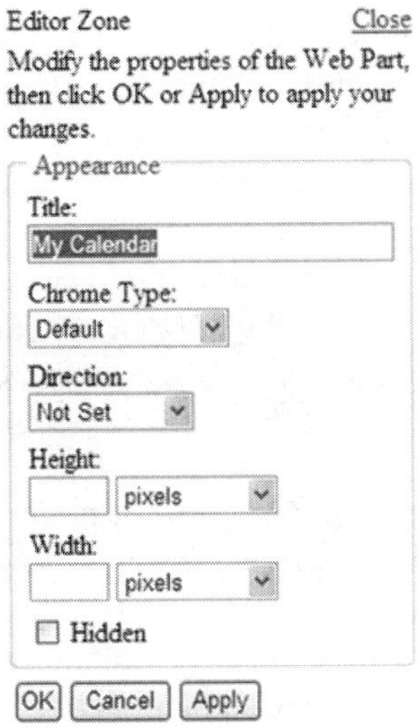

Figure 1.8 The EditorZone, with the AppearanceEditor displayed, allows you to change the appearance of the web part.

Now we'll move on to a quick summary of the major web part controls before heading into a session on data and learning about the Adventure Works Cycles business.

1.3 USING THE ASP.NET 2.0 PORTAL FRAMEWORK

Having just developed our first example, now is a good time to pause and make some sense of what we've seen. As mentioned, a great deal of functionality was achieved with very few lines of actual programming code, and I'm sure that you are probably wondering where all of that power came from. Let's start at the top and expand on the description of a portal framework that was presented in section 1.2.

What is the framework?

The portal framework is a set of controls that combine at runtime to provide an overall service. These controls are known collectively as web part controls and include the core components that we've already seen—personalization, web parts, and zones—but also include several other components that we haven't discussed in detail as yet. The most important of these is the `WebPartManager`. The `WebPartManager` control is an invisible member of the portal, but is responsible for nearly all of the major events that occur within it. For example, with our simple example from the previous section, if we were to remove the `WebPartManager`, the whole sample would just throw one great big exception—even though we only visibly used it in two lines of code!

In addition to the `WebPartManager`, we also observed web parts and zones at work. We saw how easy it is to create web parts; in fact, we even saw that standard web controls such as Calendars and Labels can be used as web parts simply by adding them to a zone. We got to see how zones assist with the layout of web parts and how the user can move the web parts freely between zones at runtime. We also caught our first glimpses of personalization when we changed the title of the Calendar web part and saw that it was automatically persisted across the browser. The fact that personalization can do this for us without our having to write any code is a very significant achievement, as it demonstrates one of the ways that the ASP.NET 2.0 architects have managed to remove the need to write code that performs common tasks.

1.3.1 Components of the framework

We'll now take a 40,000-foot view of the portal framework to get more of a high-level perspective of the functions that are contained within it. This will provide us with a full picture of the portal framework and allow us to view its breadth. I'm also going to bundle the web part controls into categories based on the functionality that they offer. Having this type of view aligns with the way that the rest of the book is laid out. In other words, if you look at the table of contents, you will see that each chapter is based on a particular functional slice of the web part framework. Within each chapter we'll be learning how to get the most out of that particular grouping of controls.

- *Web parts*—In many ways, portals only exist to display web parts. After all, it is the web part that displays what the end-user is ultimately after—whether that is a Dilbert comic, a newsfeed from Reuters, or just a simple calendar. Therefore, the web part is a very important piece of the overall portal architecture. In Chapter 2 when we examine the internal workings of the web part control you will know exactly how the Calendar and Label controls were magically turned into web parts when they were added to zones in our earlier example.

- *Connections*—Another major feature of the portal framework is web part connections. Connections allow separate web parts to communicate with one another at runtime to share information about each other. To more easily visualize this, consider a page with two web parts on it. One of these web parts displays a listing of employees and the other displays staff photographs. A connection could be used to synchronize these two web parts so that the photograph matches the employee that has been selected by a user in the other web part. Connections allow us to maintain these types of interdependencies between web parts without the need to write lots of tricky application code.

- *WebPartManager*—I mentioned the `WebPartManager` before and explained that it is the most important control in the portal framework because it manages so many of the tasks. It instantiates the zones and the web parts when the page is first viewed. It then tracks all of the state changes and monitors movements of web parts between zones. We also saw in our earlier example how it is used to change the display mode of the page to allow the user to perform editing operations on web parts. In chapter 5 we'll look at the `WebPartManger` control in detail to learn much more about each of these features. While we're at it, we'll get to see what other things the `WebPartManager` has been doing for us behind the scenes.

- *Editing*—As we saw in our initial example, the portal framework offers an `EditorZone` that can contain different editor controls. The `EditorZone` can contain any of the included `EditorPart` web controls that ship with ASP.NET 2.0 such as the `AppearanceEditor`, `LayoutEditor`, `BehaviorEditor`, and `PropertyGridEditor` parts. The requirement for the editor parts is that they inherit from the abstract `EditorPart` base class, which each of these parts does. We'll learn about these types of editor parts in chapter 5 and then explore them more fully in chapter 8 where we'll discuss how to do advanced operations with them, such as creating our own custom editor part controls.

- *Catalog*—The last of the major functional components of the portal framework is the *catalog*—or *gallery* as it is known in other applications such as SharePoint. We've mentioned that one feature of portals is how they allow users to add parts to pages at runtime. The catalog is the place where a user can go to discover which web parts are available, and then select them to add to his page. For example, a user could open the catalog and search for "weather" web parts and then, from the listing that results from this search, choose a web part and add it to his page. The workings of the catalog are discussed in chapter 5. A deeper analysis is given in chapter 9 when we totally replace the standard catalog with a custom one of our own.

This section has given us a good high-level understanding of the components of the portal framework. We've also seen what controls the ASP.NET 2.0 portal framework provides for building portals. While our knowledge of the portal framework is still fairly limited, we've established a basic, core body of knowledge to build upon. And don't worry, we'll learn much more about each of these categories of controls in the chapters that follow.

1.4 INTRODUCING ADVENTURE WORKS CYCLES DATABASE

This section opens up for you a new career—and you were ready for a change, weren't you? You've just been hired as a web application developer for Adventure Works Cycles. The section introduces you to the Adventure Works Cycles Company and its major departments, and to the database you will be working with.

Since the early 1990s, almost every book and tutorial about Microsoft technology has based its database samples on either the Northwind or Pubs databases that have shipped with SQL Server and Microsoft Access. For SQL Server 2005, Microsoft has released a new database that is based on a fictitious company named Adventure Works Cycles.

1.4.1 What is the database?

The Adventure Works database exposes a much richer set of entities than its predecessors. It also models a much more typical set of business scenarios and has groups of tables that represent the HR, sales, production, and purchasing areas of the business. Here is a quote from MSDN that describes the database.

> **NOTE** The purpose of this database is to demonstrate a complete solution for designing an integrated schema and to provide a sample database for that schema. This edition is designed to be used with Microsoft® SQL Server™ 2005.

The database schema covers many functional areas for a fictitious bicycle manufacturer. These areas include

- Customer/sales force automation and analysis
- Human resources

- Manufacturing workflow
- Engineering document management

As you can see, the main reason for using this database as the foundation for providing data scenarios in this book isn't merely for the sake of using a new technology, but because it allows the use of real-world examples when demonstrating concepts.

1.4.2 You're hired!

Throughout this book you can assume that you are a developer who is working for Adventure Works and receiving requirements from the various departments within the business, such as HR. Your "job" is to plan and implement those requests within your application where you'll be using the web parts to display data. Initially you will implement a very simple solution and then, as your understanding of the portal framework grows, you will add customizations to match the increasing complexity of the requirements. By the end of the book you will have created a highly customized portal application for the Adventure Works Cycle business.

For the remainder of this section we'll discuss the Adventure Works Cycles business to provide more context as to the nature of the departments within the company. The Adventure Works business is split up into the cost centers, each responsible for a different aspect of the business:

- *Human Resources*—The HR operating division sets company policies, and is responsible for information relating to employees, their respective departments, and historical pay data. HR also keeps track of people other than employees, such as contacts, and stores details about them, such as their address details. Naturally, quite a bit of the HR data is confidential.

- *Production*—The production center manages stock and ensures that inventory levels are always sufficient to fulfill orders that are coming through. For auditing purposes, the production systems have to store information about products, inventory, stock movements, and work orders.

- *Purchasing*—The purchasing team liaises with vendors and keeps track of the stock order details for goods that have been put on order by the production team.

- *Sales*—The sales cost center keeps track of incoming orders and runs queries over sales history data. It, obviously, has a heavy data requirement.

Reporting on day-to-day operations

To learn more about the day-to-day operations of these cost centers, let's start by creating reports about employee counts and sales figures. Open your preferred query tool for SQL Server 2005 and start by entering the query and running it.

Figure 1.9 Employee count results

```
SELECT CountOfEmployees = COUNT(EmployeeID)
FROM HumanResources.Employee
WHERE CurrentFlag = 1
```

When we run this statement in SQL Server, we can see that the Adventure Works business currently employs 290 staff as shown in figure 1.9.

Next we'll expand upon that query by grouping the staff hires by the year in which they began work. By doing this we can see how the business has grown. To create the report we still only need to query the employee table to get the data we need. Enter the SQL code and run the statement.

```
SELECT [Year Of Hire] = YEAR(HireDate),
    [Employees Hired] = COUNT(EmployeeID)
FROM HumanResources.Employee
GROUP BY YEAR(HireDate)
ORDER BY YEAR(HireDate) DESC
```

Figure 1.10 shows us the result of running this statement; and we can see from it that 1999 stands out as the company's biggest year for employee hires, with 198 employees hired.

In listing 1.3 we've altered our previous query slightly so that we can see how the 290 employees that are currently employed are distributed within the departments of the business. To present this data in a meaningful way requires us to join the `EmployeeDepartmentHistory` and `Department` tables.

	Year Of Hire	Employees Hired
1	2003	3
2	2002	4
3	2001	21
4	2000	45
5	1999	198
6	1998	16
7	1997	2
8	1996	1

Figure 1.10 Employee hires by calendar year results

Listing 1.3 Employee count by department query

```
SELECT DepartmentName = dept.[Name],
    EmployeeCount = COUNT(e.EmployeeID)
FROM HumanResources.Employee e,
    HumanResources.EmployeeDepartmentHistory hist,
    HumanResources.Department dept
WHERE hist.EmployeeID = e.EmployeeID
    AND hist.DepartmentID = dept.DepartmentID
    AND hist.EndDate IS NULL
GROUP BY dept.[Name]
ORDER BY EmployeeCount DESC
```

We can see that the `where` clause for this query specifies that the `EndDate` for the `EmployeeDepartmentHistory` entry must be null. This ensures that we are only including the current record for a given employee, and won't double-up for an employee who has multiple entries—such as an employee who was transferred between departments. Figure 1.11 shows us that, when we run the query, we can see that the production department has by far the most employees at 179.

Finally, we can write a query that allows us to see the number of sales that are made by Adventure Works Cycles to support its 290 employees. To obtain this information, we simply need to query the `SalesOrderHeader` table and add up the value of sales orders for each year. The following snippet provides the code to do this:

```
SELECT FiscalYear = YEAR(DATEADD(m, 6, soh.OrderDate)),
    SalesAmount = SUM(soh.SubTotal)
FROM Sales.SalesOrderHeader soh
GROUP BY YEAR(DATEADD(m, 6, soh.OrderDate))
ORDER BY SalesAmount DESC
```

The results for this query are shown in figure 1.12. From the results we can see that sales have grown for each of the three years that the business has been operating.

Looking at these queries helps us get a feel for the business. From these queries we can see that the sales have grown exceptionally between the years 2002 and 2005. In this time sales have more than doubled from $2.7 million to just over $6 million. It was therefore not surprising that, looking at the headcounts for each department, production and sales lead the way. In fact, of the 290 employees that the business currently employs, nearly 200 of them work in the production area.

With more than five years worth of sales, HR, production, and purchasing data, the Adventure Works Cycles business provides us with an ample scope for building interesting applications, which is lucky because that's exactly what we are about to do!

	DepartmentName	EmployeeCount
1	Production	179
2	Sales	18
3	Purchasing	12
4	Information Servic...	10
5	Finance	10
6	Marketing	9
7	Facilities and Mai...	7
8	Quality Assurance	6
9	Engineering	6
10	Production Control	6
11	Shipping and Rec...	6
12	Human Resources	6
13	Document Control	5
14	Research and De...	4
15	Tool Design	4
16	Executive	2

Figure 1.11 Employee count by department results

1.4.3 Getting our hands on data

In order to create a portal for the Adventure Works business, we will need data. Before we can use that data, our first task is to create the code that can access the SQL Server database and return it for us. This type of code is generally known as data access code and it sits within a conceptual application layer commonly referred to as the data layer. In this section we'll be creating the data access methods and the necessary logic to get data for the human resources department at Adventure Works. To do

	FiscalYear	SalesAmount
1	2004	60767644.1834
2	2003	39444013.3259
3	2002	27074681.9733
4	2005	50840.63

Figure 1.12 Sales YTD results

this we will create a project that contains all the methods needed to perform data access for each department in the Adventure Works business.

The full source code for the AW.Portal.Data project can be found on the associated source files that come with this book.

NOTE   It should be noted that the purpose of the code being shown here is to provide a simple demonstration of how to retrieve data from SQL Server and is not intended to act as a demonstration of best practices for creating data access methods. For brevity, code that would normally be included for the performance of such tasks as exception handling, security checks, and data caching has been left out.

Configuring the database connection

The application we'll be creating in this book is a web portal application, so we can store the credentials that we'll use for connecting to the database in the new `connectionStrings` section of the web configuration file. This section is a new feature in ASP.NET V2.0 and is the recommended place for storing database connection information. The `connectionStrings` section adds new security-related features to the configuration file, such as the ability to store connection strings in an encrypted form. When we add our connection string to the configuration file it looks similar to what is shown in listing 1.4.

Listing 1.4   The connection string configuration for the Adventure Works database

```
<?xml version="1.0"?>
<configuration xmlns="http://schemas.microsoft.com/.NetConfiguration/v2.0">

<connectionStrings>
  <add
    name="AdventureWorksConnectionString"
    connectionString="Data Source=.\sql2k5;
  Initial Catalog=AdventureWorks;
  Integrated Security=True"
    providerName="System.Data.SqlClient" />
</connectionStrings>

<system.web></system.web>

</configuration>
```

The configuration data shown in listing 1.4 comes from the `Web.config` file for our application and contains the connection string that we'll be using to connect to the Adventure Works database. The `connectionStrings` element of the web configuration file is the best place for connection strings that will be used within a web application. This is because there is good API support for reading from this configuration section in a strongly typed manner by using the `ConfigurationManager` class. Even better, this element can be easily encrypted when deployed into a production environment so that sensitive security information, such as usernames and passwords, are not left lying about in clear text within the configuration file.

In our application the data layer will return custom business entity classes. There are no hard and fast rules about what data types to return from a data layer and asking any two people will almost certainly result in a differing opinion. Some of your alternative options will include—but not be limited to

- Custom business entities
- Strongly typed datasets
- XML

As with almost everything in programming, the answer to the question of which data type to use will almost certainly depend on your circumstances. For example, with applications that need to expose their data to external parties you will want to use a more XML-centric approach. Likewise, if your application connects to data but it only has an occasional connection to the data source, then you may wish to use strongly typed datasets as your data type since they can help reduce the amount of code that you need to write in this scenario.

For our application, the choice of custom business entities will work just fine as we will always be connected, and using them will also ensure that we get strongly typed access to our underlying data. Custom business entities also work well with ASP.NET as they are easy to bind to controls such as the `Repeater` and the new `GridView` control.

Creating a data access layer

To get things rolling with our data layer, open Visual Studio and create a new C# library project named `AW.Portal.Data` and save it to a convenient location in your file system. Figure 1.13 shows a new C# class library project being created in a folder location named C:\Sandboxes\AdventureWorks.

When the project has been created, we want to ensure that the assembly will be created with the correct namespace and with a desirable assembly name. You can view these project settings by right-clicking on the project node in the solution explorer and choosing Properties. Notice that the assembly and namespace are set to `AW.Portal.Data`. This means that building the project will create an assembly named `AW.Portal.Data.dll` that can be referenced from other projects.

Close the properties window and add a new class file to the project named `Data-Layer.cs` by right-clicking on the project in the Solution Explorer and choosing Add file. This is the class that will contain all the individual methods for each set of data that we need to return.

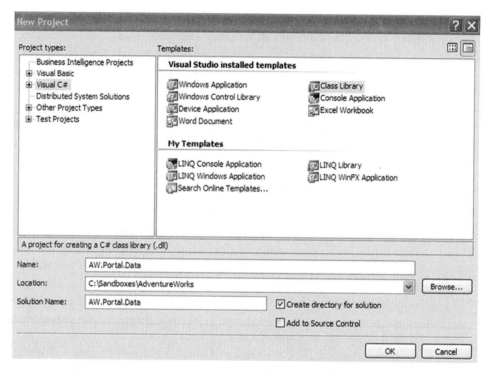

Figure 1.13   Creating a new class library project in Visual Studio 2005

Before adding the data access methods to our DataLayer class, we'll add a new property named ConnectionString to it. This property will contain the logic for specifying the connection string that is used by the DataLayer when connecting to the database. Listing 1.5 shows how this is implemented in code:

> **Listing 1.5   The DataLayer class includes the logic for retrieving the connection string information from the configuration file. This is achieved with help from the ASP.NET ConfigurationManager class.**

```
namespace AW.Portal.Data {

  public class DataLayer {

    public DataLayer() { }

      public string ConnectionString {
        get {
          ConnectionStringSettings setting =         ConnectionString
                                                      is retrieved

ConfigurationManager.ConnectionStrings["AdventureWorksConnectionString"];

          if (setting == null) {        ConfigurationManager encapsulates logic
                                            of accessing configuration data
```

```
        string errorString =
            "You must configure the connection
    ⇒string in the web config file." ;
        throw new ConfigurationErrorsException(errorString);
    }

    return setting.ConnectionString;
    }
  }
 }
}
```

Notice that we get the connection string information from the `Configuration-Manager` class. The `ConfigurationManager` is a new class in ASP.NET 2.0 that was added to help perform tasks related to accessing configuration data. The `ConfigurationManager` class is contained within the `System.Configuration` assembly. You may have to add a reference to the `System.Configuration` assembly from the `DataLayer` project if it is not already present before you can reference the `ConfigurationManager` in your code.

Figure 1.14 shows the Add Reference dialog in Visual Studio with the `System.Configuration` assembly selected and ready to be included as a project reference.

The fully qualified name of the `ConfigurationManager` class is its namespace followed by its class name, which is `System.Configuration.Configuration-Manager`. However, in listing 1.5 you can see that we have only used the class name. In order for the code to compile, we must import the namespace into our class by

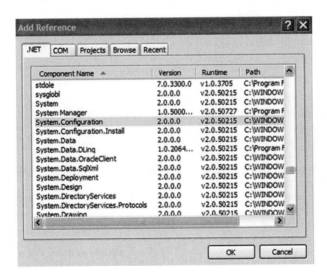

Figure 1.14
The Add Reference dialog in Visual Studio 2005 allows us to create references to shared libraries from within our .NET projects.

using the C# using directive. Add the following using directive at the top of the class file:

```
using System.Configuration ;
```

Now that the namespace has been added to the class file we are able to use unqualified type names within our code and have it compile successfully.

Defining the SQL queries

For this application we will not use stored procedures, but instead be use parameterized SQL that is embedded in the data layer as strings. Open up the AW.Portal.Data project and add a new C# class file named SQL.cs. The SQL file will contain all the SQL strings and will be accessed by the data access methods. Listing 1.6 shows some of the SQL strings embedded within a static class.

> **NOTE** For the sake of brevity, the following listing shows the code for only a few of the SQL strings. The remainder of the SQL strings can be found in the code in the associated source files that come with this book.

Listing 1.6 SQL.cs

```
public static class SQL {

  public static readonly string ListDepartments = @"
    SELECT dept.DepartmentID, DepartmentName = dept.[Name], GroupName,
      EmployeeCount = (SELECT COUNT(hist.EmployeeID) as EmployeeCount
      FROM HumanResources.EmployeeDepartmentHistory hist
      WHERE hist.DepartmentID = dept.DepartmentID
      AND hist.EndDate IS NULL)
    FROM HumanResources.Department dept
    ORDER BY GroupName, DepartmentName";

  public static readonly string ListEmployeesByDepartment = @"
      SELECT e.EmployeeID, p.FirstName, p.LastName, e.Title as JobTitle
      FROM HumanResources.Employee e,
          HumanResources.EmployeeDepartmentHistory hist,
          Person.Contact p
      WHERE hist.EmployeeID = e.EmployeeID
      AND p.ContactID = e.ContactID
      AND hist.DepartmentID = @departmentID    ◁——— Parameterized SQL
      AND e.CurrentFlag = 1
    ORDER BY p.LastName";

  public static readonly string ListJobCandidates = @"
    SELECT JobCandidateID, Resume.query('
    declare namespace                          ◁——— XQuery to query XML values
ns=""http://schemas.microsoft.com/sqlserver/2004/07/adventure-works/
Resume"";
    data(/ns:Resume/ns:Name/*)') as CandidateName,
```

```
    Resume.query('
    declare namespace  <──── XQuery to query XML values
ns=""http://schemas.microsoft.com/sqlserver/2004/07/adventure-works/
Resume"";
    data(/ns:Resume/ns:Skills)') as Skills
    FROM HumanResources.JobCandidate
    WHERE EmployeeID IS NULL";

}
```

Notice that the query named `ListJobCandidates` makes use of an XQuery expression to perform an XPATH query on the Resume field. XQuery is a language addition in SQL Server 2005 and allows you to query XML data stored in the database using the `query()` expression. In this case the Resume field in the `HumanResources.Job-Candidate` table is stored in an XML type column.

Custom business entities

The SQL strings that we've defined will allow us to retrieve data from SQL Server. This is the same data that will be displayed from within the web parts on our portal. For example, the `ListDepartments` SQL could be used by a web part whose job it is to display a listing of departments to users. To make this data usable from within our portal application, we'll make sure that the properties of our custom business entity classes align to fields in the SQL that we have defined. When data is returned from SQL Server we can load it into the properties of a corresponding business entity and return it to our portal application.

Each business entity class will have a single method named `Fill` which takes a `SqlDataReader` object that is returned from the database and reads the values from it, mapping them to the properties of the class. Because this method is common to all business entity classes we can extract its definition to an interface. Being able to reference the `Fill` method via an interface allows us to write generic code when using it—as we'll see shortly. Listing 1.7 displays the code for the interface, and also for a business entity which implements it named `Employee`.

> **Listing 1.7** The Employee class is an example of a business entity class. These classes expose a property for each field that is returned from an SQL query. Each business entity also provides a Fill method which reads the data returned from the query to its properties.

```
namespace AW.Portal.Data {

    public interface IBusinessEntity {              Method named
      void Fill( SqlDataReader reader ) ;  <────┐   Fill is defined on
    }                                            └── interface
```

```
public class Employee : IBusinessEntity {          Business entity
  private int _id;                                  implements
  private string _firstName;                        interface...
  private string _lastName;
  private string _jobTitle;

  public int ID { get { return _id; } set { _id = value; } }
  public string FirstName {
    get { return _firstName; }
    set { _firstName = value; }
  }
  public string LastName {
    get { return _lastName; }
    set { _lastName = value; }
  }
  public string JobTitle {
    get { return _jobTitle; }
    set { _jobTitle = value; }
  }

  public void Fill(SqlDataReader reader) {
    _id = reader.GetInt32(0);
    _firstName = reader.GetString(1);              ...And provides custom
    _lastName = reader.GetString(2);               implementation of
    _jobTitle = reader.GetString(3);               interface method
  }
}
}
```

Notice that the `Employee` class contains a property for each field returned by the `ListEmployeesByDepartment` SQL and that the `Fill` method is used to map the data returned from that SQL into the properties. In just a moment we'll write the generic helper method that will connect to the database and retrieve data from it. This helper code will then call the `Fill` method on the relevant business entity object, passing in the `SqlDataReader`. By having the `Fill` method defined on an interface, this helper class does not need to know about any of the actual business entities as it can communicate through the interface.

Data helper functions

The helper method that we are about to create will perform the tasks common to all data access operations. It will prepare the SQL, add it to an `SqlCommand` object, and fire the query against the database. Even though this code must be run for all business entities, it needs to be written only once because the logic is the same regardless of the business entity that it is operating over. From within the `AW.Portal.Data` project, open the `DataLayer.cs` file and add the code for the helper method shown in listing 1.8.

```
private T GetDataItem<T>(string commandText, string[] parameterNames,
object[] parameterValues)
    where T : IBusinessEntity, new() {        ◄——— Specify Generic constraints

    SqlConnection cnn = new SqlConnection(this.ConnectionString);
    SqlCommand cmd = new SqlCommand();
    cmd.CommandType = CommandType.Text;
    cmd.Connection = cnn;
    cmd.CommandText = commandText;

    if (parameterNames != null && parameterNames.Length > 0) {
        for (int i = 0; i < parameterNames.Length; i++) {
            cmd.Parameters.AddWithValue(          ◄——┐ Add parameters
                        parameterNames[i],           │ to our command
                        parameterValues[i]
                        );
        }
    }

    T dataItem = new T();

    try {
        cnn.Open();

        using (SqlDataReader reader = cmd.ExecuteReader()) {
            if (reader != null) {
                reader.Read();
                dataItem.Fill(reader);    ◄——— Read data into item
            }
        }
    } finally {
        if (cnn.State == ConnectionState.Open) {
            cnn.Close();
        }
    }

    return dataItem;
}
```

NOTE This generic method executes a statement and returns a single business entity. The completed project that comes with this book also contains a second method named GetDataItems for executing statements and returning collections of business entity objects.

As we'll illustrate, having this data access logic allows us to use a single line of code to execute SQL queries from a calling method, and ensures that all of the code for creating connections and cleaning them up is common. This in return reduces the chances of introducing logic errors in multiple places. You can also see that the code uses a new feature of the .NET Framework known as *Generics*. Generics is a powerful new addition to the .NET Framework in the 2.0 release that allows a developer to write code against types that are not defined until runtime, and provides a way to use generic constraints to constrain the types of data that can be accepted.

Notice how our `IBusinessEntity` interface allows these generic helper methods to call `Fill(...)` on an object that is merely defined as a T. This is because of the Generic constraints that are added to the method informing the compiler that T is a type of `IBusinessEntity`. Adding the `new()` constraint to the generic T item allows it to create new instances of the generic T type.

> **NOTE**   For more information about Generics, you can read the excellent article in the Msdn Magazine that can be found at the following URL: http://msdn.microsoft.com/msdnmag/issues/03/09/NET

Creating data access methods

Finally, it's time to add the data access methods that will be callable from the web application and will return the appropriate data to the web application. I'm only going to show and discuss two of the methods that return HR-related data but the actual source file and assembly that come with the book contain all the data access methods that are required to supply data for all departments within the Adventure Works business.

The following code snippet shows a method named `ListDepartments`, which calls the generic `GetDataItems` method to return a collection of `Department` business entities from the database. The `Department` class is passed as the generic argument to the `ListDepartments` method, allowing the generic code to use type information for the `Department` class.

```
public List<Department> ListDepartments() {
    return GetDataItems<Department>(SQL.ListDepartments, null, null);
}
```

The code for returning a single business entity is shown in the following snippet. This is very similar to the code used for returning a collection of business items. On this occasion the `Employee` class is passed as the generic argument.

```
public Employee GetEmployeeDetails(int employeeID) {
    return GetDataItem<Employee>(SQL.GetEmployeeDetails, new string[] {
"@employeeID" }, new object[] { employeeID });
}
```

That's it for the data access layer, and I hope that you have appreciated how simple these methods are—just a single line of code is all that is required to run statements against our `DataLayer` and obtain results. All of our hard work has been worthwhile! While creating our data access code we've seen some interesting new .NET 2.0 features. These were

- The use of generics to write algorithms that can run against any single data type
- The use of the new XQuery language to query data stored within XML data fields in SQL Server
- The new `connectionStrings` configuration setting in web applications to store connection string information

For the remainder of this book, we will be creating a web application that references this data layer to get data for the Adventure Works web portal components. The actual data layer that you'll be using is contained in the chapter 1 folder of the resources that came with this book.

1.5   SUMMARY

This chapter introduced web parts and the ASP.NET Portal Framework, and in the process we managed to come up with our own working definition of a portal. In addition, we looked at the Adventure Works Cycles database and saw how to write some basic queries against that database to retrieve a line of business data about the company. The main reason for looking at this line of business data is that throughout book we'll be working with that data and building web parts to present views of it to end users.

Upcoming chapters build on this data access code by creating a portal application for the Adventure Works business. In fact, in the next chapter the first set of requirements are issued by the HR department, and we start by creating the web application and applying the first set of web parts to it. In the process, as we use the data access layer to retrieve data for our application, we'll see the benefits of the hard work that went into building that layer.

CHAPTER 2

Web parts: the building blocks of portals

2.1 INTRODUCTION

You may already be acquainted with web parts and web part controls, and if you've worked with products such as SharePoint you have already used them quite extensively. (If these topics are not familiar, please dip into chapter 1 for a quick refresher.) Before you start this chapter, I recommend that you whet your appetite by seeing real examples of how web part controls allow users to customize the look and feel of web applications. To do so, visit http://Start.com. This is a web-based portal created by Microsoft Research. Notice how it provides a variety of methods to customize the page, by adding web parts and configuring them. For example, while at that page you could add a web part to display the current news from one of a dozen news providers, or display the weather for any city in the world. If you're like me, you could lose many hours configuring that page to exactly suit your fancy. And guess what—once you've done it, it's *your* page! Every time you visit that page, all the web parts you added, configured, and moved around will be there for you—just the way you left them.

In chapter 1 we learned that web parts are an integral aspect of a portal application. This chapter supplies a more exhaustive understanding of web parts, in particular how they are implemented in ASP.NET 2.0 portal applications.

This chapter is the first step in a journey through the properties, methods, and operations of web parts. In it we'll learn how to add custom verbs to web parts and how to customize their look and feel through themes and other customization techniques. We'll also delve a little deeper into the subject to see how web parts implement various interfaces that expose their behavior to the rest of the ASP.NET web portal framework. By the end of this chapter we'll be well on our way to understanding how the http://Start.com website achieves its magic. Let's begin!

2.2 EXPLORING WEB PARTS

Web parts are informational components, such as news updates or comics, that are added to web pages; and as such, web parts can be considered the primary building blocks of a portal application that displays dynamic content. In ASP.NET 2.0 we are provided with the `WebPart` server control for working with web parts. The `WebPart` server control comes pre-packaged with many properties and methods needed to use it in a variety of ways to show dynamic content to users.

The composition of web parts

A web part is generally rendered with a title bar, a border, and a body for displaying its dynamic content. The web part is manipulated by a web control that allows a user to work with and customize the web part. For example, users can set the web part's height or width and provide it with a title and description. Other manipulations of web parts are accessed through small menu-like items known as verbs. These operations include performing tasks such as closing the web part, minimizing it, or connecting it to other web parts on the page. Figure 2.1 shows the basic elements that make up a standard web part control.

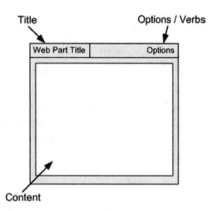

In figure 2.1 we can see the various sub-elements that combine to form a web part. Throughout this chapter we will learn more about each of these elements and see how to use the `WebPart` class to modify or affect each different element. Understanding how to gain access to each of these elements will take us a long way down the path towards having full control over how our web parts are displayed to the end-users of our portal.

Figure 2.1   The sub-elements of a Web-Part control.

Categorizing web parts

So far you've bumped into lots of buzzwords and phrases about web parts; but aside from a minor example, we have yet to learn exactly what they are. Are they simply common ASP.NET server controls? Or are they more like ASP.NET user controls? Do they ship as part of the core set of ASP.NET server controls? Answering these questions is logically the best place to begin our exploration of the ASP.NET `WebPart` control.

The simple example application that we built in chapter 1 showed that when we added standard ASP.NET server controls, the `Calendar` and the `Label`, to a web part zone, a transformation magically occurred—they became web parts. We saw that suddenly those controls had verbs, they now had titles, and they had properties that could be edited at runtime via the editor parts. To answer the question of "what is a web part?" we need to do some investigative work and discover more of the magic that turned those standard server controls into web parts!

2.2.1 Discovering the GenericWebPart control

In order to understand what happened to the `Label` and `Calendar` controls in the previous chapter, we're going to need to put our debugging skills to the test and determine how all these web part controls interact with each other. To do that we'll set up a web page and add web part controls to it. After that we'll add code to the page that will access those parts. Finally, when we attach the debugger to the code and run it we'll have a clear view of the state of those objects at runtime. Completing those steps will give us a much clearer view of how the transformation occurred.

> **NOTE** This book is designed to be very hands-on, and as such we will frequently be writing small pages to try new things as we learn about them. Therefore, it would be a good idea to create a new ASP.NET project in Visual Studio that can be used to create ad-hoc web pages for testing. For the remainder of this book I'll refer to this test project as "your test project."

Creating a web page

Open your test project and create a new web page named `GenericWebPart-Test.aspx`. This page will be used to learn how these web controls are turned into web parts. As with all web pages that contain web parts, we must start by adding a `WebPartManager` control at the top of the page. Finally, we can add a `WebPart-Zone` and add a `Label` control to it. With that, our code should look like the following snippet:

```
<asp:WebPartManager ID="WebPartManager1" runat="server" />

<asp:WebPartZone ID="WebPartZone1" runat="server">
  <ZoneTemplate>
    <asp:Label id="ctl1" runat="server" Text="I'm a label" />
  </ZoneTemplate>
</asp:WebPartZone>
```

All that we know at this stage is that at some time between now and when this page is displayed in a browser, the `Label` control that we added to the web part zone starts looking and behaving like a web part. We know this because we saw that the label gained two characteristics common to web parts—a Title and Verbs—when it was contained within the web part zone in the previous chapter. Next we'll write code that allows us to view the state of the page at runtime. Switch into the code section of the web page, enter the code, and set the debugging breakpoints that are displayed in figure 2.2.

```
 8    protected override void OnPreRender(EventArgs e) {
 9        base.OnPreRender(e);
10
11        int countOfControls = this.WebPartZone1.Controls.Count;
12        int countOfWebParts = this.WebPartZone1.WebParts.Count;
13
14        foreach (WebPart wp in this.WebPartZone1.WebParts) {
15            Type t = wp.GetType();
16            string typeName = t.Name;
17        }
18    }
19
```

Figure 2.2 Code and debugging breakpoints are used to inspect the state of controls on our page during the pre-rendering phase of the page lifecycle.

After an ASP.NET has been processing a good while, it enters into a phase that is referred to as the pre-rendering phase of the page. During the pre-rendering phase of the page, the `OnPreRender` event handler in the page is called by the ASP.NET engine, which causes code in our method to be executed. At this time, page execution will halt at the breakpoints that we've set. When the execution halts at runtime, we can inspect the state of the controls on the page at runtime. The control that we are interested in is `WebPartZone1`.

A `WebPartZone` control has two properties that are of particular interest to us because they will provide information regarding where our `Label` control is, and what type of control it is. These properties are called "Controls" and "WebParts" and, as you may guess from their names, they contain collections of controls that are contained by the web part zone. Logic would have us believe that the `Label` control will turn up in the `WebPartZone`'s "Controls" collection because it is a web control but, from what we've observed, it's pretty easy to expect that it will show up in the "WebParts" collection instead. Let's run the page and see. From the Debug menu in Visual Studio, press Start Debugging to run the page and attach the debugger to it.

Debugging the page

The page runs and stops at the breakpoints, allowing us to place our mouse over the breakpoints and inspect the state of each variable. Hovering over the `countOfWeb-Parts` variable that we declared indeed does prove that the zone now contains one web part control as shown in figure 2.3.

```
    8     protected override void OnPreRender(EventArgs e) {
    9         base.OnPreRender(e);
   10
   11         int countOfControls = this.WebPartZone1.Controls.Count;
   12         int countOfWebParts = this.WebPartZone1.WebParts.Count;
   13                            ┌─────────────────────┐
   14     foreach (WebPart       │ ● countOfWebParts 1 │ ne1.WebParts) {
   15         Type t = wp.GetType();─────────────────────┘
   16         string typeName = t.Name;
   17     }
   18 }
```

Figure 2.3   While stepping through code in debug mode you can place the mouse cursor above variables to display their state.

Similarly, hovering over the countOfControls variable will display zero for its value. This tells us that the web part zone now believes that it contains no web controls. Hover over the last breakpoint and you'll see that the name of the Type of the web part is GenericWebPart as displayed in figure 2.4.

```
    8     protected override void OnPreRender(EventArgs e) {
    9         base.OnPreRender(e);
   10
   11         int countOfControls = this.WebPartZone1.Controls.Count;
   12         int countOfWebParts = this.WebPartZone1.WebParts.Count;
   13
   14     foreach (WebPart wp in this.WebPartZone1.WebParts) {
   15         Type t = wp.GetType();
   16         string typeName = t.Name;
   17     }                         ┌──────────────────────────────┐
   18 }                            │ t.Name 🔍 ▾ "GenericWebPart" │
                                   └──────────────────────────────┘
```

Figure 2.4   Displaying the Type of the web part at runtime shows that it is no longer a Label but is now a GenericWebPart control.

With the page still in debug mode, right-click on the wp variable and choose the "Quick Watch" menu option from the resulting context menu. In response, the Quick Watch dialog is displayed for the wp variable allowing us to see the values for all of its properties. Figure 2.5 displays the Quick Watch dialog with many of the properties for the wp variable shown.

In the Quick Watch dialog we can see that the GenericWebPart has a large number of properties that do not belong to the Label class but, instead are members of the WebPart class. These properties include: "IsClosed," "Title," "CatalogIconImageUrl," and "ChromeState" to name just a few. We see that there is also a property named "WebBrowsableObject" and that it is currently displaying a value of {Text = "I'm a label"}—the very same text value that we assigned to the original label in the mark-up for the page! This is quite a significant discovery, because it tells us that the very same Label control that we added to our WebPartZone earlier has been replaced with a new Type of control and has been wrapped by the WebBrowsableObject property. We can actually still get at the underlying Label control via the ChildControl property of the GenericWebPart—as demonstrated by the

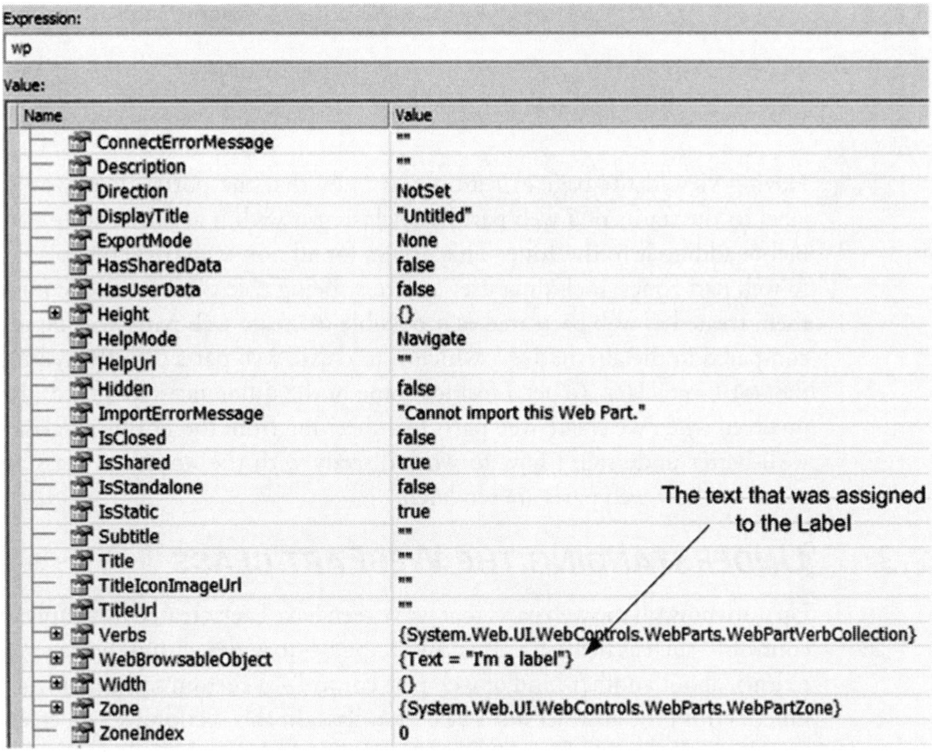

Expression:

wp

Value:

Name	Value
ConnectErrorMessage	""
Description	""
Direction	NotSet
DisplayTitle	"Untitled"
ExportMode	None
HasSharedData	false
HasUserData	false
⊞ Height	{}
HelpMode	Navigate
HelpUrl	""
Hidden	false
ImportErrorMessage	"Cannot import this Web Part."
IsClosed	false
IsShared	true
IsStandalone	false
IsStatic	true
Subtitle	""
Title	""
TitleIconImageUrl	""
TitleUrl	""
⊞ Verbs	{System.Web.UI.WebControls.WebParts.WebPartVerbCollection}
⊞ WebBrowsableObject	{Text = "I'm a label"}
⊞ Width	{}
⊞ Zone	{System.Web.UI.WebControls.WebParts.WebPartZone}
ZoneIndex	0

The text that was assigned to the Label

Figure 2.5   The Visual Studio 2005 Quick Watch window displays the runtime values of objects.

code in listing 2.1. Why would we want to get at the underlying control of the generic web part? One reason might be that we are using a control such as a Grid-View as the child control and we need to access the GridView after a page postback to re-bind it to a data source control.

Listing 2.1   The ChildControl property of the GenericWebPart provides access to the underlying web control that is wrapped by the GenericWebPart.

```
protected override void OnPreRender(EventArgs e) {
    base.OnPreRender(e);

    int countOfControls = this.WebPartZone1.Controls.Count;
    int countOfWebParts = this.WebPartZone1.WebParts.Count;

    foreach (WebPart wp in this.WebPartZone1.WebParts) {
        if (wp is GenericWebPart) {
            Type t = ((GenericWebPart)wp).ChildControl.GetType();
```

Cast the web part to a GenericWebPart to get at the ChildControl property

```
                      string typeName = t.Name;   ◁────── Returns "Label"
                  }
              }
          }
```

Having viewed the page at runtime, we saw that the portal framework elevated the label to the status of a web part by enclosing it within a `GenericWebPart` wrapper before adding it to the zone. This occurs for all non-web part controls that are added to web part zones, including user controls. Being able to create user controls and have them treated as web parts makes it possible to create web parts very rapidly and easily compared to the alternative—which is to create web parts directly by inheriting from the `WebPart` class. To get a feel for some of the differences, let's take a look at what's involved when we create web parts by inheriting from the `WebPart` class. In doing so we'll better understand how to work directly with the `WebPart` class and we'll also get to see how web parts are rendered.

2.3   UNDERSTANDING THE WEBPART CLASS

Up until now, all the web parts that we've seen have been created by simply adding server controls—such as the `Calendar` and `Label`—to zones within the page. Now it's time to learn about another kind of web part control—a custom server control that directly inherits from the abstract `WebPart` base class. In this section we will create a web part by inheriting directly from the `WebPart` class and then learn how to add our custom web part to a web page by registering our custom web part class with the page.

Dragging user controls onto zones and having them treated as web parts is fine when the web parts do not need to be shared outside a single application; but part of the power of web parts is that, by their very nature, they lend themselves well to being reused in more than just a single portal application. For reuse, user controls cannot surpass custom controls, because custom controls can be compiled into very specific assemblies and easily shared between applications. If you need to share web parts between your own applications, or indeed, package them for reuse by third parties, then you will want to create custom controls so that you can take advantage of the packaging of assemblies. To do this you will need to create custom classes that derive directly from the `WebPart` class.

The `WebPart` class lives in the `System.Web.UI.WebControls.WebParts` namespace and serves as the base class for all web part controls. In fact, if you look at the definition of `GenericWebPart`, you will see that it does in fact inherit from the `WebPart` class. The `WebPart` class itself inherits from a base class named `Part`. The `Part` class has the basic properties that are relevant for all web part "parts"— including editor parts and catalog parts such as description, title and a few others.

2.3.1   Using custom controls

We've just seen that, when creating web parts, we have two options. The first option is to create a class that derives directly from the `WebPart` class, and the second option is to drop user controls or server controls onto a web zone and have the framework place those controls within a generic wrapper known as a `GenericWebPart`. Let's now take a look at how to create web parts using each of these two methods.

The first web part that we'll build is a custom server control that inherits directly from the `WebPart` class. This will allow us to see for the first time what's involved in getting a web part up and running using that method. The web part that we will build will be a weather web part to display the weather for a variable number of days. It will have a property that allows us to specify how many days of weather to display. This is a good example of the sort of informational web part that would appear on a typical portal. Figure 2.6 displays what the weather web part control will look like when displayed in a browser.

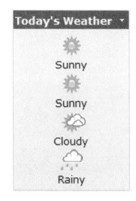

Figure 2.6   This custom web part control displays random weather information for a variable number of days.

Creating a weather web part

To start creating the weather web part, open your test web project and add a new class file named "CustomWeatherPart.cs" to the `WebPart` folder and then derive that class from `WebPart`. At this point your class should look similar to the following snippet:

```
namespace WebPartTests {

    public class CustomWeatherPart : WebPart {

            public CustomWeatherPart() { }
    }
}
```

To allow users to set the number of days of weather to be displayed, we'll add a property named `NumberOfDays`. By default we'll set it to a value of 4 so that at least that number of days of weather will be displayed—even before the user has had time to configure it to be some other value. We can store the value for this property in `View-State` so that it is persisted even after multiple trips between the browser and the web server (postbacks). The last bit of logic to be added ensures that the user cannot accidentally set the number of days to a value greater than 10 or less than 1. The code for our property is shown in listing 2.2, with all of its logic in place.

Listing 2.2   The NumberOfDays property contains the number of days of weather that should appear in the web part.

```
public int NumberOfDays {
        get {
                if (ViewState["NumberOfDays"] == null) {
                        return 4;
                } else {
```

```
                        return (int)ViewState["NumberOfDays"];
            }
    }
    set {
            if (value < 1 || value > 10) {
                    ViewState["NumberOfDays"] = 4;
            } else {
                    ViewState["NumberOfDays"] = value;
            }
    }
}
```

The NumberOfDays property can now be used to specify how many days of weather our control will display; and the constraints that were added to the property ensure that there will always be some number of days to display weather for.

Rendering custom controls

When you work with custom server controls, one of the problems you face is that user interface elements are created by using code, as opposed to standard HTML and markup. Displaying a control in code requires creating every facet of it, including its style information in code. This is not the case when using user controls because you can use Visual Studio's design-time tools to simply drag controls from the toolbox onto the surface of the user control. What's more, once the controls are on the design surface, the developer can use design time tools, such as property editors and other wizards that exist within Visual Studio, to develop and maintain the properties of the control.

You create user interface elements for custom server controls by writing code that runs during the control's Render method. The Render method is a method that is common to all web controls and is called by the ASP.NET runtime to display every web control. In the Render method you write your user interface elements directly into an HtmlTextWriter object that is passed in as a parameter to that method by the ASP.NET Framework.

NOTE   The Render method is a virtual (overridable) member of the System.Web.UI.Control class. This is a class that all server controls inherit from.

For our custom weather web part control, we'll use some logic to randomly produce a weather result for a variable number of days, and then create a weather image for each day of weather. In reality you would likely have some back-end process—such as a web service—that would return actual weather results. Add the code shown in listing 2.3 to your class and build the project to see that everything compiles.

```
private enum WeatherType {   ◁——— Create enum to use in code
    Sunny = 0,
    Rainy = 1,
    Cloudy = 2,
    Unknown = int.MaxValue
}


protected override void Render(HtmlTextWriter writer) {

    Random rand = new Random();


    for (int i = 0; i < this.NumberOfDays; i++) {          Create random
                                                           number between
                                                           0 and 3
        int weatherValue = rand.Next(1000) % 3;   ◁———
        WeatherType todaysWeather = (WeatherType) weatherValue;

                                                       Choose one of 4 images
        Image img = new Image() ;              based on result of random number
        img.ImageUrl =
            string.Format("~/images/{0}.gif", todaysWeather.ToString()) ; ◁┘
        img.AlternateText = "Today's weather";

        writer.AddStyleAttribute(HtmlTextWriterStyle.TextAlign, "center");
        writer.RenderBeginTag(HtmlTextWriterTag.Div);
        img.RenderControl(writer);
        writer.WriteBreak();                    Render weather image
        writer.Write(todaysWeather.ToString());
        writer.RenderEndTag(); // end Div
    }
}
```

In the Render method we have constructed a simple loop that will run for as many days as we have weather to display and, within each loop, a weather picture is produced and rendered.

NOTE   The HtmlTextWriter that we've used to render our weather web part is a customized text writer that simplifies the task of writing HTML and is also capable of rendering specific output based on the device that is targeted. For example, when the page is visited by an older browser, the Html-TextWriter will automatically emit down-level markup.

Adding custom controls

That completes the creation of the custom web part; all that remains is to create a web page to contain and display it—and from now on we'll refer to web pages that contain web parts as "web part pages," to distinguish them from ordinary web pages.

Add a new web page to your project named `CustomWeather.aspx` and, as with all web part pages, add a `WebPartManager` to it. You must also declare the server control to the page by using a Register directive at the head of the page as shown here:

```
<%@ Register TagPrefix="wp" Namespace="WebPartTests" %>
```

When you have registered your controls to the page you can then reference your custom web part within a `ZoneTemplate`—making sure to use the same tag prefix as declared in the register directive:

```
<asp:WebPartZone ID="WebPartZone1" runat="server">
        <ZoneTemplate>
                <wp:CustomWeatherPart
                        ID="CustomWeatherPart1"
                        runat="server"
                    Title="Weather Forecast" />
        </ZoneTemplate>
</asp:WebPartZone>
```

As we saw in figure 2.6, when this page is displayed in a browser, it will render the weather web part with the default four days' worth of weather visible. To change the number of days that are displayed you can just add the `NumberOfDays` property in the markup of the server control or set the value in code. The following snippet shows the property being set within the markup to display an entire week's worth of weather.

```
<wp:CustomWeatherPart
        ID="CustomWeatherPart1"
        runat="server"
        NumberOfDays="7"
        Title="Weather Forecast" />
```

2.3.2   Creating web parts with user controls

We've seen labels and calendars that magically morph into `GenericWebParts` and custom server controls that derive from the `WebPart` class being used to create web parts; but we haven't as yet seen a web part created using a `UserControl`. Being able to use user controls as web parts allows developers to create user interfaces employing exactly the same techniques they applied when creating web pages. This includes having the ability to drag-and-drop controls from the Toolbox onto the design surface. For this reason, user controls may also be easier to understand for someone who is relatively new to ASP.NET and who would benefit from the better design time experience that they would get when creating user controls in Visual Studio 2005. One advantage includes being able to drag controls directly from the Visual Studio 2005 Toolbox onto the surface of user controls as opposed to having to work solely in code.

The weather web part that we built had a very simple user interface and therefore the rendering code and logic were not overly complex; but as the amount of presentation code that is required for a control increases, custom server controls can become quite difficult to create and maintain because you tend to end up writing many lines of code to create the user interface layout.

Displaying calendar appointments

In this next example a user control will be used to create a web part that displays the current date and time. The web page will also display information to the users about upcoming meetings from their calendars. In our example, however, we'll again use hard-coded sample data for simplicity rather than writing the code that would be required to connect to a real calendar. Figure 2.7 shows how this web part will appear when it's complete.

From within your test web project, add a new user control file named `MyCalendar.ascx` to the project. To create the user interface elements necessary to display our control, add the markup that is displayed in listing 2.4 to the control.

Figure 2.7   A user control web part is used to display the current date and time. It also displays information about upcoming meetings for the logged-in user.

Listing 2.4   The HTML to display the calendar user interface

```html
<h3>Current Date and Time</h3>
<div>
    <span style="width: 140px">Date: </span>          ── The Date and Time
    <%= DateTime.Now.ToShortDateString() %>              interface elements
</div>
<div>
    <span style="width: 140px">Time: </span>
    <%= DateTime.Now.ToShortTimeString() %>
</div>


<h3>Upcoming Meetings</h3>
<asp:Repeater ID="rptMeetings" runat="server">
    <ItemTemplate>                                      ── The Calendar
        <p>                                                interface elements
            <b> <%# Eval("MeetingName") %></b>
            <br />
            <span style="font-size: smaller; font-style: italic;">
                <%# Eval("MeetingDateTime") %>
            </span>
        </p>
    </ItemTemplate>
</asp:Repeater>
```

Listing 2.4 creates the presentation layout for the web part. As you can see, there is a Repeater server control named `rptMeetings` that binds to some fields named "MeetingName" and "MeetingDateTime."

Binding dynamic data

I mentioned before that, in a real world situation, the data we are displaying would be coming from a live backend, line-of-business application such as a Customer Relationship (CRM) database that contains information about the contacts and customers of a business. However, in our example, those fields are going to come from some sample data held in a data table. To create the data and bind it to the repeater, switch to source code view and add the code displayed in listing 2.5 to the form:

> **Listing 2.5 Data is created and is bound to the user interface elements of our Calendar web part control**

```
protected override void OnLoad(EventArgs e) {

    base.OnLoad(e);                                    Add columns to
                                                        a DataTable to
    DataTable dt = new DataTable("MeetingData");        store data
    dt.Columns.Add("MeetingName", typeof(string));
    dt.Columns.Add("MeetingDateTime", typeof(DateTime));   Add some rows
                                                            of data to the
    DataRow row1 = dt.NewRow();                             DataTable
    row1["MeetingName"] = "AGM";
    row1["MeetingDateTime"] = DateTime.Now.AddDays(.2);
    dt.Rows.Add(row1);

                                          Add some rows of
    DataRow row2 = dt.NewRow();           data to the DataTable
    row2["MeetingName"] = "Lunch with CEO";
    row2["MeetingDateTime"] = DateTime.Now.AddDays(1.3);
    dt.Rows.Add(row2);

                                          Bind the DataTable
    this.rptMeetings.DataSource = dt;      to the user interface
    this.rptMeetings.DataBind();

}
```

The code in listing 2.5 shows that a `DataTable` is created and two columns are added to it that will contain the information about meetings. Next, dummy data is appended to the table before we finally bind the table to our repeater control, which contains the user interface logic to display the data to the user.

That completes the code for the user control. Now we can create a web page to display it in. Add a page to your test web project and, as with all web part pages, add a `WebPartManager` and a `WebPartZone` to the page.

With the page in design mode, drag the user control that we just created from the Server Explorer onto the web part zone. Listing 2.6 shows how the page appears when displayed in source view. You can see that the designer has added a Register directive for the user control and also added the correct mark-up for the user control into the body of the `ZoneTemplate`. Build and run your page in a browser to view the results. They should appear as they did in figure 2.7.

```
<%@ Register Src="MyCalendar.ascx" TagName="MyCalendar" TagPrefix="uc1" %>

<asp:WebPartZone ID="WebPartZone1" runat="server">
        <ZoneTemplate>
                <uc1:MyCalendar
                        id="MyCalendar1"
                        runat="server"
                        Title="My Calendar" />
        </ZoneTemplate>
</asp:WebPartZone>
```

Now you've seen both options for creating web part controls. That is, you can either create them by using custom server controls and by inheriting from the base `WebPart` class, or you can use user controls. In a very short time we've actually managed to build web parts by using both custom server controls and user controls. Ideally, as you've been working through these samples you've started thinking of all the different types of web parts that a real business might want to have displayed on its portal—employee information, sales data, production figures, profit and loss data, and so on. As we move further into the book, you'll learn that the portal framework comes complete with a catalog to store all these parts. Then you will see that having too many web parts never presents a problem, because they can all be stored and easily retrieved from within the catalog gallery, ready to be displayed on a user's page at any time.

2.4   UNDERSTANDING WEB PART INTERNALS

So far we've seen and created custom controls by deriving from the `WebPart` class and also created `GenericWebPart` controls by adding server controls and user controls directly to web part zones. Now it's time to zoom in on the `WebPart` class. What are the interfaces and properties that the `WebPart` class supports? How do these interfaces and properties allow other portal framework components to interact with it?

An important feature of the `WebPart` class is that it implements interfaces that allow it to describe its properties and behaviors to other members of the portal framework as described in table 2.1.

Table 2.1   The WebPart class implements three interfaces

Interface	Description
IWebPart	Describes the core properties of a web part such as its Title, Description, Height, and Width
IWebActionable	Describes how a web part provides verbs
IWebEditable	Describes a web part that provides custom editor parts for managing some of its properties

Because the WebPart class implements these three interfaces, each of the different members of the portal framework can interact with all web parts. For example, when a page is first displayed, each web part is handed to the web part manager. The manager then uses these interfaces to determine what capabilities a web part has. Therefore, when the manager was handed our weather web part, it didn't have to know anything about what properties we had given it, but by virtue of the fact that the weather web part is a web part, the web part manager knew that the control would have certain distinguishing features such as a Title and Verbs, etc.

In the sections that follow we'll spend time going over each of those three interfaces described in table 2.1 to gain a better understanding of how they are used by the portal framework, and also how we can use them to extend and customize the behavior of web parts that we create.

2.4.1   IWebPart

The IWebPart interface defines the properties that are common to all web parts. The following is a list of each of the properties that are exposed by the IWebPart interface.

- *CatalogIconImageUrl*—the URL of an image that is displayed for a web part when that part is displayed in a catalog of web parts.

- *Description*—Descriptive text about a web part that is displayed for a web part when that part is displayed in a catalog of web parts. This property is also used to display tooltip information about a web part.

- *Subtitle*—Combines with the Title property to form the complete title for a web part control.

- *Title*—the title of a web part control.

- *TitleIconImageUrl*—the URL of an image that is displayed in the web part's title bar.

- *TitleUrl*—a URL to a link containing additional information that is related to the web part.

Implementing the common web part properties

When you create a custom web part by inheriting directly from the WebPart class you will have access to each of the properties listed above in your code because the IWebPart interface is already implemented for you. However, when using user controls as web parts you will need to implement the interface for yourself to be able to code against these properties from within your control. The reason for this is that the user control does not inherit from the WebPart class, and therefore it does not have these properties associated with it. The code shown in listing 2.7 creates a user control that implements the IWebPart interface and provides a custom implementation for each property of that interface.

```
public partial class SampleWebPart : UserControl, IWebPart {

        string CatalogIconImageUrl {
                get { return "~/images/CatalogImage.png"; }
                set { return; }
        }

        string Description {
                get { return "This is the description."; }
                set { return; }
        }

        string Subtitle {
                get { return "Sub-Title."; }
        }

        string Title {
                get { return "Web Part Title"; }
                set { return; }
        }

        string TitleIconImageUrl {
                get { return "~/images/Globe.gif"; }
                set { return; }
        }

        string TitleUrl {
                get { return "~/Default.aspx"; }
                set { return; }
        }
}
```

Figure 2.8 shows how those properties would appear when rendered in a browser.
Notice that the text in the title bar is represented as a clickable link that would take
the user back to the Default.aspx page. This is due to the fact that we specified a
value for the TitleUrl property. Notice as well, that when the mouse is placed over
the title text or the image that is displayed alongside it in the title bar, the description

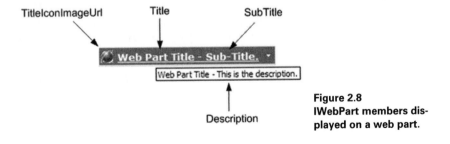

**Figure 2.8
IWebPart members dis-
played on a web part.**

is displayed as a tooltip. Each of the elements you see in the figure 2.8 web part is a direct result of the values we assigned to the interface properties in listing 2.7.

We've just seen the `IWebPart` interface in action. The `IWebPart` interface is the first of the three interfaces that are implemented by web parts. Throughout this section we've learned about the members of this interface and how they affect the look and feel of a web part at runtime. Now we'll look at the next interface that is implemented by all web parts—the `IWebActionable` interface—and see how it is used to add verbs to custom web part controls.

2.4.2 IWebActionable

Earlier in this chapter we saw that each web part has a menu, containing menu items. These menu items are referred as "verbs," and they allow users to perform operations such as closing or minimizing the web part. Every web part has a default set of verbs assigned to it by the zone in which it appears. These verbs are known as *zone verbs* and are common to all web parts—they are Close, Minimize, Restore, Delete, Edit, and Export. Which zone verbs are visible at any given time depends on the current display mode of the web page, the current user, and also the current state of the web part itself. For example, it would not make sense to display the Close verb when the web part is already closed or Restore when it is open.

Displaying custom verbs

In addition to the standard set of zone verbs that each web part is assigned, additional verbs can also be added to the web part's menu. These additional verbs would generally be for the purpose of allowing users to perform custom actions associated with the web part. This can be achieved by using the `WebPartVerb` class to create a verb, and adding that verb to the existing collection of verbs for the part. For example, we could add a verb named Copy Text to a web part that would enable users to copy text from within a web part to another control elsewhere on the page. Verbs are the perfect choice for adding these kinds of discrete operations to web parts because they are conveniently hidden away from the main user interface section of the web part, yet readily accessible to the user.

The `IWebActionable` interface is used to define a property named Verbs that appears on every web part. The Verbs property is responsible for returning all the verbs that belong to a web part, and it is here that we have the opportunity to add custom verbs to the existing collection. Let's demonstrate this by extending the `SampleWebPart` we just created, so that it implements the `IWebActionable` interface. This will allow us to add in our own custom verbs for that web part. The following snippet of code shows how to implement the interface on our `SampleWebPart` class.

```
public partial class SampleWebPart : UserControl, IWebPart, IWebActionable
{

    protected WebPartVerbCollection IWebActionable.Verbs {
```

```
            get {  }
        }
}
```

> **NOTE**   If you are using custom controls for your web parts you will not have to di-
> rectly implement these interfaces because they are already implemented on
> the base `WebPart` class. In that case, your code will differ because you will
> be overriding an existing implementation of the `IWebPart` and `IWeb-`
> `Actionable` members, as opposed to implementing one from scratch.

Next we will add code to the Verbs property to create two custom verbs for our class.
The first verb will allow the user to click on it to display the current time in a label. A
second verb will allow the user to clear the text of the label. The verbs that we add are
also associated with corresponding server-side event handlers named `DisplayTime`
and `ClearTime`. These handlers are the methods that will be called when a user clicks
on the verb. The full code for our custom Verbs implementation can be seen in
listing 2.8, while figure 2.9 shows the two verbs being displayed in a browser at runtime.

Listing 2.8   The Verbs property is used to associate custom verbs with a web part.

```
WebPartVerbCollection IWebActionable.Verbs {
    get {

        WebPartVerb timeVerb = new WebPartVerb(          Create verbs using the
            "TimeVerb1",                                  WebPartVerb class
            new WebPartEventHandler(DisplayTime)
            );

        timeVerb.Text = "Change Display Text";           Associate any text and images
        timeVerb.ImageUrl = "~/images/event.gif";        to display for the verb

        WebPartVerb clearVerb = new WebPartVerb(
            "ClearVerb1",
            new WebPartEventHandler(ClearTime)
            );

        clearVerb.Text = "Clear Display Text";


        return new WebPartVerbCollection(                Add the verbs
new WebPartVerb[] { timeVerb, clearVerb }                to a collection and
);                                                       return them
    }
}
```

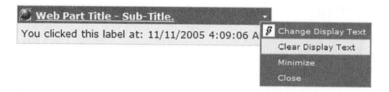

Figure 2.9 Our custom web part verbs appear in the web part's menu along with any existing zone verbs.

The verbs are created and their attributes set. This includes setting the `ImageUrl` and assigning the text that will be displayed to the user. Finally, the verbs are added to a `WebPartVerbCollection` and returned to the portal framework where they are then added to the web part for display.

When the web part is run in a browser, we can see that our custom verbs are added to the verb list along with any zone verbs. Clicking on either of our custom verbs causes the web page to post back to the web server where the associated handler method will be called. A nice enhancement might be to actually disable the Clear Display Text verb if the text has already been cleared from the display.

The WebPartEventHandler delegate

We saw that the `WebPartVerb` class is used to create verbs. When the `WebPart-Verb` class was constructed, two pieces of information were passed as its arguments. This is shown in the following snippet of code:

```
WebPartVerb clearVerb = new WebPartVerb(
    "ClearVerb1",
    new WebPartEventHandler(ClearTime)
    );
```

The first argument specifies what ID to use for the verb control, and the second argument is a `WebPartEventHandler` delegate. The `WebPartEventHandler` delegate is used to associate a method with the click event for the verb, and enforces that the specified method implements the `WebPartEventHandler` interface.

NOTE   A delegate is a special Type in .NET that allows us to specify that methods which handle events must implement a specific interface.

When the verb that we've created is clicked by a user, a postback occurs and a method named `ClearTime` is called to handle the click event. The following piece of code shows the code for the `ClearTime` method:

```
protected void ClearTime(object sender, WebPartEventArgs e) {
    this.lblText.Text = string.Empty;
}
```

Note that the `ClearTime` method implements the `WebPartEventHandler` by taking an object and an instance of the `WebPartEventArgs` class as its arguments.

Handling events in the browser

In addition to handing the click events for verbs on the server, the `WebPartVerb` class also provides a way to specify that a client-side event handler is used. Specifying a client-side event handler for verbs allows us to handle the click event for the verb in the browser, and means that there is no postback to the web server, so no page refresh occurs.

To use client-side event handlers we can simply specify the name of the client-side function when creating the verb. This process is almost identical to the previous process when we used a server-side event handler, except that the name of the handling method is passed into the verb's constructor as a string literal instead of being passed as an instance of the `WebPartEventHandler` class. Listings 2.9 and 2.10 display the code for a Verbs property, which adds a verb that is handled by a client-side Java-Script function named `ClientClickHandler`. You can see that the ID of the control is passed to the function.

Listing 2.9   Verbs can also be associated with client-side event handlers that do not require the item to post back to the web server.

```
WebPartVerbCollection IWebActionable.Verbs {
    get {
        WebPartVerb verb = new WebPartVerb(
            "Verb1",
            "ClientClickHandler('" + this.ClientID + "')"
            );

        verb.Text = "Display Web Part ID";
        verb.ImageUrl = "~/images/event.gif";

        return new WebPartVerbCollection(new WebPartVerb[] {verb});
    }
}
```

Listing 2.10   A client-side JavaScript function is written to handle the verb's click event in the browser

```
<script language="javascript" type="text/javascript">

function ClientClickHandler(webPartID) {
    alert( "You clicked the following web part: " + webPartID + "." ) ;
}

</script>
```

The use of client-side event code can help to create applications that are more dynamic and interactive, because the user is not left waiting for his operations to run while the browser performs a postback to the web server. Performing a server postback requires the entire payload of the page to be round-tripped each time that server communication is required.

Ajax, which stands for Asynchronous JavaScript and XML, is a technique that is being used increasingly by developers to create sites that are highly interactive. By using Ajax, a developer is able to send smaller packets of data through to XML web services without requiring a complete page postbox. The response from these web service calls is then processed in the browser by using client-side JavaScript. The result is twofold; first, only the part of a page that needs to be refreshed is communicated between the server and the user's browser; and second, the web pages appear more responsive because the user is not stalled while waiting for a full page refresh to occur.

I'll defer a fuller discussion about Ajax and web parts until chapter 10, when we explore ways to take advantage of this technique with the portal framework.

2.4.3 IWebEditable

The last of the three interfaces that are implemented by all web parts is IWebEditable. This interface allows developers to associate custom editing controls with their web parts. We'll look at this interface in detail in chapter 5 and again, in even greater detail in chapter 8. For now we'll just look at an example to show why you would need to use this interface. Remember from chapter 1 that we created the simple portal example and that we added an AppearanceEditorPart to an EditorZone to allow some of the properties of the web part to be edited by users at runtime. Figure 2.10 shows us the editor zone with the Appearance-EditorPart displayed.

At runtime, users of our portal can access this AppearanceEditorPart to directly manipulate the appearance of web parts on the page.

Figure 2.10 The Appearance-EditorPart provides user interface elements that allow users to manage the appearance of web parts at runtime.

Creating custom EditorParts

As you can see, the appearance editor provides us with user interface elements for managing the appearance of the web part—such as its Title, its Height, and Width. But what if you need special controls to manage a property of your web part? An example might be if we wanted to provide users of our weather web part with a map that allowed them to select their weather region visually. This is the kind of scenario that the IWebEditable

CHAPTER 2 WEB PARTS: THE BUILDING BLOCKS OF PORTALS

interface is designed to manage, as it provides us with a way of assigning custom editor controls with our web part. To implement the IWebEditable interface, two members must be implemented:

- *The CreateEditorParts method*—which allows you to return a collection of all custom editor parts that you want to associate with your control
- *The WebBrowsableObject property*—which provides a way to return a reference to the underlying control that you wish to expose to your custom editor part.

To associate a custom map editor part with our weather web part, we start by adding code to the CreateEditorParts method which returns the custom editor control that we need to manage our zip code property. The following code shows what is required to return a custom editor part named ZipCodeSelector from the CreateEditorParts method:

```
public override EditorPartCollection CreateEditorParts() {

    EditorPartCollection editorParts = base.CreateEditorParts();

    editorParts.Add(new ZipCodeSelector());
    return editorParts;
}
```

In the ZipCodeSelector editor part, we would include the rendering logic that we want to display when the part is displayed in the editor zone. As with all server controls, this is accomplished by writing some custom code in the Render method. In this case we'll add some code to display an icon and a link that the user can click to launch a larger map selection dialog. How do you do that? Figure 2.11 shows how the editor part would display in the browser when the code in listing 2.11 is executed.

Figure 2.11 shows a custom editor section appearing in the EditorZone. The

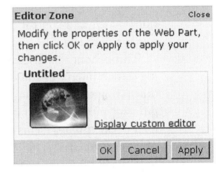

Figure 2.11 The completed editor part is displayed in the editor zone whenever the associated web part is edited.

custom editor section has a title of "Untitled" and contains an icon—a picture of the globe—and a link that allows users to launch a completely custom dialog for selecting zip codes. The custom dialog that is launched could display an interactive map that allowed users to select postcodes in a more visual manner than the standard textbox control normally offered for entering postcodes.

```
protected override void Render(HtmlTextWriter writer) {
    base.Render(writer);
    Image img = new Image();              ◄─── Create image to
    img.ImageUrl = "~/Images/Globe.jpg";       display as an icon
    img.BorderStyle = BorderStyle.None;
    img.Style.Add("margin", "0px 10px");

                                                     Write HTML to
                                                     display for the
    writer.Write(@"<span  style=""font-size:0.8em;"">")  ;  ◄─┘ control
    img.RenderControl(writer);
    writer.Write(
    ➥@"<a href=""javascript: void(0);""
    ➥onclick=""LaunchMapEditor() ;"">"
    ➥);
    writer.Write("Display custom editor");
    writer.Write("</a>");
    writer.Write(@"</span>");
}
```

We could set this up so that when the user clicks on the "Display custom editor" link, a dialog is displayed that provides the user with a simple way to make region selections—such as a control that allows the user to view a map of the world and gives him a way to make selections by clicking on areas of the map.

Throughout this discussion on web part internals, we've seen that by implementing certain interfaces and behaviors, our web parts are able to work together with the other components of the portal framework cohesively. We've also seen that having different pieces of the framework communicating via interfaces provides for a high level of extensibility. This extensibility was demonstrated when we were able to easily pass our own custom editor parts for use in the EditorZone by simply implementing the IWebEditable interface.

Although the discussion in this chapter has focused thus far on extending the functionality of controls, there is one last topic that we should cover before moving on to more work on the Adventure Works Portal. That topic is themes. While themes are not a specific feature of web parts, our discussion on web parts would not be complete without mentioning them. Themes are common to all controls in ASP.NET 2.0, and offer a very flexible way to create websites that, in turn, offer flexible visual styles and layouts.

2.5   APPLYING THEMES AND STYLES

Prior to ASP.NET 2.0, we used Cascading Style Sheets (CSSs) to create sites with highly flexible styles and layouts. We used CSS to create styles and associate them with the HTML elements in your application. This approach works well when we know exactly the sort of HTML we are producing them for. The problem that arises when using ASP.NET 2.0 is that most of the time we are no longer working directly with raw HTML, but instead are working through the abstractions of server controls. For example, consider a standard server control tag for presenting the user with an EditorZone such as the one shown here:

```
<asp:EditorZone ID="EditorZone1" runat="server">
    <ZoneTemplate>
        <asp:PropertyGridEditorPart
            id="PropertyGridEditorPart1"
            runat="server" />
    </ZoneTemplate>
</asp:EditorZone>
```

At runtime, this EditorZone server control is expanded into nearly a hundred lines of HTML markup, representing several hundred individual HTML elements. The difficulty for ASP.NET developers in the past lay in determining exactly what HTML was produced by server controls, and then mapping that to the relevant CSS styles.

Adding styles to controls

In ASP.NET 2.0, the themes feature provides a new way of creating styles for server controls. You can think of themes as style sheets for server controls. It's a good idea when developing any ASP.NET server controls—not just web parts—to extract all the style-related information contained in server controls and move it into a theme file. Having the style information separate from the presentation information provides us with the same level of flexibility that we had when using CSS alone in the past. For example, consider the Google site. It's a very simple site; but when you visit it on holidays or special occasions, it is customized for the occasion. If you go there on Easter, you are likely to see the Easter Bunny hovering just above the search text-box with his basket of Easter eggs at the ready. By grouping the style information regarding images, colors, and so forth into themes, you can easily achieve this kind of customization in your own applications. By creating several themes and applying different themes on different occasions, you could make your web parts look like pumpkins on Halloween!

Visual Studio 2005 supports the themes feature by offering new designer support for it. As shown in figure 2.12, nearly all server controls offer the developer support via the new Common Tasks feature. This feature reveals itself by offering a menu of additional features that can be accessed directly from a control when that control is viewed in design mode. In figure 2.12 we see the common tasks menu being displayed for the WebPartZone control with a single menu item that allows the user to Auto Format that control. Clicking on the menu item displays a dialog that allows the user to apply one of four named formats to that control. Figure 2.13 shows four zones, each with a different format applied to it. The name of the format is shown in the title of the web part.

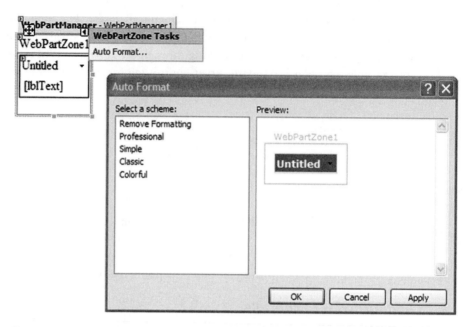

Figure 2.12 The common tasks dialog for the WebPartZone allows a developer to format that control.

When the web part zone is formatted, additional information is added to that control's declaration to describe to the ASP.NET runtime how the styles are to be applied. Listings 2.12 and 2.13 show the markup for a WebPartZone before and after it has style information added to it.

Figure 2.13 The four standard themes that come with ASP.NET 2.0.

Listing 2.12   A WebPartZone server control without any style-related attributes

```
<asp:WebPartZone ID="WebPartZone1" runat="server" />
```

Listing 2.13   A WebPartZone server control after applying a default theme

```
<asp:WebPartZone ID="WebPartZone1" runat="server"
  BorderColor="#CCCCCC" Font-Names="Verdana"
Padding="6">
      <PartChromeStyle BackColor="#EFF3FB" BorderColor="#D1DDF1"
        Font-Names="Verdana" ForeColor="#333333" />
      <MenuLabelHoverStyle ForeColor="#D1DDF1" />
      <EmptyZoneTextStyle Font-Size="0.8em" />
      <MenuLabelStyle ForeColor="White" />
```

```
                <MenuVerbHoverStyle BackColor="#EFF3FB" BorderColor="#CCCCCC"
                BorderStyle="Solid"
                BorderWidth="1px" ForeColor="#333333" />
                <HeaderStyle Font-Size="0.7em" ForeColor="#CCCCCC"
                HorizontalAlign="Center" />
                <MenuVerbStyle BorderColor="#507CD1" BorderStyle="Solid"
                BorderWidth="1px" ForeColor="White" />
                <PartStyle Font-Size="0.8em" ForeColor="#333333" />
                <TitleBarVerbStyle Font-Size="0.6em" Font-Underline="False"
                ForeColor="White" />
                <MenuPopupStyle BackColor="#507CD1" BorderColor="#CCCCCC"
                BorderWidth="1px" Font-Names="Verdana"
                Font-Size="0.6em" />
                <PartTitleStyle BackColor="#507CD1" Font-Bold="True" Font-
                Size="0.8em" ForeColor="White" />
</asp:WebPartZone>
```

As we can see, when the web part zone is formatted it becomes quite verbose because it contains so many style sub-elements. The biggest problem with having all that style information embedded in the page is that, if you decide to change the base look-and-feel for that control throughout your entire site, you have to go through all your pages and change every occurrence. If, however, you have used themes to style your controls, all style information for each of your server controls can be managed from a single place.

Creating themes

Now that we've seen the effect of having all of our style information embedded in pages, we are going to learn how to centralize this style information into a single location by using features known as Themes and Skin files. ASP.NET's feature, Themes, allows us to package style information such as style elements, images, and CSS files into folders. These folders contain

- *Skin Files*—Contain the style information for server controls—such as the style sub-elements shown in listing 1.13
- *Images*—Images that are associated with a specific theme—such as images of pumpkins for a theme named Halloween
- *CSS Files*—CSS information that compliments the colors and styles of the theme

These folders are then stored underneath a new, specially named folder called App_Themes within the application, and the names of the folders created underneath the App_Themes folder become the name of the theme. For example, we might want to create a theme for Valentine's Day, which has images of hearts and style information that is predominantly red. We could create a theme folder named "Valentine" to store the images and style information and images that are required to create the look-and-feel for that theme. This would include the style information for server controls, images that are associated with the theme, as well as any CSS files that we wish to use. Figure 2.14 shows the folder structure for a site that contains a blue Valentine.

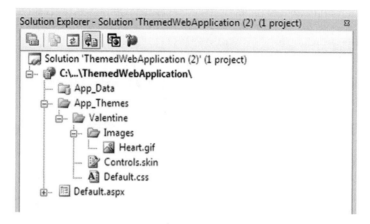

Figure 2.14   This web application contains a theme named "Valentine."

To remove the style information from the web part zone and move it into a theme folder named Valentine, follow these steps:

1   In your test web project, right-click on the solution folder and choose Add Folder, then select Theme Folder as the folder type.

2   Add a folder underneath the theme folder and name it "Valentine."

3   Right-click on the new Valentine theme folder and choose "Add Item" to add the file that will contain the style information for your server controls, and name the skin file "Valentine.skin".

The beauty of skin files is that they contain the definition of a server control in practically the same fashion as the definition would appear in a normal page, except that the theme definitions do not have an ID attribute. By the time all that style information for our web part zone is moved into the skin file, its control definition will be stripped back to its original state as shown in listing 2.12. After moving the style information into the skin file, it will as appear as it is displayed in listing 2.14:

Listing 2.14   Skin files store control definitions containing all of the style information for server controls.

```
<asp:WebPartZone runat="server" BorderColor="#CCCCCC" Font-Names="Verdana"
Padding="6">
        <PartChromeStyle BackColor="#EFF3FB" BorderColor="#D1DDF1" Font-
        Names="Verdana" ForeColor="#333333" />
        <MenuLabelHoverStyle ForeColor="#D1DDF1" />
        <EmptyZoneTextStyle Font-Size="0.8em" />
        <MenuLabelStyle ForeColor="White" />
        <MenuVerbHoverStyle BackColor="#EFF3FB" BorderColor="#CCCCCC"
        BorderStyle="Solid"
        BorderWidth="1px" ForeColor="#333333" />
```

```
          <HeaderStyle Font-Size="0.7em" ForeColor="#CCCCCC"
          HorizontalAlign="Center" />
          <MenuVerbStyle BorderColor="#507CD1" BorderStyle="Solid"
          BorderWidth="1px" ForeColor="White" />
          <PartStyle Font-Size="0.8em" ForeColor="#333333" />
          <TitleBarVerbStyle Font-Size="0.6em" Font-Underline="False"
          ForeColor="White" />
          <MenuPopupStyle BackColor="#507CD1" BorderColor="#CCCCCC"
          BorderWidth="1px" Font-Names="Verdana"
          Font-Size="0.6em" />
          <PartTitleStyle BackColor="#507CD1" Font-Bold="True" Font-
          Size="0.8em" ForeColor="White" />
</asp:WebPartZone>
```

As we can see, this skin file definition for the `WebPartZone` control looks almost identical to the `WebPartZone` control definition that we saw in listing 2.13. However, the difference is that this information is now stored in a single place—the skin file—and that all `WebPartZone` controls can now use this style without having to each have their own embedded style sub-elements. One more step is required to apply a theme within an application; you must configure the application so that it knows which theme to use. This configuration can be constructed either at page level or at application level in the `web.config` file. Both of these options are shown in listing 2.15.

> **Listing 2.15 Configuration entries for themes can be set at either page or configuration file level.**

```
<%@ Page Language="C#" Theme="Blue" %>          ◁──────   Declaring a theme
                                                          at page level

<system.web>                                     Declaring a theme
        <pages theme="Blue" />                   at configureation
</system.web>                                     file level
```

The benefit of using the web configuration file to declare themes is that you are required to declare it in only one place, whereas declaring it in each page would result in many declarations. Having the theme declared in many different places makes the code more difficult to maintain, because a developer would have to locate each place that it was declared when making changes to the theme.

Now that you better understand web parts and have worked with them a bit, let's apply your new skills to the Adventure Works Cycles business.

2.6 ADDING WEB PARTS TO THE ADVENTURE WORKS SOLUTION

In chapter 1 we created a data layer so that we could connect to SQL Server 2005 and retrieve information about the Adventure Works Cycles business. In this chapter we'll start putting that data to good use as we build the beginnings of a portal application based on the Adventure Works business. The portal that we will build throughout the course of this book will be built with small incremental steps. At the end of each chapter we'll apply a concept we've learned by integrating an implementation of that concept into the portal. While each step may, in itself seem small, by the end of the book we will have created a portal that is filled with the features that clients have come to expect of portal-style applications.

To implement the concepts you've learned in this chapter, let's get back to your job at Adventure Works. Today the HR department has asked you to develop a small website that displays some of their line of business data—such as a list of employees, departments, and information about the latest job candidates. They've specified that initially the portal should be able to display the following data:

- A listing of all departments with employee numbers listed against each one
- A listing of all employees for a given department

As an applications developer for Adventure Works you've got ASP.NET 2.0 installed and you are all geared up and ready for the task.

After discussions with the users, it is clear to you that while they have an immediate need for just these few features, their longer-term requirements are likely to be much larger. For this reason, you make the decision to use the web portal framework to build features as standalone components. Over time there will be the ability to harness the extensibility of the framework through features such as web part connections and verbs, to leverage components that we build today into tomorrow's features.

NOTE To complete this exercise you will need to create a project for the Adventure Works application. If you are comfortable with project creation and some of the new ASP.NET 2.0 features such as master pages, themes, etc., then you might just want to grab the project from the resources for this chapter that come with the book. If you would like to create the project for yourself to see how to implement these new features, you can complete the walk-through titled "Creating the Adventure Works Project" in the appendix.

Displaying all departments

We'll address the first feature request, which was to create a web part that displays a listing of all departments from the Adventure Works database. Open the Adventure Works project and create a new folder named `WebParts` and add to it a new user control file named `DepartmentListingPart.ascx`.

With the user control in design mode, add a `GridView` server control from the toolbox by dragging it onto the design surface. From the associated `GridView` tasks, choose the `<New Data Source>` option so that we can configure a data source to return the data that we need. At this time the Data Source Configuration Wizard starts up and the Choose a Data Source Type screen is displayed as shown in figure 2.15. We've already created a data access layer to perform our data operations, so from this screen we choose the Object data source type and press OK.

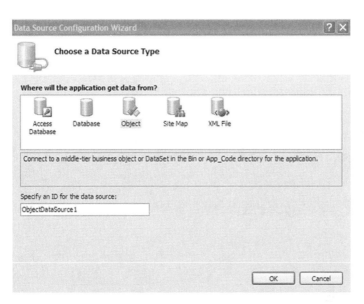

Figure 2.15   The first step in the data source configuration wizard is to specify what type of data source we are binding to.

The next screen in the wizard displays a listing of classes, allowing us to choose which business object contains the method to bind to the GridView control. This screen is displayed in figure 2.16. Select the AW.Portal.Data.DataLayer class and then press OK.

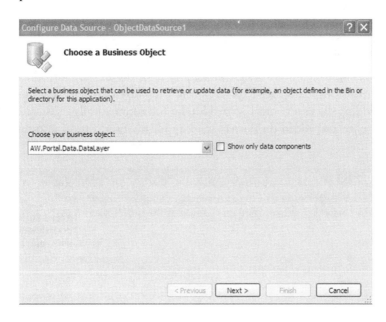

Figure 2.16
When using the object data source control, we get to specify which class will provide the data.

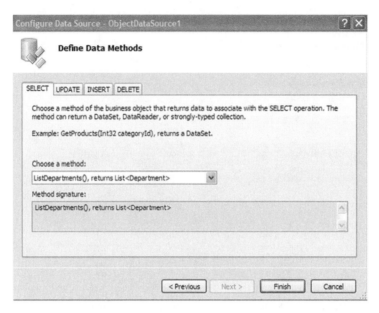

Figure 2.17 The wizard allows us to choose which methods of the object data source will perform data operations such as Select, Update, Insert, and Delete.

With the business object chosen, all that remains is to choose which method of the object will provide us with the data. The last screen of the wizard that we'll be using allows us to select the `ListDepartments` method and press Finish. This last screen is displayed in figure 2.17.

Now the wizard has all of the information it needs to create a data source control that can be bound to the `GridView`, and we can create a page in which to display our control. To add this web part to the web part page we created earlier, switch the `Default.aspx` page into design mode and drag the `DepartmentListingPart` user control from the Server Explorer on to the `WebPartZone`. Listing 2.16 shows that by adding the user control, Visual Studio has automatically registered the control with the page and added the correct markup for the user control into the zone template for us.

Listing 2.16 The DepartmentListingPart

```
<%@ Register Src="WebParts/DepartmentListingPart.ascx"
  TagName="DepartmentListingPart" TagPrefix="uc1" %>     ⟵  Added Register
                                                            declaration for
                                                            user control
...

<asp:WebPartZone ID="WebPartZone1" runat="server">
      <ZoneTemplate>
```

```
    <ucl:DepartmentListingPart
            ID="DepartmentListingPart1"
            runat="server"
            Title="Departments" />
    </ZoneTemplate>       .
</asp:WebPartZone>
```

Added user control
to zone template

The register tag that was added by Visual Studio is
known as the @ Register directive. This directive is
included in ASP.NET web pages so that a tagname
and tagprefix can be associated with user controls
and custom server controls. You can see that the
tagname (DepartmentListingPart) and tagprefix (ucl) could then be useful in declaring the
department listing user control within the page.

We can now run the application and see that
the web part is displayed with a listing of departments as shown in figure 2.18. To do this, right-
click on the Default.aspx file and choose "View
in Browser."

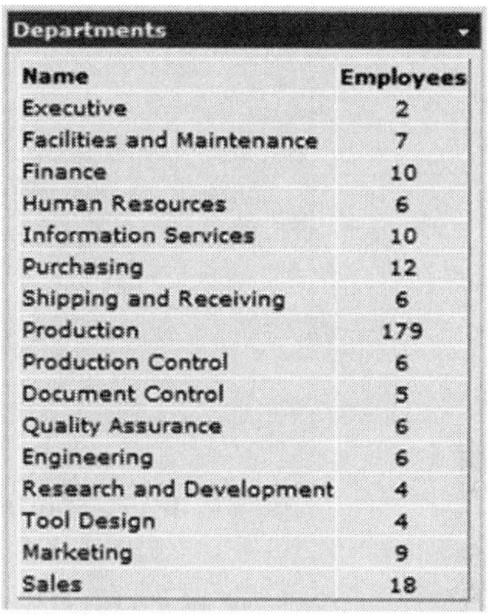

Departments	▾
Name	**Employees**
Executive	2
Facilities and Maintenance	7
Finance	10
Human Resources	6
Information Services	10
Purchasing	12
Shipping and Receiving	6
Production	179
Production Control	6
Document Control	5
Quality Assurance	6
Engineering	6
Research and Development	4
Tool Design	4
Marketing	9
Sales	18

**Figure 2.18   The DepartmentList-
ing web part shows a listing of the
departments within the Adventure
Works business with the number
of employees shown against each
department.**

Creating an
Employees web part

Now that we have a listing of all departments, we
may turn our attention to the second requirement
we were given—to display a listing of employees for a given department. We'll again
create this listing as a web part and again be using the GridView control to display
the data in a list. Right-click on the WebParts folder and add to it a new user control file named EmployeeListingPart.ascx.

With the user control in design mode, add a GridView control and choose the
<New Data Source> option. Walk through the Data Source Configuration wizard, in
a manner similar to the steps we took for the previous control, and bind the Grid-
View to the ListEmployees method of the data layer class. Finally, add the web
part to the RightZone in the web part page.

When viewed in the designer, your page should be similar to the page shown in
figure 2.19. You can now view the portal by right-clicking on the Default.aspx
file and choosing "View in Browser."

The full source code for the portal at this stage can be found in the resources that
accompany this book.

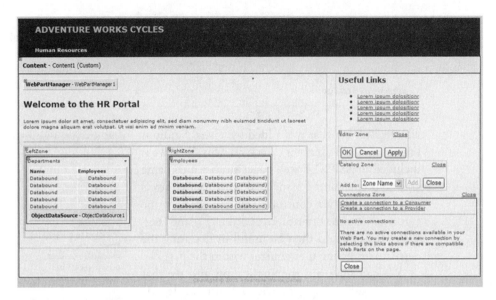

Figure 2.19   The portal when viewed in design mode within Visual Studio 2005

2.7   *SUMMARY*

In this chapter we've covered a stretch of important ground in learning about these fundamental portal components; but perhaps even more important is the fact that we now have our portal up and running. As we move through the book, in each chapter we will add small additional touches to the portal as we learn new concepts. By the end of the last chapter you will see that the sum of all these small additions is an interesting portal with many useful features.

Throughout this chapter we covered some fundamental lessons about web parts and, in particular, the `WebPart` server control, and we then added them to our own portal. We have demystified some of what happens when controls are added to web zones and learned about the special `GenericWebPart` control. We also saw how to use verbs to link additional operations to our web parts.

Finally, we started work on the Adventure Works portal application by creating the Visual Studio 2005 project and then adding our first web parts for the HR department. These web parts were simple, but we're not finished with them yet. The next chapter dips into web part connections. With this knowledge we'll be positioned to connect our two web parts and have the department part act as a filter for the employee part. This will allow us to complete the requirement that the employees be viewable by department.

CHAPTER 3

Using web part connections

3.1 DISSECTING CONNECTIONS

Connections are powerful features of the portal framework that allow data to be exchanged between web parts. Connecting web parts can be fun because it provides you with an opportunity to think up interesting ways of presenting data to end-users. In this chapter we will learn about connections and the web part controls—such as the WebPartConnection—that make it possible for connections to occur. We'll see that there are several ways to connect web parts, and we'll also learn how to create and configure transformers to connect web parts that expose different interfaces.

Let's look at an example that offers a glimpse into the power of web part connections. Suppose that you are browsing the Adventure Works portal and come across a page displaying a staff listing. When you select a row on the listing, other connected web parts on the page update their information to display data that is related to that selection. For example, the page might contain a web part that displays images. When you select employee details, the page could update to display a picture of that employee. Another web part might display the key performance indicators (KPIs) for that staff member, while yet another could display a summary of that employee's projects. Having web parts that can automatically remain synchronized with each other provides users with a more useful view of data.

All connections involve two web parts. One part provides data that can be of any type, such as fields, rows, lists, or even complex data types. This part is referred to as the *provider* web part. The other web part receives the data and is referred to as the *consumer* web part. Sitting in the middle of a connection is an optional control called a *transformer*.

Transformers provide a way to transfer data between providers and consumers that do not share a common data type. Think back to our introductory example in chapter 1—we looked at how connections allow multiple web parts to communicate. Connections work when each web part is able to communicate via data that is of a common type. When data is not common among web parts, it is the job of a transformer to transform the data into a format that can be accepted by one web part or another—thus allowing two-way data communications to occur between any web parts, regardless of whether they share common data interfaces or not.

3.1.1 The Master/Details scenario

The following section takes a look at the common scenarios that connections was designed to support, such as the Master/Details scenario and the Parent/Child scenario.

The Master/Details scenario provides a way for users to make selections from a list of items, while another part displays more detailed information about the selected item. Figure 3.1 shows the steps of this selection process.

1 A web part (A) displays a list of expenses for an employee.

2 The employee makes a selection from the list. The selected item is shown as the row, which is highlighted in grey.

3 The connection (B) passes information about the selection to another web part.

4 The other web part (C) displays the details of the expensed item—such as the date of the purchase and the name of the vendor.

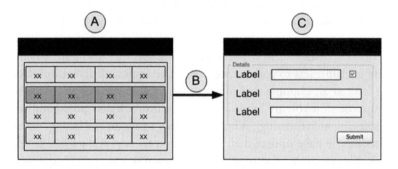

Figure 3.1   In the Master/Details scenario a row of data is selected in one web part and the details of that single item are displayed in another web part.

3.1.2 The Parent/Child scenario

The Parent/Child connection scenario is similar to the Master/Details scenario, except that for each selected item there can be more than one related record. Figure 3.2 provides an example of this.

1 A web part (A) displays a listing of departments.

2 The employee makes a selection from the list. The selected item is shown as the row highlighted in grey.

3 The connection (B) passes information about the selection to another web part.

4 A second web part (C) then displays a list of all employees for the selected department.

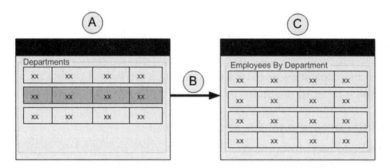

Figure 3.2   The Parent/Child scenario allows all the related rows to be shown for a single selection.

Making data easier to understand

You will often want to display different views of data to allow your users to digest it more easily. For example, applications that display accounting data often contain a great deal of information that is difficult to interpret from a single glance. Using web parts, you might allow the user to select segments of that data and then have another part that could display it in a friendlier view—such as a graph or some other more visual format. Figure 3.3 presents such a scenario.

1 A web part (A) displays profit and loss data for one of the Adventure Works departments.

2 A finance officer selects an item from the list. The selected item is shown as the row highlighted in grey.

3 The connection (B) passes information about the selection to another web part.

4 A second web part (C) presents the data from the selected row as a pie chart that is much easier to understand.

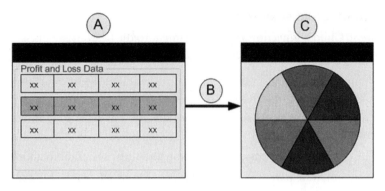

Figure 3.3 Presenting statistical data in a graphical format makes it easier to understand.

In figure 3.3, we can clearly see how the chart provides users with a simple way to understand the complex data from the web part on the left side. Separating these two displays into separate web parts simplifies the logic in each web part, and therefore makes them easier to maintain.

Creating components for specialization

To shield end users from the complexity associated with modern applications, clever people spend many hours in the difficult task of building and maintaining applications, and maintenance naturally becomes more complicated as applications grow in size. To simplify the development and maintenance of feature-rich applications, it is common to break things down into smaller components that perform specific suboperations within a larger scope of work. Having specific operations separated into individual components can make them much easier to extend and modify, because you only have to understand the behavior of a system at the component level instead of having to understand it as a whole.

Consider the example in figure 3.4 which is typical of how dynamic, data-driven applications work. It shows a page for displaying shopping cart details to a user.

The page shown in figure 3.4 might contain the following parts for displaying information relevant to data contained within the cart:

- "Related Items" that entice users to buy other goodies based on items they have already selected
- A navigational aid allowing the user to continue shopping or offering a link to proceed through to checkout, such as the component shown in the middle on the left side of figure 3.4.
- Other advanced operations offered to the user such as the ability to display images of the cart items as a slideshow, similar to the component shown at the bottom of figure 3.4.

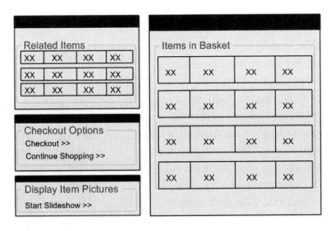

Figure 3.4 Breaking a large user interface down into smaller, individual components provides a way to reduce the complexity in a user interface.

As you can see from each of these types of information displayed to the buyer, when the overall operation is extended, things can become complicated quickly. If we were to build each of these pieces of information into our page, then the page would become very complex and would involve a great deal of presentation code and logic for synchronizing the display of each piece. Alternatively, we can separate each piece of information into individual web parts and use connections to orchestrate the data flows between the web parts. This makes it possible for each web part to perform just a single operation and remain relatively simple.

When web parts and connections are used, each separate component can feed off a single set of data, each component can respond to changes made in other components, and each component can update its display accordingly. For example, removing all items in the current basket might force the Checkout Options web part to hide the checking-out link from the user. Overall, this symbiotic relationship between components extends the usefulness of each individual part, and allows for efficient code reuse, while also extending the life of web parts.

Having seen some of the scenarios that require connections to work—the department/employee listing scenario, the financial scenario, and the shopping cart scenario—we can now appreciate the kinds of operations in which connections are used. Without connections, the code that is required to create those scenarios can be extensive, and programmers who create the requisite complex code often make mistakes. By using connections, unnecessary complexity is avoided, and we are free to focus on other requirements. It's now time to apply what we've seen so far, and learn how connections really work.

3.2 CREATING SIMPLE CONNECTIONS

To put into action the concepts from the first part of this chapter, we are going create two web parts and connect them. One web part is a provider web part that is used by an accountant to enter end-of-year financial data. This year-end data is to be used in a report being prepared for the company's board and its shareholders—for the sake of simplicity, the data is entered as a range of comma-separated numbers. This data is then exposed via a connection to a consumer web part, which displays a graphical representation of it. Figure 3.5 shows what our example will look when it is completed.

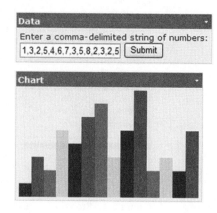

Figure 3.5 As you work through the example in this section, you will be performing steps that produce this result—a chart that displays financial data in an easy-to-read graphical format

Web part connections communicate using interfaces, which are the programmatic way of defining a contract for data that components must adhere to. How does this work? One web part provides data of a certain data type. When another web part exists that is capable of consuming that type of data, a connection between them can be made. So, the first thing that we must do for our example is to create an interface that can be used as the data contract for exchanging the data. The following snippet of code shows the interface that defines the data contract for our connection:

```
public interface INumbersInterface {
        int[] Numbers { get; }
}
```

Creating a Connection Provider

Our provider web part will be a user control named NumberProvider.ascx and, as you saw in figure 3.5, the user control has a very simple interface containing just a TextBox and a Button. To create the web part, add the user control to your sample project and give it the mark-up contained in the following code snippet.

```
Enter a comma-delimited string of numbers: <br />
<asp:TextBox ID="TextBox1"
        runat="server"
        Text="1,3,2,5,4,6,7,3,5,8,2,3,2,5" />

<asp:Button ID="Button1"
        runat="server"
Text="Submit" />
```

As you can see, this web part has a text box to allow the user to enter data, and a button that will force the web page to submit data back to the web server (a postback).

It's during this postback that the number data will be passed to the consumer web part via the connection. Switch the `NumberProvider.ascx` user control into source code view, so that the code to implement the connection provider logic can be added. To make this switch, we'll first implement the `INumbersInterface` interface that will be passed via the connection. To implement the interface, a public property named `Numbers` is added that exposes an array of integers; this data is derived from the input supplied by the user. Listing 3.1 shows how to implement the interface on the user control class.

Listing 3.1 The provider web part implements our interface, thereby exposing the Numbers property.

```
public partial class NumberProvider :
    System.Web.UI.UserControl, INumbersInterface {   ◁─┐ Implement the
                                                        │ interface
    public int[] Numbers {
        get {
            string[] strings = this.TextBox1.Text.Split(    │ Convert the user's
                new char[] { ',' },                         │ entry into an
                StringSplitOptions.RemoveEmptyEntries        │ array of strings
                );

            int[] numbers = new int[strings.Length];

            for (int i = 0; i < strings.Length; i++) {       │ Convert the array
                int tmp = 0;                                 │ of strings into an
                int.TryParse(strings[i], out tmp);           │ array of integers
                numbers[i] = tmp;
            }
            return numbers;
        }
    }
}
```

The `Numbers` property takes the text that has been entered by a user and splits it into an array of strings. The string array is then converted to an array of numbers and returned.

At runtime, the web part framework learns which web parts expose connection information by finding methods marked with a `ConnectionProvider` attribute. It is the method marked with this attribute that is responsible for returning the connection data. In our case, because we implemented the interface on the control itself, we simply return a reference to the control from the method, as you can see in the code that follows:

```
[ConnectionProvider("Number Provider", "default")]
public INumbersInterface GetProviderData() {
    return this;
}
```

That's all there is to creating the provider control, and we can now move on to create another user control.

3.2.1 Creating a connection consumer

To begin the process of creating another user control to act as the consumer web part, add another user control and name it `NumberConsumer.ascx`. This control must provide a method marked with the `ConnectionConsumer` attribute, so that the web part framework knows that it can act as the consumer within a connection. The method that is marked with the ConnectionConsumer attribute must be able to accept data of the correct type so that this web part meets its obligations to the data contract. Our class with the consumer method and a private field named _data is shown in the code that follows. Note that the field _data is used to store the data when it is received.

```
public partial class NumberConsumer : System.Web.UI.UserControl {

        INumbersInterface _data = null;

        Color[] _colors = new Color[] {        Declare some colors to
            Color.Blue,                        display on the chart
            Color.Green,
            Color.Red,
            Color.Gold
            };

        [ConnectionConsumer("Text Consumer")]
        public void SetProviderData(INumbersInterface providerData) {
                this._data = providerData;
        }
    }
```

At runtime the connection data is passed to the method marked with the `Connec-tionConsumer` attribute. In our implementation we simply grab it and store it in a field. The field will be accessed just prior to the page being rendered (the pre-rendering phase of the page) when we use the connection data to generate a bar graph to display to the user.

It's important to understand why we stored the data that was passed into the consumer web part and didn't use it until the pre-rendering phase. For any given web page, many connections could be in play. Immediately after the connections are initialized, the connection data is passed around to the web parts that are configured to receive data of the correct type. Because a web part can have multiple connections, you could be handed data from more than one connection or even handed the same piece of data more than once. Therefore, it is important not to use the data as soon as it is handed to your web part. Instead, store the data and wait until the pre-rendering phase of the page because, by this time, all the connections will have finished passing their data and the state will be finalized for that request.

If you made user interface changes at the time that you received the connection data, you would have no way of knowing whether all connections on the page had finished passing their data. This could lead to making assumptions that are incorrect; or you might end up performing the same set of operations more than once, if you received data for a second time.

To create the bar graph shown in figure 3.5 on page 70, we'll use a standard HTML table. When we loop through the numbers in the _data field we can simply color the cell if it is lower than the number we are examining. For example, if our table is 10 rows high and we want to display a bar for the number 3, we'll simply color in the bottom 3 rows of that column. Listing 3.2 shows the code for the OnPreRender override method.

```
protected override void OnPreRender(EventArgs e) {
    if (this._data != null) {

Table tbl = new Table();

        int maxNum = 0;
        for (int i = 0; i < _data.Numbers.Length; i++) {      Find the
            if (_data.Numbers[i] > maxNum)                     maximum value
                maxNum = data.Numbers[i];
        }
                                                    Cap the maximum
        maxNum = Math.Min(maxNum, 10);    <──────┘  value at 10

        for (int i = 0; i < maxNum; i++) {

            TableRow row = new TableRow();     Create a row
            tbl.Rows.Add(row);                 for each value

            for (int j = 0; j < _data.Numbers.Length; j++) {   Create a column
                TableCell cell = new TableCell();              for data item
                cell.Text = " ";

    if (_data.Numbers[j] >= (maxNum - i))  <──────  Color the cell if required
                    cell.BackColor = _colors[j % _colors.Length];

    row.Cells.Add(cell);
            }
        }

        this.Controls.Add(tbl);
    }
}
```

The method that is shown in listing 3.2 uses two loops to draw up a grid for the chart. An outer loop is responsible for writing out the rows for the grid, while an inner loop creates the cells within each row. The colored bars of the chart are achieved by applying a background color to cells.

The final task is to create the page that will host the web parts and then to wire up the connection between them. To do this, create a page named StaticConnectionsTest.aspx and open it in design view. Add a WebPartZone control and then drag the two user controls, NumberProvider.ascx and NumberConsumer.ascx, into it. The code for the web part zone should now look like the following:

```
<asp:WebPartZone ID="WebPartZone1" runat="server">
    <ZoneTemplate>
        <ucl:NumberProvider ID="NumberProvider1"
                runat="server" Title="Data" />
        <uc2:NumberConsumer ID="NumberConsumer1"
                runat="server" Title="Chart" />
    </ZoneTemplate>
</asp:WebPartZone>
```

As with all web part pages, ensure that you have a WebPartManager at the top of the page, and within it declare a StaticConnections element. The StaticConnections element can contain WebPartConnection declarations for web parts within the page. The code with the necessary connection information to create a connection between our provider and consumer web parts is as follows:

```
<asp:WebPartManager ID="WebPartManager1" runat="server">
    <StaticConnections>
        <asp:WebPartConnection ID="cnn"
                ConsumerID="NumberConsumer1"
                ProviderID="NumberProvider1"
        />
    </StaticConnections>
</asp:WebPartManager>
```

Run the example and notice that the chart is able to change its state based upon the data number that is entered into the textbox. Congratulations, you've just created your first web part connection! I'm sure that even such a simple example has sparked your interest to understand exactly what is happening, and how the data is being passed around. To begin the discovery process, let's lift the hood and take a look at the components that make up a web part connection.

3.3   SORTING OUT CONNECTION TYPES

Now you're ready to take a closer look at connections and dissect the individual pieces. Doing so will help you understand what options you have with connections and how you can work with them programmatically. We'll also learn how to connect web parts that don't even exist at design time by using connections known as dynamic connections. Before we look at dynamic connections, let's start with the other type of connection: static connections.

CHAPTER 3   USING WEB PART CONNECTIONS

3.3.1 Static connections

We saw that when we configured the static connection, we had to define information about a provider endpoint and a consumer endpoint. When the page is initialized—actually just after initialization—the WebPartManager uses the connection configuration information to activate all the connections for the page. During this activation period, the WebPartManager checks to ensure that both of the connection participants (the provider and the consumer) are enabled, and then the WebPartManager grabs the data from the provider and hands it to the consumer. To be able to pass data between the endpoints, the manager must know which method to use—which is where information provided by the ConnectionConsumer and the Connection-Provider attributes is used. With those attributes in place, the WebPartManager can determine which method should receive the data it passes. It makes this determination by scanning the web part at runtime and looking for the method.

Identifying connection endpoints

In our simple connection example where we connected the SimpleConsumer and the SimpleProvider web parts, each web part exposed just a single consumer or provider method (endpoint), but this is not a limitation. Although this is not a common occurrence, each web part can actually expose more than just one consumer or provider endpoint. In the case where a web part has multiple consumer endpoints or multiple provider endpoints, we must pass additional information to the portal framework so that it knows which endpoint to associate with a connection. To do this, we must first give each endpoint an ID. This is done by specifying an additional piece of information in the ConnectionProvider or ConnectionConsumer attribute. The ConnectionProvider attribute in the code that follows contains two arguments:

- The first argument has a value of Number Provider and represents the description of the provider.
- The second argument has a value of MyID and represents its ID. The MyID value will be referred to when creating the connection information.

The following snippet of code shows the ConnectionProvider attribute being applied to a method named GetProviderData:

```
[ConnectionProvider("Number Provider", "MyID")]
public INumbersInterface GetProviderData() {
        return this;
}
```

The ID of the connection provider can now be specified via the ProviderConnectionPointID property when you create the WebPartConnection information as shown in the code that follows. Likewise, there is a ConsumerConnectionPointID property that allows you to target a specific consumer endpoint.

```
<asp:WebPartManager ID="WebPartManager1" runat="server">
      <StaticConnections>
            <asp:WebPartConnection
                  ID="cnn"
                  ConsumerID="NumberConsumer1"
                  ProviderID="NumberProvider1"
                  ProviderConnectionPointID="MyID"
            />
      </StaticConnections>
</asp:WebPartManager>
```

If your web part does expose multiple consumer or provider endpoints and you fail to specify the identity of the endpoint when you configure the connection, the web part framework will look for an endpoint named "default," as this is the standard name given to provid-

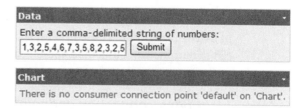

Figure 3.6   The error shown to the user when an endpoint cannot be ascertained at runtime.

ers by the web part framework when the providers are created with no specific ID. If the web part fails to locate a provider with that name, that endpoint will not be created, and the ConnectErrorMessage will be displayed on the web part associated with the endpoint created for the connection. Figure 3.6 shows how the error would appear to an end user.

All the connections we've seen so far are referred to as "static connections"—connections that are declared in the StaticConnections section of a WebPartManager. The participants of static connections are always known at design time and hardwired so that they do not change. Once they have been declared, the only attribute of static connections that can be altered is whether or not the connection is enabled. Static connections always have a shared scope—meaning that any changes made to a static connection affect every user and not just the user making the change.

Another kind of connection exists which allows connections to be discovered and created at runtime—dynamic connections. As described in the next section, dynamic connections add a great deal of flexibility to a portal because not all of their details need to be known in advance.

3.3.2   Dynamic connections

When using static connections, we saw that we needed to know the details of the web parts which were going to be participating in the connection in advance. That works well when the web parts are declared within a page, but what happens when they are not? For example, how do we connect web parts that are dynamically loaded at runtime from a CatalogZone? The answer can be found in dynamic connections.

The ConnectionsZone

Dynamic connections are not declared within the StaticConnections element, but instead require the use of their own zone called a ConnectionsZone. The ConnectionsZone provides a way for users to create and manage all the facets of connections at runtime. Like other zones—such as the EditorZone and the CatalogZone—the ConnectionsZone is only visible when the page is in a specific display mode. For the ConnectionsZone that mode is known as connect mode.

NOTE   There are five standard modes that a web page can enter into: BrowseDisplayMode, CatalogDisplayMode, ConnectDisplayMode, DesignDisplayMode, and EditDisplayMode. These are described in greater detail in chapter 4.

The purpose of the ConnectionsZone is to display all the user interface elements required to dynamically discover connection endpoints and connect them together at runtime. The code that follows shows a version of the page we used in the static connections example. In this example, however, the code has been changed to support dynamic connections instead of static connections.

```
<asp:WebPartManager ID="WebPartManager1" runat="server" />

<asp:WebPartZone ID="WebPartZone1" runat="server">
        <ZoneTemplate>
                <uc1:NumberProvider ID="NumberProvider1" runat="server" />
                <uc2:NumberConsumer ID="NumberConsumer1" runat="server" />
        </ZoneTemplate>
</asp:WebPartZone>

<asp:ConnectionsZone ID="ConnectionsZone1" runat="server" />
```

Notice that the WebPartManager no longer contains a StaticConnections element and that the page now has a ConnectionsZone added to it. If we run the page at this point, the chart that we originally saw in figure 3.5 on page 70 will no longer be displayed. This is because we removed the static connection that was providing it with data. We'll have to use the ConnectionsZone to dynamically configure the connection between the data part and the chart part before it is displayed. Remember that to display the connections tool zone, the page must first be in "connect" mode, so for the time being we'll write hard-coded logic into the load method of the page to make sure that it is. The following displays the code that is required to set the page into connect mode.

```
public partial class DynamicConnectionsPage : System.Web.UI.Page {

        protected override void OnLoad(EventArgs e) {
                WebPartManager1.DisplayMode =
        WebPartManager.ConnectDisplayMode;
        }
}
```

By re-running the page now, we see that, even though the page is in connect mode, the connections zone is still not visible. To display the connections zone we must use the verbs associated with the web part to choose the connect verb. Clicking on the connect verb will display the connections zone and allow the connection information for that particular part to be configured. If the web part cannot participate in connections then it will not have a connect verb.

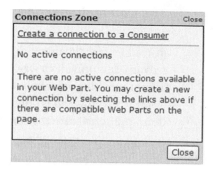

Figure 3.7   The appearance of the first screen of the ConnectionsZone depends on the connection state of the web part for which it is being displayed.

The `ConnectionsZone` has several screens that a wizard allows us to cycle through to perform connection operations. When you initially display the connections zone for a part, the appearance of its first screen will depend on whether the selected web part is currently connected to any other parts and whether it is connected as a provider, a consumer, or both. Figure 3.7 shows the first screen rendered by the connections zone. In the figure, a link is displayed for creating a connection to a consumer web part. This means that the web part being configured exposes a provider endpoint but is not currently connected.

If the web part we are configuring also exposed a consumer endpoint, there would be a second link displayed to "Create a connection to a Provider." The first screen is shown when the connection zone is in its default state. This state is known as the `ExistingConnections` mode. There are actually four possible, standard modes:

- `ExistingConnections`
- `ConnectToConsumer`
- `ConnectToProvider`
- Configuring Transformer

Each mode has its own screen to display the configuration options that are relevant for that mode. As you can probably imagine, clicking on the link titled "Create a connection to a Provider" will switch the state of the connection zone from `ExistingConnections` to `Connect-ToProvider`.

Figure 3.8 shows what happens when you click on the "Create a connection to a Consumer" link to display the connection

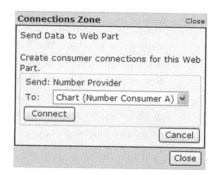

Figure 3.8   The ConnectToConsumer screen allows the user to select the web part that will be the consumer from a list of web parts.

zone in its `ConnectToConsumer` mode. You can see that Title says "Send Data to Web Part," thus indicating that we just need to select which part will be receiving the data for that part.

If we wished to provide a totally custom view for any of the wizard screens, we could do so by creating a control and deriving it from the `ConnectionsZone` class. We could then provide code in the `RenderBody` method of that class to provide our own, unique user interface views.

3.4   USING TRANSFORMERS

At this point you understand that connections rely upon both web parts—Provider and Consumer—to implement the same data contract. Now imagine yourself in a pickle—you've purchased a charting web part to display your accounting data in a visual manner from a third-party supplier, and you've purchased a custom grid web part from another vendor to display profit and loss data. It's extremely unlikely that those two vendors even know about each other, let alone share a common endpoint contract. So without the ability to pass the spreadsheet data to the charting web part, any connections that those vendors added to their parts would be useless.

Transformers provide us with a way to climb out of this hole. Using transformers, you can connect web parts that are incompatible. You can use a transformer to write code that takes data from the accounting part and exposes it as the data type that is expected by the charting web part.

Figure 3.9 shows an example of how transformers act as a bridge for connection data that is incompatible. In the diagram we see that data is received form the provider web part (A) and transformed into different data type that is expected by the consumer web part (B).

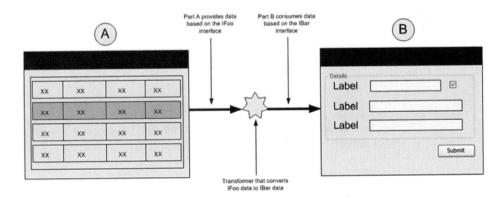

Figure 3.9   A transformer is a control that sits in the middle of a connection and transforms connection data from one type into another type.

Let's take a further look at what makes up a transformer, in order to learn more about how it manages the transformations. We'll also discover how to create our own transformers. Creating a custom transformer is something that only needs to be done when a very high level of specificity is required, because the portal framework provides us with some generic transformers that come as a standard part of ASP.NET 2.0. However, by creating our own transformer we will see exactly what is required to perform a conversion between two different types of data.

In addition to creating our own custom transformers we'll also see how to configure ASP.NET so that it is aware of our transformer and is able to automatically offer it for use when users are attempting to create new connections between incompatible interfaces.

Creating custom transformers

The portal framework provides an abstract class named `WebPartTransformer` which we can use to create our own custom transformer controls. Using the `WebPartTransformer` class requires us to implement a single method named `Transform`, which is shown in the code:

```
public override object Transform(object data) {…}
```

It's inside this method that we place the code required to transform data of one type into data of another type. To see how to implement the logic for this method, let's go back to the `INumbersInterface` interface we used earlier in this chapter. We'll take the `INumbersInterface` and change it so that it exposes its data as an array of strings rather than the array of integers that the consumer is expecting. The code that follows shows the new interface that will be the data contract for the provider:

```
namespace Samples {
        public interface IStringsInterface {
                string[] Strings { get; }
        }
}
```

The `NumberProvider` web part can now be altered so that it returns instances of string data as shown in listing 3.3.

> **Listing 3.3   The NumberProvider class provides data based on IStringsInterface.**

```
public partial class NumberProvider : UserControl, IStringsInterface {

        [ConnectionProvider("String Provider", "MyID")]
        public IStringsInterface GetProviderStrings() {
                return this;
        }

        string[] _strings = new string[0];
        public string[] Strings {
                get {
```

```
                    if (this._strings.Length == 0) {
                            this._strings = this.TextBox1.Text.Split(
                            new char[] { ',' },
                            StringSplitOptions.RemoveEmptyEntries
                            );

                    }
                    return this._strings;
                }
            }
        }
```

At this point the NumberProvider and the NumberConsumer are incompatible because their endpoints expose different contracts. The web part framework is smart enough to realize this incompatibility, and won't even provide an option to connect them when using dynamic connections. If we attempt to connect them using a static connection, we'll receive an error similar to the one shown in figure 3.10.

In order to have the NumberProvider and NumberConsumer work together we must create a transformer that can accept the IStringsInterface data and transform it into INumbersInterface data. Next we'll see exactly how to create such a transformer and learn how to configure ASP.NET so that it knows we have a way of converting between these two interfaces. Once we've done this, ASP.NET will treat these as compatible interfaces when we are configuring them within the application.

The WebPartTransformer attribute

Creating a custom transformer requires us to inherit from the base transformer class and we must also attribute our class with the WebPartTransformer attribute. This attribute is constructed by passing in the Types of the provider and consumer. The constructor for the WebPartTransformerAttribute is shown in the following code:

```
public WebPartTransformerAttribute (
      Type consumerType,
      Type providerType
)
```

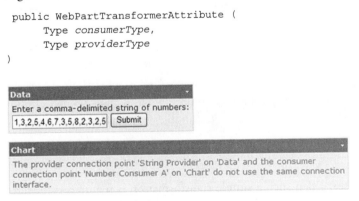

Figure 3.10 An error is displayed if you attempt to connect incompatible parts with static connections.

In our case, the consumer type (the type that we are consuming, not the type that we are sending to the consumer endpoint) will be the IStringsInterface, and we will be transforming it and exposing it as INumbersInterface. In other words, we consume strings and provide integers. The Transform method will be invoked by the web parts framework at runtime and handed data, based on the data type that you are consuming.

A simple Transform method will merely cast the incoming data to the appropriate interface and then manipulate a result based on the data type that you are providing. In listing 3.4 you can see what the code for a fully implemented transformer that changes strings data to integer data looks like.

Listing 3.4 StringsToNumbersTransformer.cs—a transformer class for transforming string arrays to integer arrays

```
namespace Samples {

    [WebPartTransformer(typeof(IStringsInterface),
typeof(INumbersInterface))]                          ◁——  Specify what data types the
    public class StringsToNumbersTransformer               transformer works with
: WebPartTransformer, INumbersInterface {

        public StringsToNumbersTransformer() { }

        int[] _numbers = new int[0];


        public override object Transform(object data) {

            string[] strings = ((IStringsInterface)data).Strings;  ◁——
            _numbers = new int[strings.Length];             Receive the
                                                            IStringsInterface data
            for (int i = 0; i < strings.Length; i++) {
                int tmp = 0;                                Convert the strings
                int.TryParse(strings[i], out tmp);          to numbers
                 numbers[i] = tmp;
            }
            return this;
        }

        public int[] Numbers {
            get { return this._numbers; }  ◁——  The INumbersInterface
        }                                        implementation
    }
}
```

As you can see, when such a simple transformation is required—converting an array of strings to an array of numbers—very little code is required to build a custom transformer class.

Configuring a transformer

The final step to perform when creating a custom transformer is to let the portal framework know about it by adding the details of the transformer to the web configuration file. This is accomplished by adding it to the system.web/webParts section of that file. The code that follows shows how that section will look after you have added an entry for our StringsToNumbersTransformer.

```
<system.web>
    <webParts>
            <transformers>
                <add
                        name="StringsToNumbersTransformer"
                        type="Samples.StringsToNumbersTransformer" />
            </transformers>
    </webParts>
</system.web>
```

Our transformer is now exposed to the web part framework and ready to act as a bridge between the strings and numbers types. We can see that our transformer has been successfully registered with the framework by inspecting the Available-Transformers property of the web part manager. The AvailableTransformers property contains a listing of all transformers currently "visible" to the portal framework, and is used when determining which web parts can be connected to other web parts on the page. The following snippet of code shows how to display a listing of available transformers:

```
TransformerTypeCollection transformers =
        WebPartManager1.AvailableTransformers;


foreach (Type type in transformers) {
        Trace.Warn(type.Name);
}
```

Figure 3.11 shows the listing of transformers that the code above created.

At the beginning of this section, I mentioned that there are pre-defined transformers that come standard with ASP.NET 2.0, as shown in figure 3.11. Although we created only one transformer class, StringsToNumbersTransformer, there are actually three transformers listed in the page trace output. The other two transformers that are shown in the output, RowToParametersTransformer and RowToFieldTransformer, ship as standard transformers with ASP.NET 2.0.

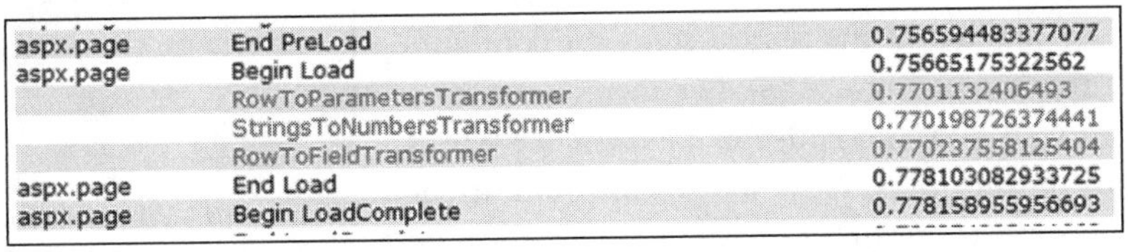

aspx.page	End PreLoad	0.756594483377077
aspx.page	Begin Load	0.75665175322562
	RowToParametersTransformer	0.7701132406493
	StringsToNumbersTransformer	0.770198726374441
	RowToFieldTransformer	0.770237558125404
aspx.page	End Load	0.778103082933725
aspx.page	Begin LoadComplete	0.778158955956693

Figure 3.11   The list of available transformers as displayed in the page trace output.

3.4.1 Using pre-defined transformers

The custom transformers we created in the previous sections have limited use. By contrast, having a set of pre-defined transformers is handy because they are common and can be used by all third parties. This means that they can be used as guidelines for vendors so that their web parts can be interoperable with other parts. This also means that the number of transformers required can be limited to just a few, as opposed to having to create new transformers every time we need to connect incompatible web parts.

RowToParametersTransformer

The `RowToParametersTransformer` is one of the existing ASP.NET transformers that allows us to take data from a provider implementing the `IWebPartRow` interface and connect it to a consumer which is expecting to receive data based on the `IWebPartParameters` interface. `IWebPartRow` and `IWebPartParameters` are both standard ASP.NET interfaces, and can be found in the `System.Web.UI.WebControls.WebParts` namespace.

When a user connects two parts using the `RowToParametersTransformer`, a wizard step will appear within the connections zone to guide users through the configuration. During this step the user can map each column in the `IWebPartRow` data source to a parameter within the control. This screen is displayed when the connections zone is in `ConfiguringTransformer` mode. Figure 3.12 shows the first screen of the wizard for configuring a transformer being displayed within the connections zone.

We can go back and edit the connection configuration at any time by switching the web part into connect mode and using the Edit button that appears when a transformer is present on the connection, as shown in figure 3.13.

By looking at the wizard steps for configuring the `RowToParametersTransformer`, we have seen how the end-user's experience works with transformers. Now we can turn our attention towards creating two web parts that can be used with this type of transformer. We will need

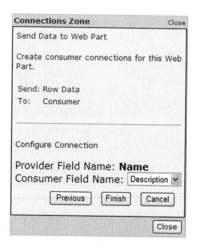

Figure 3.12 The screen for configuring the RowToParametersTransformer walks users through each field in the provider row, and allows them to map that field to a parameter in the consumer.

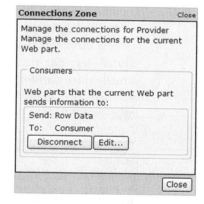

Figure 3.13 When the connection contains a transformer, the edit button is enabled to allow the user to enter ConfiguringTransformer mode.

one web part that provides `IWebPartRow` connection data, and another web part that receives `IWebPartParameters` connection data.

Providing IWebPartRow data

To create a web part that will provide data to the connection, we must provide a data type which implements `IWebPartRow`. Implementing the `IWebPartRow` interface requires our web part to implement two members—`Schema` and `GetRowData`. The `GetRowData` method is called by the transformer when it needs to get the actual row of data from the connection.

The other property, `Schema`, returns a `PropertyDescriptorCollection`—which is a collection of items that describes each field within the row of data returned by the `GetRowData` method. The items returned via the `Schema` property are used by the transformer at runtime to create the configuration screen. This explains how the configuration screen knew that the provider had a field called "Name" in the image displayed in figure 3.12. Listing 3.5 shows a full implementation of a class that exposes a provider endpoint for the `IWebPartRow` interface.

Listing 3.5 The transformer communicates with our web part via its IWebPartRow interface.

```
public partial class RowProvider : UserControl, IWebPartRow {

    private DataTable _table;

    public RowProvider() {
        _table = new DataTable();

        _table.Columns.Add(new DataColumn("ID", typeof(int)));
        _table.Columns.Add(new DataColumn("Name", typeof(string)));

        DataRow row = _table.NewRow();
        row.ItemArray = new object[] { 1, "Item 1" };
        _table.Rows.Add(row);
    }

    public void GetRowData(RowCallback callback) {
        callback(_table.DefaultView[0]);
    }

    public PropertyDescriptorCollection Schema {
        get {
            return TypeDescriptor.GetProperties(_table.DefaultView[0]);
        }
    }

    [ConnectionProvider("Row Data")]
    public IWebPartRow GetProviderData() {
        return this;
```

Annotations in listing:
- `_table.Columns.Add` / `row.ItemArray` block — **Create some initial dummy data**
- `callback(_table.DefaultView[0]);` — **Called by the transformer to get the data**
- `return TypeDescriptor.GetProperties(_table.DefaultView[0]);` — **Called by the transformer to get schema information**
- `[ConnectionProvider("Row Data")]` — **The connection endpoint**

```
        }

        protected override void Render(HtmlTextWriter writer) {
            writer.Write("This part is the provider.");    ◁──┐ Render some
        }                                                       trivial interface
}                                                               for the web part
```

In the example we see that ConnectionProvider endpoint does indeed return an IWebPartRow data type—and in this case we can simply return an instance of the user control itself, as it already implements that interface. The control in the example returns hard-coded sample data; but, in a real application, this row could be dynamic. For example, in a real application, this row could be the row from a SelectedIndex of a data grid or such.

Consuming IWebPartParameters data

We have a web part that provides the IWebPartRow data to the RowToParameters-Transformer, and all that we need before we can use the transformer is a web part that consumes the IWebPartParameters data that the transformer will be providing. Like the IWebPartRow interface, the IWebPartParameters interface serves a dual purpose:

1 It provides a method for exposing its schema information to the transformer, which can then be used to create the configuration screen.

2 It provides a method for the interchanging of data.

To enable the transformer to retrieve information about the properties of the consumer web part, the IWebPartParameters interface provides us with a method named SetConsumerSchema. This method must be called by the consumer to let the transformer know for which parameters it expects to receive data. This is the information that the transformer uses when rendering the wizard to match properties to columns. Listing 3.6 shows an example of how to call SetConsumerSchema on the provider and pass it the details of two of its properties named TempID and Description.

NOTE   The item that is passed to the consumer is not the actual provider class, but an instance of the RowToParametersTransformer class which implements the IWebPartParameters interface.

> **Listing 3.6   The consumer calls the SetConsumerSchema on the transformer to pass to it the properties available for mapping.**

```
[ConnectionConsumer("Parameters Data")]
public void SetProvider(IWebPartParameters provider) {
        if (provider != null) {
                PropertyDescriptorCollection props =
                    TypeDescriptor.GetProperties(this);
```

```
PropertyDescriptor p1 = props.Find("TempID", false);
PropertyDescriptor p2 = props.Find("Description", false);

PropertyDescriptorCollection schemaProps =
        new PropertyDescriptorCollection(
                new PropertyDescriptor[] {p1, p2}
            );

provider.SetConsumerSchema(schemaProps);      Pass the
                                              properties to
this._provider = provider;                    the transformer
    }

}
```

As usual, the consumer stores the provider data in a local field for use during the pre-rendering process, and at that time the consumer must call the GetParameters-Data method on it. When that method is called, a reference to a callback method is passed as an argument, and it is this callback method that will be invoked and have the actual data row passed to it. Importantly, the callback method must match the signature of the ParametersCallback delegate. The code that follows provides an example of how to do this:

```
protected override void OnPreRender(EventArgs e) {
    if (this._provider != null) {
        this._provider.GetParametersData(
            new ParametersCallback(SetProviderData)
            );
    }
    base.OnPreRender(e);
}

public void SetProviderData(IDictionary dict) {
    this._data = dict;
}
```

When we have the data, it's simply a matter of using it during the rendering phase. The following code shows a simple example of displaying the provider data by writing out each value:

```
protected override void Render(HtmlTextWriter writer) {
    if (this._provider != null && this._data != null) {
        foreach(DictionaryEntry de in this._data) {
            writer.Write(
                string.Format("{0} : {1}<br />",
                de.Key,
                de.Value
                )
            ) ;
```

```
            }
    } else {
            writer.Write("No data here!");
    }
}
```

In this example, we are simply displaying the data that was received from the provider directly to the user. In a real example, we might use the data that we receive to do something more interesting. For example, the data we receive could hold a value for a city and another value for a country. These values could then be passed to a weather service that returns the weather information for the specified city.

RowToFieldTransformer

The other pre-defined transformer within the ASP.NET web part framework is the `RowTo-FieldTransformer`. As its name suggests, this transformer also works with `IWebPartRow` provider data, but it is looking for a consumer that expects to receive `IWebPartField` data—which is like a single field version of the previous transformer.

The configuration user interface provided by this control displays all the column definitions from within the `IWebPartRow` source in a dropdown list as shown in figure 3.14. This allows the user to choose which single column from the row will provide it with its data.

Now that we've learned a great deal about transformers and how they work, we will look at one further area of working with transformers

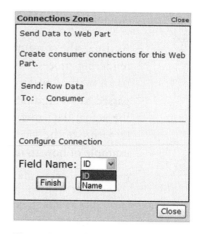

Figure 3.14 The transformation screen for the RowToFieldTransformer.

that can be customized and that is the user interface that the user works with when configuring a transformer during the connection process. Next we'll learn how to completely customize that part of the user experience by providing the user with a custom piece of user interface that allows him to manage the transformation mapping.

Customizing the transformation experience

The two ASP.NET transformers we've seen in this section have both provided the user with configuration screens that guide him through the configuration process at runtime. We are able to create configuration screens for our own custom transformers by implementing the `CreateConfigurationControl` method in our custom `Web-PartTransformer`. In this method we can simply return any control that we'd like to present to the user that will allow the user to perform the configuration. The only caveat to this is that the control we return must implement the `ITransformerCon-figurationControl` interface.

The `ITransformerConfigurationControl` interface has two simple events that must be exposed by our control to allow it to communicate with the containing connections zone. The events I'm referring to are the `Cancelled` and `Succeeded` events, and we raise them to indicate to the connections zone that the user has finished configuring the transformer. When the connection zone receives a notification from either the `Cancelled` or `Succeeded` event, it can change its user interface to display a new view to the user. The following code represents the bare minimum amount of code for a control that implements the `ITransformerConfigurationControl` interface. Note that this control would not actually display any user interface, nor would it have any way to raise its two events. Implementing this rendering logic is left as an exercise for the reader.

```
public class MyControl :
        Control, ITransformerConfigurationControl {

    public event EventHandler Cancelled;
    public event EventHandler Succeeded;
}
```

That's all there is to creating a unique configuration experience for our transformers. By supplying an `ITransformerConfigurationControl` with our transformers, we can simplify the experience of the end-user when working with our data, especially when the mapping might be more advanced than a simple field-to-field mapping. For example, a more advanced mapping might see several address fields mapped to a single address field property. In such an advanced scenario the user would certainly require a custom interface to manage the mapping.

Planning for interoperability

Having a common set of interfaces that are defined for working with connection data means that third-party web part providers will have a set of guideline interfaces to use. Using these interfaces when we are writing our own custom web parts applications makes it likely that our controls will work with vendor-supplied controls without requiring the writing of any code. For example, when creating a web part that exposes connection information, we should attempt to provide the connection data as an `IWebPartRow` data type instead of exposing it as a custom interface type. Likewise, ensuring that when we are consuming connection data, we use either the `IWebPartParameters` or `IWebPartField` data types will make our web parts more interoperable with other web parts.

The next section pulls together the theory and practice of web part connections, as you put them into action for Adventure Works.

3.5 ADVENTURE WORKS— IMPLEMENTING CONNECTIONS FOR HR

At the end of chapter 1 we created a portal for Adventure Works Cycles. In that exercise we created two parts: a part to display a listing of departments, and a part to display a listing of employees. In this exercise we will apply our new knowledge of connections to join these two parts to one another, so that the employee list can be filtered by a selected department in the department list. Figure 3.15 shows how the two web parts will appear when this connection has been made. The image shows the Finance department as the selected department with the employees for that department shown in the employees list.

The IT department at Adventure Works has decided that, whenever possible, we should increase the extensibility of our controls and use the standard connection interfaces that work with the pre-defined ASP.NET transformers. To do this we will ensure that the DepartmentListing web part exposes its data via the IWebPartRow provider interface, and have the EmployeeListingPart web part consume the department identifier via the IWebPartField consumer interface.

NOTE   If you don't have a copy of the project from chapter 2 you can grab it from the chapter 2 section of the resources website for this book at http://manning.com/neimke.

Adding the provider endpoint

We'll start the process of implementing the standard transformer interfaces within our application by altering the DepartmentListingPart.ascx control to make it expose a connection endpoint based on the IWebPartRow interface. Open that control

Departments			Employees	
Name	**Employees**		Barber, David	(Assistant to the Chief Financial Officer)
Select Executive	2		Kahn, Wendy	(Finance Manager)
Select Facilities and Maintenance	7		Liu, David	(Accounts Manager)
Select Finance	10		Moreland, Barbara	(Accountant)
Select Human Resources	6		Norman, Laura	(Chief Financial Officer)
Select Information Services	10		Poe, Deborah	(Accounts Receivable Specialist)
Select Purchasing	12		Seamans, Mike	(Accountant)
Select Shipping and Receiving	6		Sheperdigian, Janet	(Accounts Payable Specialist)
Select Production	179		Spoon, Candy	(Accounts Receivable Specialist)
Select Production Control	6		Tomic, Dragan	(Accounts Payable Specialist)
Select Document Control	5		Walton, Bryan	(Accounts Receivable Specialist)
Select Quality Assurance	6			
Select Engineering	6			
Select Research and Development	4			
Select Tool Design	4			
Select Marketing	9			
Select Sales	18			

Figure 3.15   Adding a connection between the two web parts will allow the user to make a selection in the Departments web part and have the employees for that department be automatically displayed in the Employees web part.

in design view, and configure the `GridView` to allow users to select items and modify them so that the fill color of the selected row is highlighted. You can do this by adding the attributes listed in the following code to the `GridView` control declaration:

```
AutoGenerateSelectButton="True"
SelectedRowStyle-BackColor="Yellow"
```

Now switch the control into source code view and add the `IWebPartRow` interface definition to it. At this point the code for your class should look like this:

```
public partial class DepartmentListingPart : UserControl, IWebPartRow {

        public void GetRowData(RowCallback callback) {
                // implementation goes here
        }

        public PropertyDescriptorCollection Schema {
                get {
                        // implementation goes here
                }
        }
}
```

The `Schema` property requires us to return a collection of `PropertyDescriptor` objects for each property that we want to expose to the transformer; in other words, how many properties do we want to expose for dynamic configuration? We could expose just the ID of the selected department—which is all that is needed for this example; but in the future, we may create other parts that can utilize other properties of a department, such as its name or description. So let's return a `Property-Descriptor` for each property of the selected `Department` item to keep things uncomplicated. The code to accomplish this turns out to be simple, as seen in the following listing. The `TypeDescriptor` class already knows how to extract these descriptors based on a type, so we can relegate the hard work to it.

```
public PropertyDescriptorCollection Schema {
    get {
        PropertyDescriptorCollection props =
            TypeDescriptor.GetProperties(typeof(Department));
        return props;
    }
}
```

The logic for our provider is contained within the `GetRowData` method. This is the method that will be called by the transformer when it needs to get the data to send to the consumer. This method is responsible for creating the data we described in our `Schema` property, and passing it back to the caller via the callback that is passed to the method. The code to do this follows:

```
public void GetRowData(RowCallback callback) {

    int index = this.GridView1.SelectedIndex;
    int departmentID = (int)GridView1.DataKeys[index].Value;

    DataLayer datalayer = new DataLayer();
    Department department = datalayer.GetDepartment(departmentID);

    callback(department);
}
```

To complete this control we simply need to expose a provider endpoint that exposes the `IWebPartRow` data. The provider endpoint returns the instance of the class because the class implements the interface. The following shows the code for the provider endpoint:

```
[ConnectionProvider("Department Provider Data")]
public IWebPartRow GetProviderData() {
        return this;
}
```

Our `DepartmentListing` web part is now set up to provide its data in accordance with the `IWebPartField` interface.

Adding the consumer endpoint

Now we can configure the consumer endpoint on the employees web part so that it accepts data based on the `IWebPartField` interface. Open the `EmployeeListing-Part` in design mode and remove the `DataSource` control from the page and the `DataSourceID` from the `GridView`. We'll now be implementing the binding logic in code because we have to decide whether we are connected or not. Open the control in source code view so that we can create the consumer endpoint logic.

As we've seen with all the connection consumers we've created so far, the first step is to add a method and mark it with the `ConnectionConsumer` attribute as shown in the code that follows. In this method, we simply take the data that is handed to us and assign it to a private field. Remember that we do this because we have to wait until the pre-rendering phase of the page before we use it, so that we are sure we have the latest connection data to work with.

```
public partial class EmployeeListingPart : UserControl {

        IWebPartField _provider;
        int _data = 0;

        [ConnectionConsumer("Department Field Consumer")]
        public void SetProviderData(IWebPartField provider) {
                this._provider = provider;
        }

}
```

During the pre-render phase we must call a method named `GetFieldValue` on the `IWebPartField` provider to get the value of the field from the provider. In the next code snippet we can see that this method is called and a `FieldCallback` delegate is passed to it as the argument. This is the consumer's way of asking to receive its data from the transformer. The transformer will invoke the callback—which must take an object as its only argument—and the consumer can then work with the data. You can see that our callback method named `GetFieldData` simply stores the value in a local variable named _data so that it can be used in the rendering phase.

```
protected override void OnPreRender(EventArgs e) {
        if (this._provider != null) {
                this._provider.GetFieldValue(
                        new FieldCallback(GetFieldData)
                );
        }
        base.OnPreRender(e);
}


private void GetFieldData(object data) {
        int.TryParse( data.ToString(), out this._data) ;
}
```

By the end of the pre-rendering phase, the _data field will contain the value from whatever provider we are connected to—in our case this will be the ID of a department which has come from the `DepartmentListingPart` control. In listing 3.7 we see the logic to either display a full listing of employees if we are not connected, or to display a filtered listing if we are connected and a department ID has been passed through to us.

> **Listing 3.7   When we render our control we check the connection data to determine whether to display a filtered list or a full listing of employees.**

```
protected override void Render(HtmlTextWriter writer) {

    DataLayer datalayer = new DataLayer() ;
    List<Employee> employees ;

    if (_provider != null && _data > 0) {
        employees = datalayer.ListEmployeesByDepartment(_data);
    } else {
        employees = datalayer.ListEmployees();
    }

    GridView1.DataSource = employees;
    GridView1.DataBind();

    base.Render(writer) ;
}
```

The code in our render method will now check to determine whether a connection exists before fetching the employee data. If a connection does exist, it will use the data from the connection to limit the employees that it gets to a specific department; otherwise it will fetch the employees for all departments.

Adding the ConnectionsZone

The last thing to do is to go back to the web part page—`Default.aspx`—and add a `ConnectionsZone` control and set the page into connect mode—as shown in the code that follows. This will allow us to add and configure a dynamic connection between the two web parts at runtime.

NOTE   In chapter 4 we will see how to set the `DisplayMode` of the `WebPart-Manager` dynamically, instead of hard-coding it as we have done so far.

```
protected override void OnLoad(EventArgs e) {
        base.OnLoad(e);
        WebPartManager1.DisplayMode = WebPartManager.ConnectDisplayMode;
}
```

Right-click on the `Default.aspx` file and choose View in Browser to view the portal. Notice that initially the employee listing is still unfiltered. Choose the connect verb from either of the web parts and then walk through the configuration process. Be sure to configure the transformer to pass the `DepartmentID` field as shown in figure 3.16.

After configuring the connection, the employees listing will be connected to the departments web part and will have its items filtered by the selected department. Run the page in a browser and check to see that it appears as shown in figure 3.17.

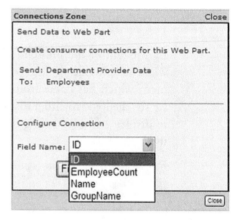

Figure 3.16   The provider data is displayed in a dropdown list so that you can choose which field will supply the data for this connection.

With the page displayed, make some selections in the departments listing and verify that the employees displayed are correct for the department that is chosen. As you make those selections, think of the underlying mechanics that made this possible. The department's listing is providing data based on the `IWebPartRow` interface, and the employee's listing is consuming connection data based on the `IWebPartField` interface. What's more, once we implemented those two interfaces on our web parts, there was no need to write any code to manage the transformation between the two.

As we continue through the book, we'll be able to leverage the connection data exposed by these web parts by adding other web parts that also work with the pre-built

Departments		
	Name	Employees
Select	Executive	2
Select	Facilities and Maintenance	7
Select	Finance	10
Select	Human Resources	6
Select	Information Services	10
Select	Purchasing	12
Select	Shipping and Receiving	6
Select	Production	179
Select	Production Control	6
Select	Document Control	5
Select	Quality Assurance	6
Select	Engineering	6
Select	Research and Development	4
Select	Tool Design	4
Select	Marketing	9
Select	Sales	18

Employees	
Barber, David	(Assistant to the Chief Financial Officer)
Kahn, Wendy	(Finance Manager)
Liu, David	(Accounts Manager)
Moreland, Barbara	(Accountant)
Norman, Laura	(Chief Financial Officer)
Poe, Deborah	(Accounts Receivable Specialist)
Seamans, Mike	(Accountant)
Sheperdigian, Janet	(Accounts Payable Specialist)
Spoon, Candy	(Accounts Receivable Specialist)
Tomic, Dragan	(Accounts Payable Specialist)
Walton, Bryan	(Accounts Receivable Specialist)

Figure 3.17   The two parts are now connected, and the Employees web part is filtered by selections made in the Departments web part.

transformers. As you can imagine, it won't be long before our pages are full of dynamic information.

3.6   SUMMARY

Our knowledge of web parts is rapidly expanding. In chapter 2 we covered the different types of web parts and saw that they can help to break down and simplify the task of creating complex, information-centric portals. In this chapter we discussed the concept of connecting web parts so that we can share data from different sources; and that by using common patterns, such as the Summary/Detail and the Parent/Child, we can present data to users in an effective manner. We also saw that connections can assist in breaking user interface components down into simpler, more manageable pieces.

We also introduced the WebPartConnection control and saw how it works within the framework to provide us with the ability to create connections, both statically and then dynamically.

Finally, we discussed transformers and how they can be used to create connections between different types of web parts. We saw the interfaces that they work with, and then finished by implementing a Parent/Child style of connection between the web parts we created in chapter 2.

There are still many important members of the web part framework to learn about; and in the next chapter we'll look at the most important member—the Web-PartManager—and see what it's been doing for us all this time, unbeknownst to us.

C H A P T E R   4

The Web Part Manager

4.1   INTRODUCTION

At this point, your knowledge of the portal framework is rounding out. At the beginning of our journey, we peeked in from the top of the portal and saw that web parts can be created to show different views of information. We've now descended through several layers of the portal framework, down through connections and into the realm of the web part manager. It is here that we've seen the essential services of the framework—such as authentication and page mode management—and how those services are managed by the WebPartManager. Learning to leverage these services is the key to understanding how to create truly custom portal applications. By combining WebPartManger customizations with the physical structures of portals such as zones, connections, and web parts, we can extend the portal framework to suit almost any need.

In chapters 1 through 3, we've added a WebPartManager control to the top of every web page we've written. Without a WebPartManager, web part controls won't work at all; they'll just throw big, ugly exceptions. It's interesting to note that although the WebPartManager has been chugging away under the covers managing operations, we've only touched it once. For example, in chapter 3, we saw that the WebPartManager determined whether the "connect" verbs were added to the web parts. In addition, it's the WebPartManager that guarantees that when you make a single visit to a page and close a web part, the web part remains closed on the next visit to the web page. It's the WebPartManager that turns ordinary controls into GenericWebParts, that initializes connections, and that moves web parts between zones when the user drags them across a page. In short, the WebPartManager does a heck of a lot.

By the end of this chapter, you'll have a respectable grasp of the WebPartManager, and be fairly adept at both working with it and customizing it.

4.1.1 A control with many hats

What are the many hats a WebPartManager can wear? Tracking, managing personalization, controlling lifecycle events, switching page displays, and importing and exporting web parts, to name a few. That's a stack of hats. To get some sense of the importance of the WebPartManager's role, consider the following five categories of tasks and activities that are displayed in table 4.1.

Table 4.1 The WebPartManager is a versatile control that manages a wide range of activities

Category	Activities
Tracking web parts	Adding web parts to zones; closing web parts; moving web parts; tracking which web parts belong in which zones.
Managing Personalization Data	Initializing web parts; loading personalization data; saving personalization data.
Controlling Lifecycle Events	Creating web parts; initializing connections.
Switching Page Display Modes	Switching the mode of the page.
Importing and Exporting Web Parts	Serializing and de-serializing web parts for the export process.

The WebPartManager manages each of these activities and exposes event notifications when they occur. As you can see, there's really not a great deal that goes on without the involvement of the WebPartManager. Let's take a high-level tour through each of these categories to get a better sense of them.

Keeping track of web parts

At any given moment, the webpartmanager knows exactly what web parts are on a page, which zones they belong to, and whether or not the user is authorized to view them. The webpartmanager also performs operations that require a web part to be added to or removed from a page. Moving a web part between two zones is also achieved via the manager. The code that follows lists an example of how the WebPartManager adds a web part to a page at runtime.

```
CustomWeatherPart weatherPart = new CustomWeatherPart();
weatherPart.ID = "CustomWeatherPart1";
weatherPart.NumberOfDays = 6;

WebPartManager1.AddWebPart(
       weatherPart,
       WebPartZone1,
       WebPartZone1.WebParts.Count
);
```

Adding a generic web part such as a user control to the page is slightly different from adding a custom web part, because the WebPartManager must first create a GenericWebPart from whatever control is being used at the time. The following snippet of code demonstrates how the WebPartManager creates a GenericWebPart:

```
TextBox textbox = new TextBox();
textbox.ID = "TextBox1";
GenericWebPart gwp = WebPartManager1.CreateWebPart(textbox);

WebPartManager1.AddWebPart(
       gwp,
       WebPartZone1,
       WebPartZone1.WebParts.Count
);
```

Notice that WebPartManager first creates a GenericWebPart control, which can then be passed into the AddWebPart method. This is similar to what occurred under the covers when the Label control was turned into a GenericWebPart in the previous chapter.

Managing personalization data

The WebPartManager also manages the loading and saving of web part personalization data. At the beginning of the page lifecycle the WebPartManager is handed a blob of data from the personalization system, which it then distributes to each of the relevant web parts. At the end of the page lifecycle, the WebPartManager gathers up the personalization data from each of the web part controls, packages that data into a single blob, and hands it back to the Personalization system for saving. This process allows user customizations to persist across browser restarts. Personalization is a very broad topic, so I'll defer further discussion about it until chapter 6, when we can devote an entire chapter to it.

Controlling lifecycle events

All of the events that occur during the web part page lifecycle are tracked and exposed by the WebPartManager. For example, if you want to receive notifications about when connections are initialized, you will get them from the manager. Likewise, if you want to receive notifications whenever a user is attempting to move a web part between zones, it's the WebPartManger that will notify you of that event. The code snippet that follows is an example of how you might listen for such events and disallow the move based on some condition. For example, you could have zones within your application that can only contain five web parts. When a user attempts to drag a sixth web part into the zone, you could use the WebPartMoving event to cancel the move.

```
protected void WebPartManager1_WebPartMoving(
    object sender, WebPartMovingEventArgs e) {

    bool isMoveCancelled = true;

    // implement some custom logic here

    e.Cancel = isMoveCancelled;
}
```

This code shows us a skeleton implementation of handling the WebPartMoving event of the WebPartManger. Typically, code would be included within this event handler that would perform logic and set the value of the e.Cancel property based on that logic. Overall there are 20 lifecycle events exposed by the WebPartManager that can be used to provide custom behaviors and control the lifecycle within our applications.

Switching page modes

In chapter 3 we briefly discussed the five standard modes that a web part page can enter into—BrowseDisplayMode, CatalogDisplayMode, ConnectDisplay-Mode, DesignDisplayMode, and EditDisplayMode. We also saw that we were able to set the current mode of a page when we forced the page to be in "connect" mode in chapter 3. These modes are set by the WebPartManager and provide us the means to perform powerful operations on web parts—such as connecting them or editing them.

Importing and exporting web parts

Web part controls can be exported from and imported into pages at runtime. SharePoint has a feature similar to this which allows users to discover web parts stored in a central gallery on the internet and to import them into the page. You can use the import/export capability exposed by the WebPartManager to add this SharePoint feature to your own applications. For example, you could expose methods on a web service to accept and retrieve the web part definitions that can be created by the WebPartManager.

This section has presented an overview of the five categories of tasks that are performed by the WebPartManager. Throughout this chapter we will learn more about the WebPartManger by digging deeper into the inner workings of these five tasks. Understanding how to extend and control the behavior of these tasks is the key to creating truly unique portal applications.

4.2   THE PAGE LIFECYCLE

Whenever an ASP.NET web page is requested, a class is created on the web server to handle that request. It's this class that we refer to as the Page class. When the page has finished handling the request, it is destroyed and ceases to exist—at least until that page is requested again. Between the time the page is created and destroyed, it goes through a sequence of events that are known as The Page Lifecycle. The Page Lifecycle is the event model that dictates when things occur—such as when controls are initialized or when postback events take place.

Before we start writing code to work with the `WebPartManager`, it's important to take the time to see when its events occur and map them to the lifecycle of the page so that we have a full picture of what to expect, and when. Table 4.2 displays the events that occur on the `Page` class and overlays those events with events occurring at portal framework level.

Table 4.2   Knowing when things occur in the lifecycle of a page is critical for understanding how to customize the behavior of portal components

Lifecycle Stage	Description
Init	WebZones register themselves with the `WebPartManager` by making a call to `RegisterZone` on the current `WebPartManager` for the page. All static `WebParts` are loaded via the `WebPartZoneBase` making a call to `GetInitialWebParts`.
InitComplete	Dynamic Connections and dynamic `WebParts` are loaded from Personalization data. Personalization data is applied to all `WebParts`.
LoadComplete	Connections are activated and connection data is transformed and exchanged.
PreRender	Typically where page logic is written to deal with connection information.
SaveStateComplete	Personalization data is saved.

By examining the stages in table 4.2, it is easy to see the effects of misunderstanding the lifecycle. The snippet that follows shows the code that is required to dynamically add a `WebZone` to a page. Notice that the code runs during the `OnInit` phase of the page lifecycle. The `OnInit` phase occurs just prior to the `InitComplete` stage of the page lifecycle—which is when web parts are first loaded.

```
protected override void OnInit(EventArgs e) {
        base.OnInit(e);

        EditorZone zone = new EditorZone();
        zone.ID = "EditorZone1";
        this.Controls.Add(zone);
}
```

One of the first things that a zone does when it is created is to register itself with the `WebPartManager` control that exists for the current page. The `WebPartManager`

Server Error in '/TestWebPartApplication' Application.

A Zone can only be added to the Page in or before the Page_Init event.

Description: An unhandled exception occurred during the execution of the current web request. Please review the stack trace for more information about the error and where it originated in the code.

Exception Details: System.InvalidOperationException: A Zone can only be added to the Page in or before the Page_Init event.

Source Error:

```
Line 10:          EditorZone zone = new EditorZone();
Line 11:          zone.ID = "EditorZone1";
Line 12:          this.Controls.Add(zone);
Line 13:      }
Line 14:
```

Figure 4.1 **Attempting to add a zone to a page after the initialization phase will result in an error.**

then checks whether the initialization phase has completed and, if so, it throws the InvalidOperationException. For this reason, if we attempt to perform the same operation any time after the initialization phase of the page lifecycle, an error will result. This can be seen in figure 4.1.

Just as we wouldn't attempt to add a zone to the page after the InitComplete phase, there would be no point in attempting to read data that you were expecting to receive via a connection prior to the PreRender phase, because the connections are not activated until just before then.

4.3   PAGE DISPLAY MODES

Understanding the page lifecycle for web parts leads us onto another important concept—that of page mode management. In the previous chapter, we saw that a web page can have several different display modes and that changing between the modes is done by setting the DisplayMode property of the web part manager instance like so:

```
WebPartManager1.DisplayMode = WebPartManager.ConnectDisplayMode;
```

There are five standard modes that the page can enter into, and with each state there are different user interface elements that allow the user to perform a specific set of operations—such as managing connections or editing the properties of web parts. Table 4.3 lists each of the display modes and details the operations that are associated with them.

We've already seen that the mode of the page is affected by setting the Display-Mode property of the current WebPartManager instance to one of the modes listed above. The manager class also exposes a property named SupportedDisplay-Modes that allows us to obtain a listing of all modes available at any particular

Table 4.3   Each Display Mode exposes certain operations.

Mode	Operations
BrowseDisplay-Mode	This is the default state of a web part page. In this state users can view the web parts on the page.
CatalogDisplay-Mode	In this mode the user can drag parts between the zones. There are also special user interface elements present that allow the user to choose web parts from a gallery, and to add them to the page.
ConnectDisplay-Mode	In this mode special user interface elements are displayed to users that allow them to connect web parts together. There is also a "connect" verb added to all web parts that are capable of being connected.
DesignDisplay-Mode	Similar to browse mode, except that it allows users to drag web parts between zones.
EditDisplayMode	This mode allows users to edit the properties and attributes of web parts. To do this, special user interface elements are displayed. In this mode users can also drag web parts between zones.

moment. In a typical web part application we would display a list of the available modes to the user, allowing them to switch modes so that they could perform a specific set of tasks. For example, it might be desirable for the administrators of a portal to be able to log in and change certain features of the web parts, such as the back color or their display title. By picking from a list of available modes, the users could switch their web page from its default browse mode and into edit mode. Once in edit mode, the user can make changes to web parts and then switch back into browse mode to continue using the site as normal. Listing 4.1 illustrates how to present a list of valid modes in a dropdown list.

Listing 4.1   Using the SupportedDisplayModes property of the WebPartManager to present the user with a list of modes to choose from.

```
foreach (WebPartDisplayMode displayMode in
  WebPartManager1.SupportedDisplayModes) {

    if (displayMode.IsEnabled(WebPartManager1)) {        Check that the
        DropDownList1.Items.Add(                          mode is enabled
            new ListItem(displayMode.Name)
            );
    }
}
```

NOTE   Prior to the load phase of the Page Lifecycle, the WebPartManager's SupportedDisplayModes property will only contain the Browse and Display modes. For this reason it's important that the code shown in listing 4.1 is run during an event that occurs during or after the load phase, so that all of the supported modes are able to be included in the list.

Notice that in the code listing we check to see whether a mode is enabled before adding it to the list. You might be surprised to find a method on the display mode because you are expecting each mode to be a simple string value or an enumerated data type. This is not the case. All display modes are actually derived from the abstract `WebPartDisplayMode` base class.

The WebPartDisplayMode class

The `WebPartDisplayMode` class contains several properties that are used by the web part framework to determine what controls should be available to the user at any given point in time. The following list details some of the properties of the `WebPartDisplayMode` class.

- `AllowPageDesign`—A value for determining whether users can change the layout of a web parts page when the page is in a certain display mode.
- `AssociatedWithToolZone`—A value that indicates whether a certain display mode is associated with a class that derives from the `ToolZone` class. For example, the `ConnectDisplayMode` would return true here, as it is associated with the `ConnectionZone`.
- `Name`—The name of a display mode.
- `RequiresPersonalization`—A value indicating whether a particular display mode requires personalization before it can be enabled.
- `ShowHiddenWebParts`—A value that indicates whether controls that have their `Hidden` property set to true should be displayed.

By querying these properties, members of the portal framework can ascertain the current state of the page and adjust themselves accordingly.

In addition to the five standard modes, we can actually create our own custom display modes. Creating a custom mode would allow us to create a special state for the pages in our portal, and then give our web parts the ability to detect that state and act accordingly. As an example, a web part could be created to display its editing views inline when the page was in a special mode without having to display the editor zone to change certain properties.

To create a custom display mode we create a class and derive it from the `WebPartDisplayMode` base class. Then we override the properties that we need to achieve a desired state. The snippet that follows shows a class that inherits from `WebPartDisplayMode` and provides a custom implementation for the `IsEnabled` property:

```
public class CustomDisplayMode : WebPartDisplayMode {
    public CustomDisplayMode() : base("CustomDisplayMode") { }

    public override bool IsEnabled(WebPartManager webPartManager) {

        if( Roles.IsUserInRole("Administrator") ) {
        return (webPartManager.Personalization.IsModifiable);
```

```
        }
            return false;
        }
}
```

To add the custom display mode to the list of `SupportedDisplayModes` for a given page, we must override the `CreateDisplayModes` method of the `WebPartManager` for it to be added to the list. Figure 4.2 shows our custom display mode appearing with the other modes in a dropdown list; while in the code snippet, a custom web part manager is used to show the code required to add the custom mode to the `WebPartManager`'s list of display modes.

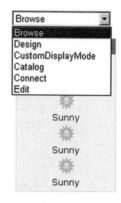

```
public class CustomWebPartManager : WebPartManager {

        protected override WebPartDisplayModeCollection
          CreateDisplayModes() {
          WebPartDisplayModeCollection modes =
            base.CreateDisplayModes();
                modes.Add( new CustomDisplayMode() );
                return modes;
        }
}
```

Figure 4.2 The custom display mode would be presented to users in the Administrator role.

It's worth noting that the order in which the list of available display modes is displayed is the same as the order in which they were added. To change the order of the list we simply change our code a little. For example, changing our code to match the following snippet would cause the `CustomDisplayMode` to be displayed first in the dropdown list:

```
protected override WebPartDisplayModeCollection CreateDisplayModes() {
    WebPartDisplayModeCollection modes = base.CreateDisplayModes();
        modes.Insert(0, new CustomDisplayMode());
        return modes;
}
```

Now that we've seen some of the heavy-duty tasks that are performed by the `WebPartManger` such as display mode filtering, lifecycle management, and keeping track of web part movements, it's time to turn our attention to another important role played by the `WebPartManager`: security. In the next section we will learn what role the `WebPartManager` plays in securing access to web parts.

4.4 WEB PART AUTHORIZATION

The `WebPartManager` provides a mechanism that allows web parts to be displayed or hidden based on a filter that can be set on a web part at design time. Using this authorization feature, web parts can be designed to target a particular audience or group of users within a certain application role. For example, the HR department might have a web part for displaying a list of employees who accumulated the most sick leave for the current year. This is certainly a web part that should not be viewed by employees outside of the HR department. Using an authorization filter, you could specify that users must be members of the HR department to view the sick leave web part. The following snippet shows a web part with its `AuthorizationFilter` set to allow only users in the role of Administrator to view it:

```
<asp:WebPartZone ID="WebPartZone1" runat="server">
        <ZoneTemplate>
                <wp:SecretPart
                        ID="CustomWeatherPart1"
                        AuthorizationFilter="Administrator"
                        runat="server"
                        Title="Sssshh, it's a secret!"
                        />
        </ZoneTemplate>
</asp:WebPartZone>
```

The `AuthorizationFilter` is a property that is exposed by the base `WebPart` class and exists to expose authorization information. However, contrary to what you might suspect, simply setting its value to a non-empty value will not cause the framework to automatically hide it from users that are not in an appropriate role. To force the authorization checks to occur we must write code, as explained in the section that follows.

Performing authorization checks

The `WebPartManager` provides us with a method named `IsAuthorized` that is used to indicate whether the current user is authorized to view any given web part. Internally, the web part manager calls the `IsAuthorized` method for each web part that it adds to a web page prior to making the web part available to the user. When the method is called, a public event named `AuthorizeWebPart` is raised and exposes information about the web part that is being added.

To manage the web part authorization process, we can write code to run when the `AuthorizeWebPart` event is raised and return a value that will be used for the `IsAuthorized` value. The bit of code that follows shows how to use the `OnAuthorizeWebPart` attribute of the `WebPartManager` to wire up an event handler for this event:

```
<asp:WebPartManager ...
OnAuthorizeWebPart="wpm_AuthorizeWebPart" />
```

IMPORTANT! When you subscribe to the `AuthorizeWebPart` by wiring up the event handler in code, you will never receive the authorization event notifications for static web parts. This is because static web parts are created and added to the zones prior to the Init phase of the page, and the Init phase is the first chance you have to create code to wire up the event. For this reason you should only use the declarative syntax for event wiring when using the `AuthorizeWebPart` event.

The `AuthorizeWebPart` event exposes the `WebPartAuthorizationEventArgs` class. This class provides information about the web part that is currently being evaluated by exposing the following properties:

- `AuthorizationFilter`—Gets the string value assigned to the `AuthorizationFilter` property of a `WebPart` control; used for authorizing whether a control can be added to a page.

- `IsAuthorized`—Gets or sets the value indicating whether a web part control can be added to a page.

- `IsShared`—Gets a value that indicates whether a web parts control is visible to all users of a web part page.

- `Path`—Gets the relative application path to the source file for the control being authorized, if the control is a user control.

By handling the `AuthorizeWebPart` event, we can use these properties exposed by the `WebPartAuthorizationEventArgs` class to make decisions about whether the user is authorized, based on the `AuthorizationFilter`. In listing 4.2 we see how to use the `AuthorizationFilter` from the `EventArgs` which are passed in and then return a value that indicates whether or not the current user has permission to view the web part being evaluated at the time:

Listing 4.2 Within the AuthorizeWebPart event handler, code is written to check the users' role memberships.

```
void wpm_AuthorizeWebPart(object sender, WebPartAuthorizationEventArgs e) {

        bool isAuthorized = false;

        string[] roles =
                e.AuthorizationFilter.Split(      Split filter for
                    new char[] { ',' }            listing of roles
                );

        for (int i = 0; i < roles.Length; i++) {
            if (IsUserInRole(roles [i])) {        Check each
                    isAuthorized = true;          role for user
                    break;                        membership
            }
        }

        e.IsAuthorized = isAuthorized;
}
```

In the code we see that the `AuthorizationFilter` property is checked against roles held by the users to determine whether or not they have access to the web part. You can see that, although the code we wrote here used the `AuthorizationFilter` to perform checks against the role membership of the user, we are not limited to using it in this way. By exposing the authorization of web parts in this manner, the ASP.NET team has left it open for us to choose how web parts are authorized within our applications. This is preferable to having web parts hard coded against user roles, for example. By having such an extensible mechanism for performing authorization checks it would even be possible to create web parts that should only be displayed at certain times of the year. For example, a department store might have a web part that displayed special items for its website visitors at certain times of the year. This could be achieved by using the `AuthorizationFilter` to store a list of seasons for which that web part was valid:

```
<wp:DiscountShoppingPart
       ID="DiscountShoppingPart1"
       AuthorizationFilter="Winter, Summer"
       runat="server"
       Title="View today's specials"
/>
```

Of course, if we are only interested in using the `AuthorizationFilter` to perform checks against application roles, why have to include event handling code in all of your web part pages? In this case, what makes more sense is creating a custom `Web-PartManager` and adding the custom role checking within it as a standard operation. To do this we can either override the `IsAuthorized` method, or we can override the `OnAuthorizeWebPart` method and include our code in that method. By having this common code held within the manager class, there is no chance that we'll forget to add the event handler when creating new pages and our logic will all be in one place, making it easier to maintain. The snippet that follows shows how to override the `OnAuthorizeWebPart` method to perform common authorization logic:

```
public class SecureWebPartManager : WebPartManager {

       public SecureWebPartManager() { }

       protected override void OnAuthorizeWebPart(
              WebPartAuthorizationEventArgs e) {

       }
}
```

We can now add code that performs common authorization checks into the body of the `OnAuthorizeWebPart` method so that all of our authorization checks are performed from a single place. If an application were simply checking against the application roles of a user, this code would look just like the code shown in listing 4.2.

Another important service offered by the `WebPartManager` is the importing/exporting service, which allows web part definitions to be imported from, and exported to, an external XML format.

4.5　IMPORTING AND EXPORTING WEB PARTS

So you've got your web portal up and running and it's being used throughout the organization. One day one of your key developers tells you that he has just created a clever new web part to expose lines of business data—such as a listing of new customer prospects that the sales people have added to the customer list this month. Now you'd like to make the new web part available to all users of the portal. How do you do that? Does adding the new web part to the site require a deployment of the entire application? You know that deployment of the entire application would involve writing deployment notes, testing the entire application, and recruiting people for the actual deployment.

Breathe a sigh of relief—deployment of the entire application is not required, because the portal framework allows web parts to be transported in and out of web applications via XML definition files known as Control Description Files. There's even a standard catalog part known as the `ImportCatalogPart` that allows users to browse for these XML definition files and import them at runtime.

This section explains the actual mechanics of how the web part manager imports and exports these definition files. This will leave us free to concentrate more specifically on the `ImportCatalogPart` in the next chapter when we look at the `CatalogZone` in greater detail.

The XML format of a web part allows it to be highly portable, thereby enabling us to use it to create certain useful scenarios within our applications. For example:

- An organization might have more than just a single web application. For example, they could have a web application that was used by HR staff to manage staff information, and another web application that was used by all staff to view company announcements, and which allows employees to offer feedback to management. When there is more than one web application within an organization, it makes sense to separate web parts so that they can be shared. Each application then needs to contain only the web parts that are specific to the function of that application. Parts that are more general can then be contained within a central repository so that they can be accessed by all applications. These web parts might include parts that expose information about company news, world news, weather, humor, horoscopes, etc. These general parts would be exposed as XML via the central service by using either a web service or a central file share.

- Applications can be created that allow advanced users to customize complex web parts and then have those customizations saved out to an XML file. This file would contain information reflecting the changes that had been made, and could then be sent to other users or imported into a central repository so that those customizations were available for all users. An example of this might be a web part for configuring a complex report. An administrator could make changes to a report's configuration, such as specifying a date range to use when filtering the data, and then save those changes into a reporting gallery using names that help to define the data that the new report shows, such as Weekly Sales Report, Sales MTD, and Sales YTD.

Now that we've looked at a couple scenarios for using importing and exporting, let's jump in and take a look at the mechanics of it so that we can see how to enable importing and exporting in our own portal.

Requirements for exporting

Before web parts can be exported, two conditions must be met. The first of these requires that the portal framework be configured to allow exporting. This is done by setting the `enableExport` attribute to true on the `webParts` element in the web configuration file.

```
<system.web>
    <webParts enableExport="true">    ◁────┐  The enableExport
                                           │  attribute is set to "true"
    </webParts>
</system.web>
```

The second condition is that the web part that is targeted for export must have its `ExportMode` property set to a value other than None. The values for the `Export-Mode` come from the `WebPartExportMode` enumeration and can have any of the following three values:

- `All`—All the properties and settings of the web part can be extracted.
- `None`—This is the default, and is the most secure setting. When a web part has its `ExportMode` set to this value, an exception will occur if an export operation is attempted upon it.
- `NonSensitiveData`—Only properties and settings that are not marked as sensitive data can be extracted.

Sensitive data are personalized properties that have their `IsSensitive` property set to true. Listing 4.3 shows a class with a single property that is marked as sensitive.

> **Listing 4.3   WebPart properties can be marked as sensitive by specifying so for the isSensitive argument of the Personalizable attribute.**

```
public class SecretWebPart : WebPart {

    string _secret = "";
    [Personalizable(PersonalizationScope.User, true)]  ◁──┐ Pass true as the
    public string Secret {                                 │ second argument
        get {                                              │ for sensitive data
            return this._secret;
        }
```

```
        set {
            this._secret = value;
        }
    }
}
```

If this web part were to be exported, the value of the `Secret` property would only be persisted to the XML format if the `ExportMode` for that part were set to `All`, or if the current page were in shared personalization mode.

Simple import/export example

To help better understand the mechanics of importing and exporting, let's work through a simple example. In this example we'll create a web part that allows users to enter their personal information. The web part will have four fields: Name, Department, SSN, and Date of Birth. The first two fields will have a shared personalization, so changes that are made to them will be visible to all users of the portal. The last two fields, SSN and Date of Birth, will have a per-user personalization use, so changes that are made to them will be visible only to the user who made the changes. Finally, the last two fields will also be marked as sensitive data, so that their values are not persisted during an export operation. When complete, this control will look similar to the one displayed in figure 4.3.

Figure 4.3   The EmployeeDetails web part allows users to enter their personal information while protecting the sensitive SSN and Date of Birth fields from export operations.

NOTE   As I've mentioned already, there is actually an easy way of extracting the XML from a web part by simply using the Export verb that is present on web parts when the requirements for exporting have been met. The reason for deliberately taking the longest route to obtain the XML in this exercise is that along the way we will gain a solid understanding of how the underlying process works. We'll be applying this knowledge later in the book when we learn how to build highly customized web part galleries. So, as you work through this example, just remember, it's really just a baby step towards things to come!

We'll get started by adding a new user control named `EmployeeDetails.ascx` to our test project and adding the user interface code that is shown in the snippet that follows.

```
<div>
    <b>Name:</b> <%= this.Name %><br />
    <b>Department:</b> <%= this.Department %><br />
```

```
    <b>SSN:</b> <%= this.SSN %><br />
    <b>Date of Birth:</b> <%= this.DOB %>
</div>
```

The web part will have a property for each of the four fields it exposes. As you can see, code blocks are interspersed with the HTML markup so that the values of these properties are written into the page. We need to mark each of these properties with the correct attributes to ensure that their data is persisted by the personalization system. We must also ensure that our two private fields are marked as having their data stored on a per-user basis, and that the personalization system treats them as sensitive data for export operations. Listing 4.4 shows the code required to add the four properties and configure their personalization properties correctly.

Listing 4.4 The EmployeeDetails control with properties for each of the four fields it exposes marked appropriately for personalization.

```
public partial class EmployeeDetails : UserControl {

    private string _name;
    [Personalizable(PersonalizationScope.Shared)]      ◁──  Mark as shareable
                                                            data for personalization
    [WebBrowsable]                                      ◁──  Mark as browsable
    public string Name {                                     to appear in
        get { return _name; } set { _name = value; }        property editor
    }

    private string _department;
    [Personalizable(PersonalizationScope.Shared)]
    [WebBrowsable]
    public string Department {
        get { return _department; } set { _department = value; }
    }

    private string _ssn;
    [Personalizable(PersonalizationScope.User, true)]  ◁──  Set scope for
    [WebBrowsable]                                           personalization
    public string SSN {
        get { return _ssn; } set { _ssn = value; }
    }

    private string _dob;
    [Personalizable(PersonalizationScope.User, true)]
    [WebBrowsable]
    public string DOB {
        get { return _dob; } set { _dob = value; }
    }
}
```

That's all that there is to creating this web part. The attributes we've used will ensure that the data is persisted and protected correctly by the personalization system. We can now move on to creating the page that will host our web part. We are going to use this web page to personalize the fields of the web part, and then to export the XML for the web part so that we can view it. When completed the page will have a structure similar to that shown in figure 4.4.

Create a page named `DisplaysMy-Details.aspx` and open it in design view. Add a `WebPartManager` and a `WebPartZone` control and then drag the `EmployeeDetails.ascx` user controls into the zone. At this time we can also create a layout for the page and add controls for our buttons and the XML viewer. The code to create the entire page is shown in listing 4.5.

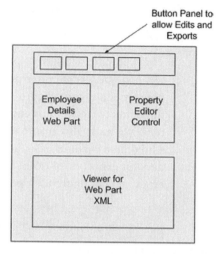

Button Panel to allow Edits and Exports

Employee Details Web Part

Property Editor Control

Viewer for Web Part XML

Figure 4.4 The web page that will host the EmployeeDetails web part will provide an editor to manage the values of the control and a viewer for displaying the exported XML.

Listing 4.5 The markup and server controls required to create the user interface for the page described in figure 4.4.

```
<div id="buttonpanel">
    <asp:Button ID="btnResetPersonalization" runat="server"
            Text="Reset" />
    <asp:Button ID="btnEdit" runat="server" Text="Edit" />
    <asp:Button ID="btnToggleScope" runat="server" />
    <asp:Button ID="btnExport" runat="server" Text="Export" />
    <asp:Button ID="btnImport" runat="server" Text="Import" />
</div>

<div id="webcontrolspanel" style="width:700px">
    <div style="width:320px; float: right">
        <asp:EditorZone ID="EditorZone1" runat="server">
            <ZoneTemplate>
              <asp:PropertyGridEditorPart
                ID="PropertyGridEditorPart1"
                runat="server" />
            </ZoneTemplate>
        </asp:EditorZone>
    </div>
    <div style="width: 300px">
        <asp:WebPartZone ID="WebPartZone1" runat="server">
            <ZoneTemplate>
              <uc2:EmployeeDetails
                ID="EmployeeDetails1"
                runat="server"
                Title="Employee Details"
```

Buttons that drive functionality of page

Property Grid to manage properties of Employee Details

EmployeeDetails web part

```
                    ExportMode="NonSensitiveData"      ↑ EmployeeDetails
                />                                      | web part
            </ZoneTemplate>
        </asp:WebPartZone>
    </div>
</div>

<div id="xmlviewerpanel">                   A TextBox to display
    <asp:TextBox ID="txtWebPart"    ◁───┘   exported web part XML
        runat="Server"
        TextMode="MultiLine"
        Rows="37"
        Columns="90"
        />
</div>
```

Now that we have the web part and the layout for our web page sorted out, it's time to wire up the buttons that we added to the button panel to get our page working. There are five buttons and they serve the following purposes:

- *Reset*—Allows all personalization details for controls on the page to be reset. Clicking on this button will cause any dynamic web parts that have been imported into the zone to be removed, and any values that have been assigned to the web part properties to be removed as well.
- *Edit*—Switches the DisplayMode of the web part manager to Edit. This allows us to edit the properties of the web part.
- *ToggleScope*—Switches the personalization scope between "per-user" and "shared." When the page is in per-user scope the sensitive properties will not be exported, whereas when the page is in shared scope they will.
- *Export*—Exports the XML for our web part causing it to be displayed in the text box.
- *Import*—This button is enabled whenever there is XML in the text box, and causes that web part to be imported into the zone as a new, dynamic web part.

Before we add the code for those buttons, we need to add logic, based on the current state of the page, that will determine issues such as whether the Import button is enabled and deciding what text to display on the Edit and Toggle buttons. Listing 4.6 displays the code we should add to run during the PreRender phase, to keep those button properties synchronized with the current state of the page.

We can now go ahead and wire up the code for the buttons. The Reset, Edit, and Toggle buttons are actually quite straightforward, so we can proceed to add the code for those straight away. The code for them is covered in the listings that follow on pages 114 through 116.

```
protected override void OnPreRender(EventArgs e) {
    base.OnPreRender(e);

    if(WebPartManager1.DisplayMode == WebPartManager.EditDisplayMode){
        this.btnEdit.Text = "Browse" ;          Toggle Edit/Browse
    }else{                                       button
        this.btnEdit.Text = "Edit" ;
    }

    if(WebPartManager1.Personalization.Scope ==
        PersonalizationScope.Shared){
        this.btnToggleScope.Text = "User Scope" ;
    }else{                                       Toggle user
        this.btnToggleScope.Text = "Shared" ;    scope button
    }

    this.btnImport.Enabled = this.txtWebPart.Text.Length > 0;
}
```

The Reset button simply makes a call through to the personalization service and calls the ResetPersonalizationState method. This has the effect of resetting any personalization changes that have been applied to the current page—including any controls on it.

```
protected void btnResetPersonalization_Click(object sender, EventArgs e) {
    this.WebPartManager1.Personalization.ResetPersonalizationState();
}
```

It is the job of the Edit button to switch the page in and out of Edit mode. Clicking this button will toggle the DisplayMode between Browse and Edit. When the page is in Edit mode an Edit verb will appear on the web part, and clicking it will display the EditorZone, allowing the web part to be edited.

```
protected void btnEdit_Click(object sender, EventArgs e) {
    if (this.WebPartManager1.DisplayMode ==
        WebPartManager.EditDisplayMode) {
        WebPartManager1.DisplayMode = WebPartManager.BrowseDisplayMode;
    } else {
        WebPartManager1.DisplayMode = WebPartManager.EditDisplayMode;
    }
}
```

The next task is to write the code for the Toggle Scope button. When we click on this button, the "personalization scope" for the page will be toggled between two values: Shared and Per-User. We'll be learning a lot more about personalization scope throughout the book, but for now just understand that any personalization scope affects certain users when changes are made to web parts. Any changes that are made to web parts when the page is in shared scope apply to all users of a site—even unauthenticated ones. Changes made to web parts when a page is in per-user scope only apply to the user who made them. Also, when web parts are exported on a web part and the page is in shared scope, then all of the properties of that part will be exported, whereas if the page is in per-user scope, then only non-sensitive properties are persisted.

```
protected void btnToggleScope_Click(object sender, EventArgs e) {
    if (WebPartManager1.Personalization.CanEnterSharedScope)
        WebPartManager1.Personalization.ToggleScope();
}
```

We can now write the code for the actual import and export operations. The Web-PartManager class provides two methods which we'll be using to perform these operations, and they are shown in the snippets that follow:

```
public virtual void ExportWebPart (
        WebPart webPart,
        XmlWriter writer
)

public virtual WebPart ImportWebPart (
        XmlReader reader,
        out string errorMessage
)
```

WARNING! Exporting web parts can allow potentially sensitive data to be imported and exported. As such, this feature should be handled with care—especially when importing XML that is external to your application.

Using the methods provided by the WebPartManager makes writing the code to perform these operations straightforward. We simply grab the web part that we want to serialize and pass it to the ExportWebPart method along with an XmlText-Writer that we create. The code to do this is explained in listing 4.7.

> **Listing 4.7   Clicking the Export button causes the web part to be serialized and the resulting XML to be displayed in the viewer text box.**

```
protected void btnExport_Click(object sender, EventArgs e) {

    StringBuilder sb = new StringBuilder();
    WebPart partToExport =
        WebPartManager1.GetGenericWebPart(EmployeeDetails1);

    if (partToExport.ExportMode != WebPartExportMode.None) {    ◁┐ Check that
                                                                 │ web part can
        using (StringWriter sw = new StringWriter(sb))          │ be exported
        using (XmlTextWriter xw = new XmlTextWriter(sw)) {
            WebPartManager1.ExportWebPart(partToExport, xw);    ◁┐ Export
        }                                                        │ web part
```

```
        string partXML = sb.ToString();
        this.txtWebPart.Text = partXML;   ◄——— Display XML in viewer
    }
}
```

After you have extracted the XML definition for the web part, you can choose where to store it. It doesn't matter where the XML is stored, just as long as it can be accessed for importing at a later time. Typically, if the web part definitions are not going to be made available outside the current application, they may be stored in either the file system or in a database. If they are going to be accessed by more than a single application, it would make sense to abstract the storage and retrieval of web part definitions behind a web service façade so that any application can access them. Regardless of where we choose to store the XML for our web part definitions, importing a web part simply means retrieving the XML. When we have the XML for a web part, it can be passed to the ImportWebPart method of the WebPartManager to create a web part instance. Once we have our web part instance, we simply use the WebPartManager again to add the web part to the page. Code listing 4.8 shows the code needed to perform an import operation:

> **Listing 4.8   Clicking the Import button causes a dynamic web part to be created based upon the XML in the viewer text box.**

```
protected void btnImport_Click(object sender, EventArgs e) {

    string partXML = this.txtWebPart.Text;

    if (!string.IsNullOrEmpty(partXML)) {
        using (StringReader sr = new System.IO.StringReader(partXML))
        using (XmlTextReader tr = new XmlTextReader(sr)) {
            string errorMessage;
            WebPart webPart =                             Import web part XML
                WebPartManager1.ImportWebPart(tr, out errorMessage);   ◄┘

            WebPartManager1.AddWebPart(
                webPart,
                WebPartZone1,              Add part to
                WebPartZone1.WebParts.Count   the page
                );
        }
        this.txtWebPart.Text = string.Empty;
    }
}
```

That's all the code that is required to be able to run the example. Before we run the code, however, we must make two final checks. Earlier when we looked at the requirements for being able to export web parts, it was mentioned that the exporting functionality must first be enabled in the web configuration file. In our example we are switching the personalization scope into Shared scope; and doing so also requires a configuration entry. Open the `Web.Config` file and make sure that you have a `webParts` section which contains the entries shown in this snippet:

```
scope.
<system.web>
    <webParts enableExport="true">
            <personalization>
                <authorization>
                    <allow
                        verbs="enterSharedScope"
                        users="*" />
                </authorization>
            </personalization>
        </webParts>
</system.web>
```

Configuring the authorization for personalization in this way allows us to switch the personalization scope of web pages into shared scope. Using the star (*) for the users' attribute simply means that all users can set the scope of web pages into shared scope. Other options here include limiting the ability to make scope changes to certain users or enforcing restrictions based on the users' role within the application.

When you run the example it should appear in a browser, and look similar to the image shown in figure 4.5.

Notice the XML that is produced when the Import button is clicked. Try changing the scope between Shared and Per-User to see how it affects the XML that is produced.

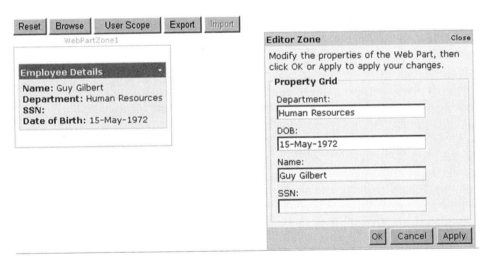

Figure 4.5 The completed page allows the properties of the web part to be managed within the standard PropertyGrid Editor part.

Notice also that changes that are made in Per-User scope are not visible when you are in Shared scope mode. You might also notice that the web part has an Export verb that provides a way of automatically creating the XML. We'll see this again in the next chapter when we take a closer look at the `ImportCatalogPart`. Before we move away from the exporting feature, let's finish by taking a brief look at the format of the XML that was exported.

XML format of web part description files

The web part description files that we've been exporting contain all of the information required to create an instance of the underlying web control, and to set all of the property information for it. The file is basically split into two sections named `meta-Data` and `data`. The `data` section contains all of the information about the state of the web part, whereas the `metaData` section contains some additional information about the underlying assembly and also what error message should be displayed to the user in the event of an import failure. Listing 4.9 shows an abbreviated version of the web part description file from our example.

Listing 4.9 The web part description file contains details about the state of a web part and also its type information.

```
<webParts>
    <webPart xmlns="http://schemas.microsoft.com/WebPart/v3">
        <metaData>
            <type src="~/WebParts/EmployeeDetails.ascx" />      ← Assembly
            <importErrorMessage>                                    type or
                    Cannot import this Web Part.      ←            path to
            </importErrorMessage>                                  user control
        </metaData>                            Message to display
        <data>                                 for import errors
            <properties>   ←──  Properties
                            of web part
                <property name="Name" type="string">Guy Gilbert</property>
                <property name="DOB" type="string">15-May-1972</property>
                <property name="SSN" type="string" />
                <property name="Department" type="string">
                    Human Resources
                </property>
            </properties>
            <genericWebPartProperties>   ←──  User control
                                              configuration
                <property name="AllowClose" type="bool">True</property>
                <property name="Width" type="unit" />
                <property name="ExportMode" type="exportmode">
                    NonSensitiveData
                </property>
            </genericWebPartProperties>
        </data>
    </webPart>
</webParts>
```

Getting to this point has been quite an intense learning experience, but in the process we've gained important knowledge. We've learned how to serialize and de-serialize web parts, and seen how doing so provides a way to store and share them among applications. We've also scratched the surface of personalization. Personalization may appear a little confusing for the moment but don't despair; chapter 6 explains it more fully. The last item we'll look at in this chapter involves web parts and master pages. We'll learn a bit about master pages and see how to manage interactions between web parts and the `WebPartManager` when using master pages.

4.6 USING WEBPARTMANAGER WITH MASTER PAGES

At your first meeting with master pages, you'll do little more than shake hands, but you'll see how to use them and also gain an understanding for the effect that they have on the interactions between web parts and the `WebPartManager`, and that's a good start. Master pages are new in ASP.NET 2.0 and will be a very popular feature because they enable us to easily apply a consistent layout to an entire web application. To achieve this, one or more master pages is created that defines the layout for the common user interface elements. If you've ever used master pages in PowerPoint presentations, this should sound familiar, because an ASP.NET master page also contains behaviors that are common to all pages. Each actual page contains only unique content; and all the common elements such as menus, headers, and footers are contained within the master page file.

In addition to the base HTML markup, the master page also contains one or more content placeholders. These placeholders define regions within the template that are substituted with the page content at runtime. The snippet that follows shows a simple master page template:

```
<%@ Master Language="C#" %>

... HTML, HEAD AND BODY TAGS WOULD GO HERE

<table>
<tr>
        <td>
                <asp:contentplaceholder id="MainContent" runat="server" />
        </td>
        <td>
                <asp:contentplaceholder id="SideContent" runat="server" />
        </td>
</tr>
</table>
```

A content page references the master page by using the `MasterPageFile` attribute of the `Page` directive and then creates a `Content` control for each `ContentPlace-Holder` control in the master page that it wants to provide content for. The content within the Content controls is merged with the master page content at runtime. The snippet that follows shows the markup for a content page that references a master page:

```
<%@ Page Language="C#" MasterPageFile="~/Default.master" %>

<asp:Content ID="Content1" ContentPlaceHolderID="MainContent"
  Runat="Server">
        ... Main content would go here
</asp:Content>

<asp:Content ID="Content1" ContentPlaceHolderID="SideContent"
  Runat="Server">
        ... Other content would go here
</asp:Content>
```

For web part applications, we can use master pages and content placeholders to declare the WebPartManager and other common controls within the master page file—this could include controls such as the EditorZone and CatalogZone controls as well. When the WebPartManager is declared in a master page, it cannot declare the StaticConnections for parts within content pages. As you will remember from the last chapter, the WebPartManager allows you to explicitly declare static connections between two parts on a web page within the body of the WebPartManager tag itself through the use of a StaticConnections element:

```
<asp:WebPartManager ID="WebPartManager1" runat="server">
        <StaticConnections>
                <asp:WebPartConnection
                        ID="cnn"
                        ConsumerID="NumberConsumer1"
                        ProviderID="NumberProvider1"
                        />
        </StaticConnections>
</asp:WebPartManager>
```

So that static connections can be declared when the web part manager is contained within a master page, the web part framework provides us with the ProxyWebPart-Manager which can be declared in the content pages and used to define the static connections. You actually create the ProxyWebPartManager in the same way that you would create a WebPartManager, and at runtime the ProxyWebPartManager communicates information through to the WebPartManager on our behalf. If you don't actually have any static connections to declare, then you can get away without having to add a ProxyWebPartManager.

```
<asp:ProxyWebPartManager ID="ProxyWebPartManager1" runat="server">
        <StaticConnections>
                <asp:WebPartConnection ... />
        </StaticConnections>
</asp:ProxyWebPartManager>
```

Well that's it; well done. It's been quite a journey exploring the `WebPartManager`; but it's time well spent because you've shored up the knowledge you need to dig in and work the deep behavioral customizations that your customers will demand. Armed with this knowledge, let's re-visit the Adventure Works portal to see how the application of these `WebPartManager` customizations will affect our code base.

4.7 ADVENTURE WORKS— ADDITIONS TO THE HR CODE

At the end of chapter 3 the Adventure Works portal was starting to shape up. At that point, we had web parts displaying lists of departments and employees to users. In addition, a connection allowed users to select departments and to have those selections change the employees shown in the other web part. The HR management is cheering the progress that you've made with the portal, but has highlighted some potential concerns. Their biggest concern is security; they are concerned that as the number of web parts on the portal grows and more users start using the portal, unauthorized users might be able to view sensitive information.

Another feature that the HR management has asked us to investigate is how we can allow their users to perform certain customization tasks on the portal, such as repositioning web parts on pages and dynamically adding or removing web parts from pages.

In this section we are going to add two new features to our Adventure Works portal application that will help us to meet the requests from the HR management. First we'll add a control that allows users to change the display mode of the page at runtime. Having the ability to dynamically change the display mode is essential to allowing portal users to perform the kinds of tasks HR wants—namely, moving web parts around and adding or removing web parts.

After we've created the control for changing display modes, we'll implement a custom `WebPartManager`. The custom `WebPartManager` will contain code for performing authorization checks on all web parts from a central place and in a consistent manner.

> **NOTE** If you don't have a copy of the project from chapter 3 you can grab it from the chapter 3 section of the resources website for this book.

Creating a DisplayMode picker control

In chapter 3 we added code to the `Default.aspx` page that allowed us to manage connections. To achieve this, we had to hard-code the page so that it was set in "connect" mode. As we've learned in this chapter, we can fix that by implementing a mode changer control that allows users to dynamically change the page mode at runtime. Open the `Default.aspx` page in code view and remove the following line of code:

```
WebPartManager1.DisplayMode = WebPartManager.ConnectDisplayMode;
```

To allow the users to change the mode we'll create a user control that displays a list of available modes and allows them to make a selection that changes the current mode. Additionally the control should pre-select the current mode within the list. Create a new user control named ModeChanger.ascx and add a DropDownList control to it. Set the AutoPostBack property of the dropdown list to true so that events are fired whenever the selected item is changed. The code for the dropdown control should now look like this:

```
<asp:DropDownList ID="DropDownList1" runat="server" AutoPostBack="True" />
```

There are two aspects to creating our mode changer control. The first of these is loading the control with data. We saw this earlier in the chapter when we looked at the page display modes. In that section we saw that WebPartManager exposes a property which contains a list of the display modes available to us. We'll use this property when the page is initializing and add the names of each one as a list item in the DropDownList control. The following snippet displays the code to do that:.

```
protected override void OnInit(EventArgs e) {
    base.OnInit(e);

    WebPartManager wpm =
        WebPartManager.GetCurrentWebPartManager(this.Page);

    foreach (WebPartDisplayMode displayMode in wpm.SupportedDisplayModes) {

        if (displayMode.IsEnabled(wpm)) {
            DropDownList1.Items.Add(
            new ListItem(displayMode.Name)
            );
        }
    }
}
```

The key functionality here is that we use the IsEnabled property of the WebPart-DisplayMode to ensure that only display modes available for the current state of the page will be added to the list. For example, if EditorZone is not on the page, the EditDisplayMode will not be enabled, so there is no point in offering the user the option to switch into that mode.

The second issue we confront is what code we must write to change the modes. The code that manages the mode changing will be wired up to handle selection changes in the dropdown list. This means that whenever the user changes the selected item in the list, an event will be raised and our code will be run. In the code that handles the event we will grab the text from the selected item in the list and then check to ensure that it is a supported mode value. We'll use that value to set the current display mode on the WebPartManager.

```
protected void DropDownList1_SelectedIndexChanged(
    object sender, EventArgs e) {
```

```
    WebPartManager wpm =
        WebPartManager.GetCurrentWebPartManager(this.Page);

        string modeName = DropDownList1.SelectedValue;
    WebPartDisplayMode mode = wpm.SupportedDisplayModes[modeName] ;
    if( mode != null )
        wpm.DisplayMode = mode ;
}
```

All that remains is to ensure that whatever display mode the page is currently in also appears as the selected item in the dropdown list. To set the selected item of the dropdown list, add the code shown in the snippet that follows to our master page:

```
protected override void OnPreRender(EventArgs e) {

    WebPartManager wpm =
        WebPartManager.GetCurrentWebPartManager(this.Page);

    WebPartDisplayMode currentMode = wpm.DisplayMode;

    DropDownList1.ClearSelection();
    DropDownList1.Items.FindByText(currentMode.Name).Selected = true;

}
```

We can now add the user control to the web part page and press run to see the results. You should receive a result similar to the picture shown in figure 4.6.

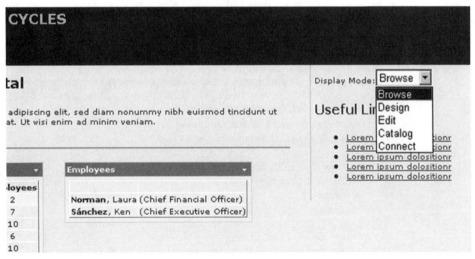

Figure 4.6   The ModeChanger control as it appears within the Adventure Works Portal application.

NOTE You can add a `PropertyGridEditorPart` to the `EditorZone` and a `PageCatalogPart` to the `CatalogZone` to make the Edit and Catalog modes appear within the list.

Adding a custom WebPartManager

The next feature we want to implement is a custom `WebPartManager` to handle all our web part authorization checks. The code we'll be implementing to perform authorization checks is similar to the code we saw earlier in the chapter when we discussed using `AuthorizationFilter` strings to store authentication information. In the section on web part authorization I mentioned that it is good for authorization logic to be standard across the entire application. The logic for the authorization checks we'll be performing is all the same—checking to find which roles a user is a member of—so moving all of the authorization logic for displaying web parts into the web part manager makes sense: single point of implementation, single point of failure!

To create our custom `WebPartManager`, add a class file to the project named `PortalWebPartManager.cs` by right-clicking on the `App_Code` folder and choosing `Add File`. When the file is created ensure that the `PortalWebPartManager` class inherits from `WebPartManger`.

There are two pieces of code that need to be added to our custom `WebPartManager`. We need one method that will perform a role-based check for the current user and another method to handle the `AuthorizeWebPart` events. The code that handles the authorization events will get the `AuthorizationFilter` string for each web part and then split it up into individual roles. Once we have the individual roles for each web part we can loop through them and check each role to determine whether or not the user has access to that web part. Listings 4.10 and 4.11 contain the code for handling the event and for the helper method which checks the users' roles.

> **Listing 4.10 When web parts require authorization, we compare the roles in the AuthorizationFilter with the users' roles to see if they match.**

```
protected override void OnAuthorizeWebPart(
    WebPartAuthorizationEventArgs e) {

    if (string.IsNullOrEmpty(e.AuthorizationFilter)) {      ◁── Role restrictions
        e.IsAuthorized = true;                                    on this part?
        return;
    }
                                                            ┌─ Convert filter
    string[] authorizedRoles =                              │  to array of
        e.AuthorizationFilter.Split(new char[] { ',' });  ◁┘  role strings

    for (int i = 0; i < authorizedRoles.Length; i++) {
        if (IsUserInRole(authorizedRoles[i])) {  ◁─ Check each
            e.IsAuthorized = true;                    role string
            return;                                   individually
        }
```

```
        }
        e.IsAuthorized = false;   <———— No match, return false
}
```

Role membership is checked in two places as shown in listing 4.11. First we determine whether the application is configured to use the new ASP.NET 2.0 Roles feature and, if so, we check with that feature to see if there's a match. If the Roles feature is not enabled, we simply check the user attached to the current thread to determine whether it has a valid role membership. We have not configured the Adventure Works portal to use the Roles feature, so our code will refer to whatever user is attached to the current context when performing authorization checks.

Listing 4.11   Check the role membership of the current user.

```
bool IsUserInRole(string roleName) {
    if (Roles.Enabled) {
        return Roles.IsUserInRole(roleName);
    } else {
        return Context.User.IsInRole(roleName);
    }
}
```

By adding this code to our custom WebPartManager, we now have a single point for managing all the web part authorization logic in the portal, and also a single place from which to fix any bugs that arise within the code.

4.8   SUMMARY

This is a core chapter as it has provided us an understanding of how the portal framework works. That understanding will prove invaluable as we start customizing our portal application in the upcoming chapters. When you combine the concepts you've mastered in this chapter with the knowledge of personalization you will gain in the next chapter, you will find that you have unraveled many of the key concepts of the portal framework. Chapter 5 will put you in good standing because it covers the last of the web part controls—Zones. Then, chapter 6 wraps up discussions on personalization. So as you start chapter 7, your ability to produce a uniquely customized portal will be limited only if you withhold your creativity or have limited time and energy to expend.

You should come away from this chapter with several key points. First, you've seen that a close relationship exists between the WebPartManager and personalization. We witnessed how the power of that relationship works when we created the EmployeeDetails control and saw that users were able to change its property values and have those changes persisted without our needing to write any code to do so. In that same exercise we saw how the WebPartManager can extract an XML definition from a web part and then recreate the web part from that same definition at a later point in time. This feature will become increasingly important to us later in the book when we extend the Adventure Works Catalog to facilitate portal users in choosing web parts from a web service catalog.

This chapter demonstrated another important point—how the `WebPartManager` manages the current mode of a page and how this determines what controls are visible. This behavior brings home the symbiotic nature of all the controls within the framework. It's this oneness that I find most appealing as it enables rich functionality to be provided with a minimum of implementation code.

The final concept from this chapter that I'd like you to hold onto is the Page Lifecycle. Understanding the Page Lifecycle is crucial to determining how the components in web applications work. Failure to observe important events such as page initialization and pre-rendering occurring within our page can lead to unexpected and oftentimes unwanted behavior—as we saw when we added a zone to the page and it caused an exception to be thrown.

CHAPTER 5

Working with zones

5.1 INTRODUCTION

Now that you have reached the half-way mark of this book, it may be helpful to stand back for a minute and see where you are. The previous three chapters have been reference chapters for the major web part controls within the portal framework. Each of those three chapters was written to provide a solid understanding of the major building blocks used when developing portal applications. To re-cap a bit, we first learned about the WebPart control and saw that it provides a way to display data that users can personalize to suit their own preferences. We also saw that users can move web parts around at runtime within the regions of the page known as zones. After learning about web parts we saw how to use web part connections to extend the usefulness of web parts by allowing them to interoperate with other web parts on the page. And then, in the previous chapter dealing with the WebPartManager control we gained insights into how the WebPartManager control orchestrates the inner workings of the portal. We saw that the WebPartManager control scrutinizes nearly all events and provides the events that supply the portal framework with its lifecycle. Such events include controlling when personalization data is gathered up and sent off for storage.

In this chapter—the fourth and last of the web part control reference chapters—we will explore the topic of zones. As we hike through the chapter we'll gain an appreciation that zones are much more than rectangular areas that web parts can be dragged in and out of. In fact, we'll see that zones play a very fundamental role in determining the character of our portal. We'll start by learning how zones are classified and then look into traits that are common to all zones.

5.2   CLASSIFYING ZONES

Within the portal framework all zones are categorized as being either WebPart zones or Tool zones. This classification is based on two concerns: first, what type of child controls the zones contain; and second, what purpose the zones serve. WebPart zones contain web parts as their child controls, whereas Tool zones contain the child controls consisting of editor parts, catalog parts, or connections.

The purpose of WebPart zones is therefore to contain web parts while it is the role of the ToolZone to contain controls that offer tasks complimentary to web parts, such as catalog controls, editing controls, and connection controls. WebPart zones should seem familiar to us by now, because they are the main type of zone we've used so far, but let's take a look at both types of zones and explore their differences.

5.2.1   WebPart zones

Throughout the book so far we've used WebPart zones extensively to provide a place where our web parts can live on a web page. We've seen that web parts can be added to a WebPartZone control either at design time or dynamically at runtime. To allow web parts to be added at design time, the WebPartZone exposes a special ZoneTemplate to declare web parts within. An example of this is shown in listing 5.1:

> **Listing 5.1   A WebPartZone that contains a single web part declared within its zone template.**

```
<asp:WebPartZone ID="WebPartZone2" runat="server">
    <PartTitleStyle BackColor="Black" Font-Bold="True"
        ForeColor="White" />
    <PartStyle BackColor="LightGray" />
    <ZoneTemplate>
        <uc2:EmployeeDetails
            ID="EmployeeDetails3"
            runat="server"
            Title="Employee Info" />
    </ZoneTemplate>
</asp:WebPartZone>
```

The code listing shows a WebPartZone with some declarative elements that control certain style elements. Also declared within the WebPartZone is the ZoneTemplate section; it's within the zone template that the EmployeeDetails web part is declared and will inherit the styles that we see declared within the WebPartZone definition.

Figure 5.1 shows how the part styles that are contained within the `WebPartZone` would affect the `EmployeeDetails` web part when it is rendered within a browser.

Figure 5.1 shows that styles declared within the `WebPart` zone apply to all web parts displayed within this particular zone. On this occasion, the `PartTitleStyle` element ensures that each web part has a title with a black-colored background and its title is displayed in white, emboldened text. The `PartStyle` element provides the web part a gray-colored background.

Figure 5.1 The Employee Info web part shows the effects that have been applied by the style elements contained within the WebPartZone.

5.2.2 Tool zones

Tool zones provide the controls that allow users to manage web parts within the portal. For example, we saw how the `ConnectionsZone` provides a place for configuring and maintaining connections between web parts. Likewise, we've seen that the `EditorZone` provides controls for managing the properties of web parts within a web page. Three types of tool zones come as a standard part of the ASP.NET 2.0 control set: `EditorZone`, `ConnectionsZone`, and `CatalogZone`.

Both the `EditorZone` and the `CatalogZone` have a `ZoneTemplate` similar to the one in the `WebPartZone`, allowing a user to declare child controls at design-time. However, unlike the `WebPartZone`, any controls contained within the `ZoneTemplate` of these zones cannot be `WebPart` controls. In the case of the `EditorZone`, any controls declared within its `ZoneTemplate` must inherit from a base class called `EditorPart`, whereas any controls contained by the `CatalogZone` must inherit from a base class named `CatalogPart`. Listing 5.2 shows the declarative syntax for creating a `CatalogZone` as well as an `EditorZone`.

> **Listing 5.2 The CatalogZone and EditorZone both have zone templates that contain their "parts" and also have similar style elements.**

```
<asp:CatalogZone ID="CatalogZone1" runat="server">
    <PartTitleStyle BackColor="#507CD1" ForeColor="White" />
    <FooterStyle BackColor="Red" ForeColor="White" />
    <HeaderStyle BackColor="Red" ForeColor="White" />
    <ZoneTemplate>
        <asp:PageCatalogPart ID="PageCatalogPart1" runat="server" />
    </ZoneTemplate>
</asp:CatalogZone>


<asp:EditorZone ID="EditorZone1" runat="server">
    <PartTitleStyle BackColor="#507CD1" ForeColor="White" />
    <FooterStyle BackColor="Red" ForeColor="White" />
    <HeaderStyle BackColor="Red" ForeColor="White" />
    <ZoneTemplate>
```

```
            <asp:AppearanceEditorPart ID="Part1" runat="server" />
            <asp:BehaviorEditorPart ID="Part2" runat="server" />
      </ZoneTemplate>
</asp:EditorZone>
```

Each of the "part" controls contained within the template zones of the `EditorZone` and `CatalogZone` exist to provide a specific piece of functionality. Within the `EditorZone`, the `AppearanceEditorPart` control allows users to manage certain appearance aspects of web parts, such as their title, height, and width. The `BehaviorEditorPart` enables administrators to control other web part properties such as the `TitleUrl` or the `CatalogIcon` for the web part. In the `ZoneTemplate` of the `CatalogZone`, a `PageCatalogPart` is declared that provides users with a way to manage which web parts are displayed on the page at any given time.

Noting that each of the zones shown in listings 5.1 and 5.2 has had a `ZoneTemplate` provides insight into the similarities that exist between them. Not only do the zones each have a `ZoneTemplate`, but we can see that each of the three zones shown in these examples—`WebPartZone`, `CatalogZone`, and `EditorZone`—has contained an identical set of style elements. So while I've told you that zones fall into two camps—`WebPart` zones and `Tool` zones—it's clear that quite a few similarities exist across all zones. The section that follows explores the inherent similarities in zones because all zones are derived from a common base class.

5.2.3   WebZone—the common base class

Now that we've seen how all zones fall into one of two categories, it's important to understand that both the `ToolZone` and `WebPartZone` classes themselves inherit from a common base class named `WebZone`. The inheritance hierarchy for all zones can be seen in the following code snippet:

- `WebZone`
  - `ToolZone`
    - `CatalogZoneBase`
      - `CatalogZone`
    - `EditorZoneBase`
      - `EditorZone`
    - `ConnectionsZone`
  - `WebPartZoneBase`
    - `WebPartZone`

This hierarchy listing shows us that, regardless of whether a zone is a `WebPart` zone or a `Tool` zone, all zones are ultimately derived from the `WebZone` class, and it's this class that provides the zones with common attributes—such as their styles and their rectangular appearance within a page.

Learning about the common inheritance of zones and the two classifications of zones has been an important step toward truly understanding them. Now let's take a closer look at the common style elements that are provided for all zones by the `Web-Zone` class.

5.2.4   Zone appearance

Listings 5.1 and 5.2 offered a glimpse at the common styles of zones and how each zone was declared in a similar manner. Because they derive from the `WebZone` class, all zones share the following common features:

- The style settings for the zone
- Zone layout

The layout for zones is provided by a set of common rendering methods that exist on the `WebZone` class, which we'll cover in a short while. For now, however, concentrate on the styles for zones to see what they cover and how we can work with them.

Common styles are exposed to zones via a vast set of style properties on the `Web-Zone` class. This explains why each of the zones in the earlier listings contained the same named style settings for properties such as `PartTitleStyle`, `HeaderStyle`, and `FooterStyle`. These style properties are responsible for determining how borders are displayed, what colors and fonts are used, and how the headers and footers of zones are presented to users. We can use these style properties to customize the rendered appearance of controls within the zones on our pages. In figure 5.2 we see a `CatalogZone` with callouts showing various areas and regions within that zone which can be affected by styles.

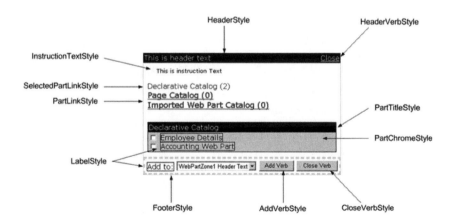

Figure 5.2   The style elements can be used to affect the appearance of a wide range of elements within the zone.

The use of style elements allows us to apply font settings, background and foreground colors, and even images to all the major regions within our zones. Not all the styles called out in figure 5.2 are properties of the base `WebZone` class. Rather, the `WebZone` class supplies only the styles that are common to all zones, such as `HeaderStyle`, `FooterStyle`, `PartStyle` and `PartChromeStyle`. Other style properties specific to a specific zone are added by that zone. For example, the `InstructionTextStyle` property is added by the `CatalogZone`, as it is the only zone to supply such text.

Listing 5.3 contains the declarative syntax necessary to create the `CatalogZone` shown in figure 5.2

Listing 5.3   This CatalogZone contains style elements that are used to control the visual appearance of the zone and its child controls.

```
<asp:CatalogZone ID="CatalogZone1" runat="server"
     Font-Names="Verdana"
     Padding="10"
     InstructionText="This is instruction Text"
     HeaderText="This is header text"
     BorderColor="lightgray"
     BorderWidth="1px">

     <HeaderVerbStyle ForeColor="White" />
     <HeaderStyle BackColor="Black" ForeColor="White" />
     <CloseVerb Text="Close Verb" />
     <AddVerb Text="Add Verb" />                    Style elements provide the
     <VerbStyle Font-Size="Smaller" />                visual characteristics
     <PartLinkStyle ForeColor="Blue" />
     <SelectedPartLinkStyle ForeColor="Blue" />
     <InstructionTextStyle Font-Size="Small"
          CssClass="instruction-text" />
     <LabelStyle BorderColor="Black" BorderWidth="1px" />
     <PartChromeStyle BackColor="Control" />
     <PartLinkStyle Font-Size=Large />
     <PartTitleStyle BackColor="Black" ForeColor="White" />
     <FooterStyle BorderStyle="Dashed" />


     <ZoneTemplate>
       <asp:DeclarativeCatalogPart ID="DeclarativeCatalogPart1"
         runat="server">
         <WebPartsTemplate>
           <uc2:EmployeeDetails ID="EmployeeDetails2"
             runat="server" Title="Employee Details" />
           <wp:AccountingPart ID="AccountingPart"
             runat="server" Title="Accounting Web Part" />
         </WebPartsTemplate>
       </asp:DeclarativeCatalogPart>
     <asp:PageCatalogPart ID="PageCatalogPart1"
```

```
       runat="server" />
       <asp:ImportCatalogPart ID="ImportCatalogPart1"
          runat="server" />
    </ZoneTemplate>

 </asp:CatalogZone>
```

As we see in this listing, there are many attributes that can be affected by the style. Each of these style elements actually inherits from the base `System.Web.UI.WebControls.Style` class, which means that each style element allows the user to define fonts, colors, borders, and CSS styles for a particular area within the control's user interface. Having the ability to define a CSS style through the style elements is important because there is much that can be controlled through CSS which cannot be managed by a style. In listing 5.3 the `InstructionTextStyle` declares a CSS style named "instruction-text" so that it can control the padding on its left side. This is how the instruction text is made to appear indented in figure 5.2.

Although styles provide us with a great deal of flexibility in customizing the rendered output of zones, you sometimes require a finer level of control, such as when you need to add totally new elements within the zone. The next section describes how to deal with this type of situation.

5.3 CUSTOM RENDERING OF ZONES

The tools described in this section enable us to customize zone output to a greater degree than you can using styles. To view this higher degree of customization, take a look at figure 5.3, which shows the `CatalogZone` from SharePoint.

The SharePoint gallery is similar to the ASP.NET `CatalogZone`, in that it lists each gallery (Catalog) in the top half of the zone and allows a user to select a gallery. When a gallery is selected, the web parts contained within the gallery are displayed in the lower half of the zone. The SharePoint Gallery contains some unique features that cannot be achieved purely through the use of styles, such as

Figure 5.3 The CatalogZone in SharePoint provides elements for paging and filtering which cannot be achieved by simply specifying styles.

- Web Parts appear in a pageable list.
- A Filter allows web parts to be filtered.
- There is even spacing between the name of each gallery and the number of parts contained.

In order to achieve these types of effects within our own zones, we must resort to customizing the rendering process of the zone rather than simply applying styles. Throughout the next section we'll learn which methods must be overridden to custom render zones, and we'll see some code samples for doing so.

5.3.1 The structure of zones

Before the discussion on styles I mentioned that, in addition to providing common styles for zones, the `WebZone` class also provides methods to control the rendering of specific areas within a zone; because of this all zones share the layout shown in figure 5.2.

As we can see in figure 5.4, all zones actually have a header, footer, and a body section. The header generally displays the title, the body contains the parts exposed by the zone, and the footer contains additional controls. Looking at figure 5.5, we can see how this layout is applied to a `Catalog-Zone` control.

The `CatalogZone` shown in figure 5.5 is a good example of how zones use their header and footer space to render titles, verbs, and optionally any other helper controls that may be useful to serving the needs of the zone. In the case of the `CatalogZone`, we see that the title of the zone and a Close verb are rendered in the header, while the footer contains a selector control which lists the zones contained on the page and two verbs: one for adding web parts to the selected zone and one to close the catalog zone.

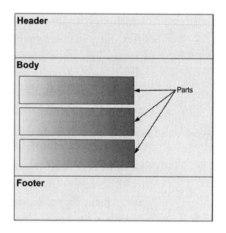

Figure 5.4 Each zone has three major sections which are enforced by rendering methods contained within the base WebZone class.

Figure 5.5
The CatalogZone uses its footer section to provide controls that allow the user to choose where to add web parts on the page.

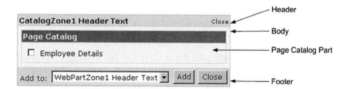

5.3.2 Rendering the header, body, and footer

The `WebZone` base class provides the following methods that can be overridden to control the rendering of zones:

- `RenderContents`
- `RenderHeader`
- `RenderBody`
- `RenderFooter`

By overriding any or all of these methods we can provide complete customization over the appearance of zones by directly emitting our own custom HTML as the rendered output. To fully understand this, consider what happens when we do not customize these methods and therefore get the base implementation of them. In the base implementation of the `RenderContents` method, an outer table is created and then the `RenderHeader`, `RenderBody`, and `RenderFooter` methods are called to display those sections of the zone within the table. This gives us the structure shown in figure 5.4.

When customizing zones by using custom rendering, we first choose which section of the zone we are customizing and then override the relevant method. For example, let's say we wanted our zones to exist within HTML DIV elements rather than HTML tables. By overriding the default behavior of the `RenderContents` method, a different HTML tag could be used to contain the zone such as a DIV. Likewise, if we have some special requirements for displaying custom user interface elements to the user from within our zone, we can override any of the rendering methods to insert our logic. For example, to create a totally custom footer section within a zone we simply create a class that inherits from the zone type that we want to customize, and then override the `RenderFooter` method this way:

```
public class ListCatalogZone : CatalogZone {

        protected override void RenderFooter(HtmlTextWriter writer) {
            // Custom footer rendering code goes here...
        }
}
```

By overriding the `RenderFooter` method in this manner we are free to use the `HtmlTextWriter` to add any rendering code we please—or even to not render anything, and therefore remove the footer rendering from the `CatalogZone` altogether.

Although taking ownership of the render process for sections of the zones makes it possible to provide a totally unique interface for our zones, taking ownership can also be an onerous task. For example, if we overrode the `RenderBody` method for the `CatalogZone`, we would be undertaking the responsibility of rendering the following:

- Instruction text
- Links for each gallery
- Links for each web part for the selected gallery

All of this adds up to quite a bit of work. We have to ensure not only that we do the right thing when adding our custom user interface elements, but also that we re-create the existing user interface elements correctly. When re-creating the existing user interface elements, care must be taken to ensure that it is done in a manner consistent with their normal appearance. This means that we are not only creating HTML to contain and display text, but also applying any styles that the user has added via the zone declaration.

Having looked at the structure of zones and examined the rendering process of them, it's time to get our hands dirty by writing code that allows us to perform custom rendering of our own zone.

5.3.3 Displaying the galleries in a DropDownList

To see how to customize the appearance of our galleries we will now create a custom `CatalogZone` and override its `RenderCatalogPartLinks` method so that each of the galleries are displayed within a dropdown list as opposed to being listed as individually clickable links. The tasks involved in creating this customization are

- Override the `RenderCatalogPartLinks` method of the zone to insert custom rendering logic to insert a dropdown list at the top of the zone.
- Create code that displays the instructional text of the zone and apply styles that have been supplied by the developer.
- Create a method that handles the postback event of the dropdown list and use the selected value of the list to set the selected gallery.

Figure 5.6 shows how our custom catalog zone will appear at runtime.

Notice that the galleries in our custom `CatalogZone` are now contained within a dropdown list and that only galleries containing web parts are displayed. Let's see how this custom rendering is performed. In your test project, create a new class named `ListCatalogZone` and derive it from the `CatalogZone` class. Next, override the `RenderCatalogPartLinks` method to display the instructional text and create a dropdown to display the galleries. The code to do this is displayed in listing 5.4.

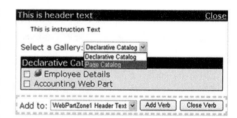

Figure 5.6   Custom rendering is used to display the available galleries within a Drop-DownList control instead of listing them as individual links.

```
protected override void RenderCatalogPartLinks(HtmlTextWriter writer) {

        this.RenderInstructionText(writer);  ◁——— Display Instruction Text

        DropDownList galleryList = new DropDownList();
        galleryList.ID = this.ClientID + "_GallerySelector";      Create
        galleryList.Page = this.Page;                            DropDownList
        galleryList.ClearSelection();
        galleryList.AutoPostBack = true;


        foreach (CatalogPart gallery in this.CatalogParts) {

                WebPartDescriptionCollection parts =
                    gallery.GetAvailableWebPartDescriptions();

                if (parts.Count > 0) {
                        galleryList.Items.Add(
                            new ListItem(gallery.Title, gallery.ID)
                            );                          Add Galleries to
                }                                       DropDownList

        }

        if (galleryList.Items.Count == 0) {
                writer.Write(
                  "There are no galleries that contain web
                parts."
                    );
        } else {
                writer.Write("Select a Gallery:");
                if (!string.IsNullOrEmpty(this.SelectedCatalogPartID)) {
                        galleryList.Items.FindByValue(
                                this.SelectedCatalogPartID).Selected = true;  ◁
                }
                                                        Select Gallery
                galleryList.RenderControl(writer);
        }
}
```

The code for our custom gallery rendering logic, shown in listing 5.4, first calls a helper method to display the instructional text. The reason for separating this code into a helper method is that we not only write the instructional text, but apply any InstructionTextStyle styles that have been specified as well. If we didn't separate the logic for displaying the instructional text into its own method, the RenderCat-alogPartLinks method would become overly long and cumbersome to maintain. After rendering the instruction text, our code then creates a DropDownList control and assigns it a unique ID. It is important to note that we also set the `AutoPostBack` property to true. This ensures that when the user makes a selection in the list a postback will occur, and we can set the selected catalog part to whatever gallery the user has selected. Setting the selected catalog part ensures that when the remainder of the `RenderBody` logic is run for the `CatalogZone`, the web parts that will be displayed will reflect the selected gallery.

The last part of the custom rendering code shown in listing 5.4 checks whether any galleries have been added to the dropdown list. If no galleries were added—either because there were none or because there were no galleries that contained web parts—the user is notified. If galleries were added to the dropdown list, a label is added and the currently selected gallery is pre-selected in the dropdown list. You can see that the code for pre-selecting a gallery within the dropdown list uses the `SelectedCatalogPartID` property of the `CatalogZone` to work out which item to select.

The following code snippet shows the code for the `CatalogZone` helper method:

```
protected virtual void RenderInstructionText(HtmlTextWriter writer) {
        if (!string.IsNullOrEmpty(this.InstructionText)) {
                Label lbl = new Label();
                lbl.Text = this.InstructionText;
                lbl.Page = this.Page;
                lbl.ApplyStyle(base.InstructionTextStyle);
                lbl.RenderControl(writer);
                writer.WriteBreak();
                writer.WriteBreak();
        }
}
```

Notice here that in the `CatalogZone` helper method one of the lines of code applies the `CatalogZone` to the label. Doing this adds the styles that were specified in the declaration of the control to the Label that we're creating to display the instructional text. By applying styles during custom rendering, we allow our custom catalog to offer a consistent experience and allow developers to use our control exactly as if it were one of the standard `CatalogZone` controls.

Now that we've completed the `CatalogZone` logic and added in our own dropdown list, we must write the code that will handle the postback event from the dropdown list and use it to set the `CatalogZone` property to reflect whatever item the user has chosen. To handle the postback event we can write code to run during the `CatalogZone` phase of page processing which occurs just prior to the page load event. This is an event that occurs just prior to the page load event during a page postback and allows controls to update their state based on values that have been posted back from the client. In our case this will involve looking for a value in the postback data collection that corresponds with the unique ID that we gave to our dropdown control. The following code shows the code required to handle the postback event and to update the `CatalogZone`:

```
protected override bool LoadPostData(
        string postDataKey,
        NameValueCollection postCollection
        ) {

        this.SelectedCatalogPartID =
                postCollection[this.ClientID + "_GallerySelector"];
        return base.LoadPostData(postDataKey, postCollection);
}
```

The `LoadPostData` method for our control is actually called by the ASP.NET runtime. The ASP.NET runtime calls this method for every control on a page that implements the `IPostBackDataHandler` interface, which the `CatalogZone` class does. In our implementation of `CatalogZone` we retrieve the value that is contained within the post collection for the dropdown list that we added. In our case the value that we retrieve from the post collection for the dropdown list will be the ID of a gallery because that is what we assigned as the value for each dropdown item that we added to the dropdown list.

Add the custom `CatalogZone` to a web page and run the page within a browser to see how the custom gallery that we created here works.

We've now seen that we can customize the appearance of our zones by using either styles or by directly customizing the rendered output. However, as we saw in the section on custom rendering, taking control of rendering a section such as the body section of a zone can be a significant undertaking. This is particularly true if we are interested only in making small customizations. For example, we saw that Share-Point gallery body contains a control for filtering the web parts in the list. If we attempted to apply this small enhancement to the body of the ASP.NET `Catalog-Zone` by overriding the `RenderBody` method, we'd have to custom render the entire body, including the gallery links. To assist with rendering only specific elements within zones, the portal framework provides us with another piece of architecture known as chrome.

5.4   USING WEBPARTCHROME

Chrome is a rendering element used by the `WebPartZone`, `EditorZone`, and `Cat-alogZone` as a specific way to render parts that are contained within those zones. The chrome acts as a visual container for the parts in the zones. In this way, chrome enables us to perform rendering tasks on the parts that are contained within the body of a zone without having to custom render the entire body of each part.

5.4.1   Defining chrome types

At this point we'll drill in and examine the types of chrome that exist and write some examples that allow us to gain an understanding of what effect chrome has on the overall rendering process. To do this we will

- Look at the different types of chrome that exist
- Create our own custom chrome
- Write samples against our own custom chrome to see how to implement chrome
- Use the samples that we write to examine what rendering can be affected by chrome

The best place to start when looking at chrome is to learn the different types of chrome that exist. Each different zone uses a specific type of chrome which has special rendering methods that match the features exposed by the zone. Table 5.1 lists the types of chrome that are used by the three zones and also lists the methods exposed by the chrome that can be used to assist with custom rendering:

Table 5.1 Zones each use specific chrome types which have rendering methods that are useful for controlling the appearance of certain areas of the zone.

Zone	Standard Chrome Types	Chrome Rendering Members
WebPartZone	WebPartChrome	GetWebPartVerbs, RenderPartContents, RenderWebPart
EditorZone	EditorPartChrome	RenderEditorPart, RenderPartContents
CatalogZone	CatalogPartChrome	RenderCatalogPart, RenderCatalogPartContents

The standard chromes—WebPartChrome, EditorPartChrome, and Catalog-PartChrome—give us the default look and feel that we experience as we browse a portal and view zones and their parts. For example, WebPartChrome uses its RenderWebPart method to perform the following tasks:

- Creates the styles that will be used for the outer area of the part
- Draws the outer table that contains the part
- Adds the appropriate ID to the table to allow client scripts to interact with the part—for dragging, etc.
- Renders the Title for the part
- Calls RenderCatalogPartContents so that the parts contents can be drawn within the chrome template that has been created

As shown by this list, chrome is responsible for rendering the outer parts of the zone as opposed to the inner area where the main content of the zone is contained. Because of this, it can be useful to customize how chrome is rendered when we need to change the appearance of the outer area of our zones beyond what we can achieve by simply using styles. An example of this would be if we wanted to provide our zones with unique, rounded corners—such as those Valentine's Day hearts that were mentioned in chapter 2.

5.4.2   Customizing chrome

At times we'll want to create a custom look for the outer area of our zones—a look that will give all our pages a distinctive feel or flair. To do so, we create our own custom chrome class and write code within that class that performs custom rendering logic to suits our needs. To allow us to use custom chrome in the portal, each zone has a method that is responsible for returning the chrome type that should be used for rendering its parts. The methods for each of these three zones that return their chrome are

- `WebPartZoneBase.CreateWebPartChrome`
- `EditorZoneBase.CreateEditorPartChrome`
- `CatalogZoneBase.CreateCatalogPartChrome`

Overriding these methods provides us with an interception point we can use to return our own chrome classes which contain custom rendering logic for rendering parts and their contents. To see how this works, take a look at listing 5.5 and notice the logic contained within its `RenderPartContents` and `RenderWebPart` methods:

> **Listing 5.5   This custom chrome class uses its RenderWebPart and Render-PartContents methods to display the user interface of web parts for a web zone.**

```
public class CustomWebPartChrome : WebPartChrome {

        public CustomWebPartChrome(WebPartZone zone, WebPartManager wpm) :
              base(zone, wpm) { }

        public override void RenderWebPart(
              HtmlTextWriter writer,                         Render outer
              WebPart webPart                                    area of
              ) {                                              web part

              writer.Write("Outer section of the web part");  ←
              writer.WriteBreak();
              this.RenderPartContents(writer, webPart);
              writer.WriteBreak();
              writer.Write("End of outer section");
        }                                                 Render web
                                                          part content
        protected override void RenderPartContents(  ←
              HtmlTextWriter writer,
              WebPart webPart
              ) {
              writer.Write("Part contents");
        }
}
```

This custom chrome class shown in the preceding segment inherits from Web-PartChrome and can therefore be returned as the chrome to be used by the Cre-ateWebPartChrome method of a WebPartZone. In order for the chrome to be used by a zone, we must associate the chrome with the zone. In the case of a WebPartZone, we accomplish this by overriding the CreateWebPartChrome method and returning an instance of our custom chrome class. The following snippet shows a custom Web-PartZone using our CustomWebPartChrome to perform web part rendering:

```
public class CustomWebPartZone : WebPartZone {

        protected override WebPartChrome CreateWebPartChrome() {
                return new CustomWebPartChrome(this, this.WebPartManager);
        }
}
```

At runtime when the zone is rendering its body section, it will loop through each of its contained web parts and actually use the chrome to do the rendering of that part like so:

```
WebPartChrome chrome = this.WebPartChrome;
foreach (WebPart part in this.WebParts) {
        chrome.RenderWebPart( writer, part ) ;
}
```

This final snippet shows us that every web part within the WebPart zone is rendered through the chrome, and not through the zone itself.

5.4.3   Viewing the results of custom chrome

To appreciate the additional level of control gained over the rendering process by creating our custom chrome, we can now use the CustomWebPartZone to host some web parts and view the rendered output. Add the following markup to a page in your test project and run it to view the output.

```
<wp:CustomWebPartZone ID="CustomWebPartZone1" runat="server">
        <ZoneTemplate>
                <asp:TextBox ID="part1" runat="server" Title="Part One" />
                <asp:TextBox ID="part2" runat="server" Title="Part Two" />
        </ZoneTemplate>
</wp:CustomWebPartZone>
```

Here our CustomWebPartZone class is declared within a page, and as we can see, it contains two web parts declared within its zone template. At runtime the Render-WebPart method of our custom chrome class will be called twice—once for each web part contained within the zone. Figure 5.7 shows the results of the page being run in a browser.

As we see, the text rendered from the RenderWebPart and RenderWebPart-Contents methods is displayed instead of the textbox web parts we'd normally expect

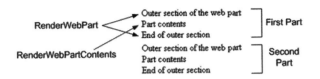

Figure 5.7
This figure shows how the RenderWebPart and RenderWebPartContents methods affect the rendered output of web parts contained within a zone.

to see. To further highlight what's going on, we can remove the overridden `Render-WebPart` method we added to the custom chrome class. Removing this method from our custom chrome class means that the base class implementation of that method will be called at runtime and do all of its normal rendering of borders, titles and verbs so at least our parts will look like the web parts we've seen in the past. Our custom `RenderWebPartContents` code will still run and render the body of the part as the text that we emitted: Part Contents. Figure 5.8 shows the output rendered when we remove the implementation we added for the `RenderWebPart` method.

Working through the chapter to this point has provided a good look at the three main rendering methods for zones and we've seen how the level of control from the combination of styles, zone rendering, and chrome rendering simplifies the task of creating the exact look and feel we want for parts within our portal. We've also seen that each of these three methods of affecting the rendered output comes with a different level of difficulty. Using styles is relatively straightforward, while overriding the rendered sections within zones is much more difficult because then we are attempting to create a lot of visual elements and functionality.

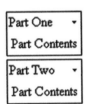

Figure 5.8 By removing the code we wrote for the RenderWebPart method, we make the web parts regain their familiar look as the verbs and title texts are also rendered in the header area.

Now that we've learned about the makeup of zones and seen how to affect their visual elements, it's time to take a closer look within the `EditorZone` and the `CatalogZone`.

5.5   EXPLAINING PARTS

From what we've seen and read about zones so far, it should be clear that the main function of zones is to act as containing areas for part controls. After all, it is the part controls contained within the zone that provide the user with the real functionality to accomplish various tasks. For example, in the case of the `EditorZone`, a user would call on the `AppearanceEditorPart` to maintain the appearance of web parts on a page. In this section we'll see that each zone contains parts of a specific type. Finally, once we understand how parts work, we'll take a closer look at the parts contained by the `EditorZone` and the `CatalogZone` to learn about the functionality provided those zones. These are the last of the major web part controls that we need to cover in detail.

Within the body of a zone, the parts that are rendered give the zone its distinct purpose. For example, while the `WebPartZone` itself is quite useful for providing the layout and visual styles for web parts contained within it, having a `WebPartZone` without web parts would really be of little use. The same goes for the `EditorZone` and the `CatalogZone`. Can you imagine an `EditorZone` with no editor parts? It would be practically useless!

Each type of zone contains only a certain kind of part within its body. In the case of a `WebPartZone`, these parts are web parts that are derived from the `WebPart` class, whereas in the case of the `CatalogZone` control they would be parts derived from the `CatalogPart` class. Table 5.2 lists the types of parts contained within the standard ASP.NET 2.0 zones.

Table 5.2 Zones each contain parts of only a certain type.

Zone	Base Part Type	Specific Part Types
WebPartZone	WebPart	GenericWebPart, WebPart
CatalogZone	CatalogPart	DeclarativeCatalogPart, PageCatalogPart, ImportCatalogPart
EditorZone	EditorPart	AppearanceEditorPart, BehaviorEditorPart, Layout-EditorPart, PropertyGridEditorPart
ConnectionsZone	N/A	N/A

The items in table 5.2 highlight the fact that each type of zone accepts only a specific set of part types that can be contained within its body, and that each of the part types for a zone derive from a specific base part type. This is why the `CatalogZone` is able to happily accept any of either the `DeclarativeCatalogPart`, `PageCatalog-Part`, or `ImportCatalogPart` controls within its body—because they all derive from `CatalogPart`. It's also worth noting that each of these part classes—`WebPart`, `CatalogPart`, and `EditorPart`—are derived from the same base class: `Part`.

Let's now take a closer look at each of the standard parts that can be accepted by the `CatalogZone` and the `EditorZone`. By learning about the functionality exposed by these two zones we'll get to see how they are used to personalize web pages and thereby satisfy our portal users.

5.5.1 EditorZone parts

As we've just seen, an `EditorZone` can contain any of the four standard editor parts that inherit from the `EditorPart` class. The four standard editor zone parts are `AppearanceEditorPart`, `BehaviorEditorPart`, `LayoutEditorPart`, and the `PropertyGridEditorPart`. This section describes how users work with the standard editor parts to personalize the properties, layout, appearance, and behavior of web parts on their web pages.

AppearanceEditorPart

The `AppearanceEditorPart` provides controls that allow a user to modify several of the visual elements of a web part. With this editor part a user can dynamically modify the text that is displayed for a web part or set the width and height for the web part. The Chrome Type control allows the user to specify certain chrome-related style settings. With this property the user can specify whether the web part has a border and whether or not the title should be displayed for the web part. Figure 5.9 shows the user interface that is presented by the `AppearanceEditorPart`.

The `AppearanceEditorPart` is displayed within the `EditorZone` whenever the page is in edit mode and a web part on the page has been selected for editing.

Figure 5.9 To modify the visual elements of a web part, users make use of the AppearanceEditorPart interface to begin the task.

BehaviorEditorPart

Another editor part control is the `BehaviorEditorPart`, which provides the ability to manage the behavior properties of a web part. Unlike the `AppearanceEditorPart`, the `BehaviorEditorPart` is only visible under certain circumstances. In addition to the page being in edit mode and a web part being selected, the `BehaviorEditorPart` requires that the page be in shared personalization scope before it is visible. This is because the web part properties affected by the `BehaviorEditorPart` apply to all users rather than just the user making the changes. Figure 5.10 shows the user interface that is presented for the `BehaviorEditorPart` control.

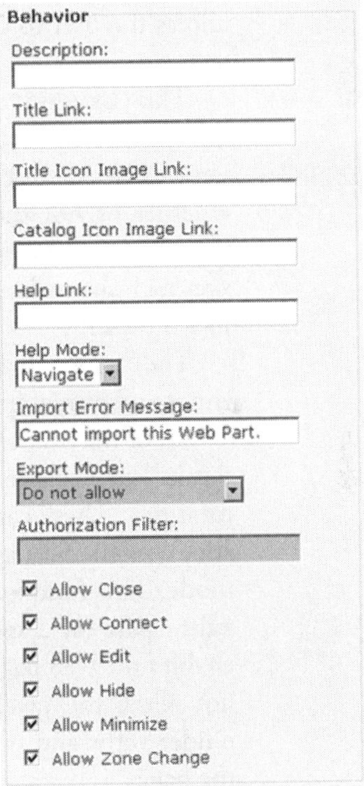

As we can see, the `BehaviorEditorPart` allows the user to alter the description for a web part. The description is used to display extra information about a web part to users, and is commonly displayed in a tooltip. The next set of properties governed by this part are several hyperlinks that allow icons to be associated with the web part and also allow users to navigate to pages that display more information about the web part. For example, when the Help Link property is set to a URL, a help verb is displayed for the web part, allowing the user to navigate to a web page that provides help information about the web part. The Help Mode property allows the user to select one of three values,

Figure 5.10 The BehaviorEditorPart allows authorized users to change the features exposed by certain web parts.

Modal, Modeless, and Navigate, that dictate how the help URL is displayed when the user clicks on the help verb. If the Help Mode is set to Modal, the help URL is displayed in a modal dialog window that the user must close before the web part page can continue, whereas if the Help Mode property is set to Navigate, then the contents of the web part page are replaced with the contents of the help URL.

Other behaviors manageable by the `BehaviorEditorPart` include authorization settings. The user can select an `ExportMode` which determines whether a web part can be exported and whether sensitive data is contained within the exported data. The user can also change the Authorization Filter which, as we have seen, supplies a way to determine which users the web part should be displayed for.

LayoutEditorPart

The `LayoutEditorPart` is displayed under the same circumstances as the `AppearanceEditorPart`; that is, whenever the page is in edit mode and a web part is selected for editing, it allows the user to change the layout settings of a web part.

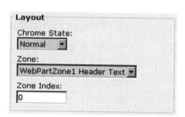

The `LayoutEditorPart` has a property called Chrome State which has two possible values—Normal and Minimized—that determine whether or not the web part is fully visible or whether it is rendered in a minimized mode. Figure 5.11 shows how this editor part is rendered in a browser.

Figure 5.11   When a user is unable to use or enable JavaScript and is therefore unable to dynamically drag web parts around in the browser, he must use the LayoutEditorPart to change the position of web parts within zones on the page.

The Zone and ZoneIndex properties allow the user to move a web part between zones and to manipulate its position within the zone.

All of the properties governed by the `LayoutEditorPart` can be managed without it. For example, web parts contain a verb that allows their minimization and restoration. They can also be dragged between zones when the page is in either edit or design mode. This functionality is embedded within an editor part for a specific reason: the embedding enables the web page to cater to browsers that do not allow the JavaScript behaviors required to render verbs and to drag and drop web parts on the page.

PropertyGridEditorPart

The last of the standard editor parts is the `PropertyGridEditorPart` which is displayed in figure 5.12.

Figure 5.12   The PropertyGridEditorPart allows users to maintain the values of custom properties on web parts.

The `PropertyGridEditorPart` allows a user to manage custom properties that have been associated with a custom web part control. The properties displayed by the `PropertyGridEditorPart` are dynamically generated, based on custom properties of the web part marked with the `WebBrowsable` attribute:

```
[Personalizable(PersonalizationScope.Shared)]
[WebBrowsable]
[WebDescription("The name of the employee.")]
public string Name {
        get { return _name; }
        set { _name = value; }
}
```

Other attributes can be used to influence how the custom properties are rendered within the `PropertyGridEditorPart`. The `WebDisplayName` attribute allows us to specify the value that appears within the label for the control and the `WebDescription` attribute can be used to supply additional information about a property that will be displayed as a tooltip for the property in the `PropertyGridEditorPart`.

The `PropertyGridEditorPart` is somewhat clever in the controls it displays by default for custom web part properties. Table 5.3 presents a list of the controls that allow users to manage properties of differing types:

Table 5.3 Controls used by the PropertyGridEditorPart

Property Type	Control Used
String	TextBox
Numeric	TextBox
DateTime	TextBox
Enum	DropDownList
Boolean	CheckBox

By looking at table 5.3 we can see what I mean when I say that the `PropertyGridEditorPart` is clever. While it's great that this editor part knows to use a Checkbox control to represent a Boolean and a `DropDownList` control to represent an enum, the choice of a `TextBox` control to display a `DateTime` value is sub-optimal. This raises a valid reason to create a customized `PropertyGridEditorPart` control, in that we can use better controls to display and validate certain values. For example, it would be preferable to associate a calendar control with `DateTime` properties for the purpose of ensuring that only valid values are entered.

That's it for the `EditorZone` and its editor parts. As we've seen, by combining the four editor parts that we've covered throughout this section, the user is provided with a great deal of flexibility and power to customize the look, feel, and behavior of a portal at runtime. When you see this type of flexibility that comes as standard behavior in ASP.NET, you can really begin to appreciate just how successful the

ASP.NET team has been in ensuring that the minimum bar for web applications has been truly raised.

5.5.2 CatalogZone parts

The `CatalogZone` parts that come as standard parts within the portal framework are the `DeclarativeCatalogPart`, the `PageCatalogPart`, and the `ImportCatalogPart`. Each of these parts displays web parts which are stored in different areas known as catalogs. Each catalog stores and retrieves its associated web parts in a different format; users can select parts from these catalogs and add them to a page at runtime.

PageCatalogPart

The `PageCatalogPart` shown in figure 5.13 contains all the web parts that the user has previously closed from `WebPart` zones on a page. This mechanism provides a way for users to re-add web parts to a page that they have previously closed, including web parts that have been dynamically added and then closed.

In Figure 5.13, the Page Catalog contains the Employee Details web part. This part would have been closed by a user at some stage. Closing a web part is not the

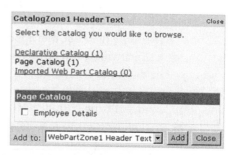

Figure 5.13   The user interface of the Page-CatalogPart is displayed within the lower portion of the CatalogZone.

same as deleting it. Deleting a web part from the page removes it forever whereas closing it simply adds it to the Page Catalog where it can be re-added.

DeclarativeCatalogPart

The `DeclarativeCatalogPart` stores its web parts in a declarative syntax within the web page. When a `DeclarativeCatalogPart` has been added to a `CatalogZone`, users are able to use it to add web parts to the page. This is done by selecting the `DeclarativeCatalogPart` from within the `CatalogZone`. When the user selects the `DeclarativeCatalogPart` from within the `CatalogZone`, a list of all parts that have been added to that catalog part are displayed in the bottom half of the `CatalogZone` body as shown in figure 5.14.

To add web parts to the `DeclarativeCatalogPart`, a page author simply embeds the web control declaration for the web parts directly within the body of the `DeclarativeCatalogPart` section of the `CatalogZone`. The following snippet of code shows a web part being added to the `DeclarativeCatalogPart` catalog.

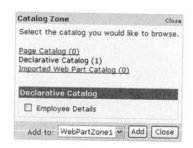

Figure 5.14   The user interface of the DeclarativeCatalogPart is displayed within the lower portion of the CatalogZone.

```
<asp:CatalogZone ID="CatalogZone2" runat="Server">
        <ZoneTemplate>
                <asp:DeclarativeCatalogPart ID="DeclarativeCatalogPart2"
                  runat="server">
                <WebPartsTemplate>
                        <uc2:EmployeeDetails ID="EmployeeDetails2"
                                runat="server"
                                Title="Employee Details" />
                </WebPartsTemplate>
                </asp:DeclarativeCatalogPart>
        </ZoneTemplate>
</asp:CatalogZone>
```

In the code snippet above we see the markup used to create the `CatalogZone` shown in figure 5.12. The code shows that the Employee Details web part is contained within the `WebPartsTemplate` of the `DeclarativeCatalogPart`.

It is worth noting that web parts that are declared in the `DeclarativeCatalog` can be "instanced" on a web page any number of times. For example, let's say that you open the Declarative Catalog shown in figure 5.14 and add the Employee Details part contained within it to `WebPartZone1`. After you do so, the Employee Details web part will still appear within the Declarative Catalog, and can still be added to the page. Therefore a page can contain many instances of web parts that are declared within this type of catalog. The DeclarativeCatalog is therefore an ideal place for web parts that you'd like to add multiple times such as a web part which allows images to be added to a page or a web part that allows a user to enter and display arbitrary chunks of HTML on a page.

ImportCatalogPart

The last of the `CatalogParts` is the `ImportCatalog`. The ImportCatalog provides users with a way to import web parts into a web application by browsing for web part description files and then importing them. The web part description files are the XML files we discussed in chapter 4 when we looked at the import/export process from the `WebPartManager` perspective. In addition to enabling users to search for web part definition files and import them, the `ImportCatalogPart` also lists web parts previously imported by a user. Existing web parts are displayed in the lower part of the interface for the `ImportCatalog-Part` as shown in figure 5.15.

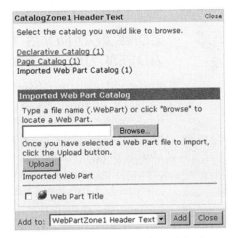

Figure 5.15 The user interface of the ImportCatalogPart is displayed within the lower portion of the CatalogZone.

In figure 5.15 the `ImportCatalogPart` is shown with a single web part listed near the bottom of the control. As in the declarative catalog, web parts that have been imported can be added to the web page any number of times. Users can customize the text that is displayed on the interface for this catalog part by setting one of two properties: the `BrowseHelpText` and the `UploadHelpText`. The `BrowseHelpText` property is used to set the text displayed above the "Browse" control, while the property named `UploadHelpText` can be used to set the text that appears just above the "Upload" button.

In addition to the standard zone parts we've seen for the `EditorZone` and the `CatalogZone`, it is possible to create our own custom parts. By inheriting from the right base classes, we can actually create our own specialized part controls that can be added to zones. For example, by inheriting from `CatalogPart` we could create a special catalog part control. This catalog control part could allow users to import web parts that are stored somewhere other than where they are stored by the existing catalog parts—such as a web service or the file system. Having a `CatalogPart` that could store and retrieve web parts from outside of the current web application opens the door to the possibility of sharing web part definitions between multiple web applications. SharePoint actually does something similar to this with its gallery where it allows users to search for web parts from an online repository of parts which are stored on the Microsoft.com website.

If learning about the parts contained by zones and the various ways to render them felt like a bit of a technical slog, don't be too discouraged because there was a lot of information to cover. The advantage is, armed with the knowledge gained from this chapter, you are now fully ready to start creating zones that provide users with a unique experience. In fact, why don't we start by using our new knowledge to create some cool zone additions to the Adventure Works portal?

5.6 ZONE ADDITIONS TO THE ADVENTURE WORKS PORTAL

At the end of chapter 4 we added some architectural features to the Adventure Works Portal for authorizing web parts and allowing users to dynamically change the display mode of the page. In the time that has elapsed since the last chapter, we've had more discussions with the HR management team to discover which features to build next. During the talks the HR department clamored for many more web parts so that users of the portal could gain access to a wider range of business information. Additionally, HR gazed at its crystal ball and glimpsed a need in the future to share web parts between the current portal and some smaller, more specific sub-portals that would suit the needs of smaller project-specific teams. After the talks, it was decided that the functionality of the standard ASP.NET `CatalogZone` should be enhanced to make it easy for administrators to add web parts to the portal, as well as make it simple to share web parts between portal applications.

NOTE   If you don't have a copy of the project from chapter 4 you can grab it from the chapter 4 section of the resources website for this book.

5.6.1   Planning the CatalogZone extensions

To create the agreed upon enhancements, we will need to provide a way for web parts to be shared easily between web applications. From earlier sections of this chapter, you will recall that the existing `CatalogZone` parts allow web parts to be loaded from three separate places, but that none of them allowed web parts to be shared concurrently between separate applications. For our requirements, web parts should be storeable in a central location and loaded from there into more than one application in a manner similar to that shown in figure 5.16.

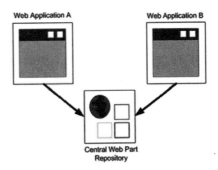

Figure 5.16   Our custom gallery (Central Web Part Repository) can be accessed by multiple web applications.

Storing web part definitions centrally will allow administrators to pre-configure web parts with specific customizations and upload them for use. This will be useful for ensuring that the parts in the central gallery have the most common settings already applied, and most users will typically not be required to make any customizations of their own before using them. Such settings might include the default number of rows to display on a web part with a pageable interface or ensuring that a news web part is pre-configured to read news from the most commonly selected news channels.

5.6.2   Creating a custom catalog part

To achieve our result we will create a custom catalog part that will be able to store and retrieve web parts from a configurable location which, in our case, will be a fileshare location on the network. The catalog part we create will be derived from the `CatalogPart` base class, which means it can be added to the standard `CatalogZone` just like any of the existing three catalog parts. Figure 5.17 shows how our catalog part named Central Gallery will appear when displayed within the `CatalogZone`:

To create our catalog part, add a class file to the Adventure Works project named `CentralGalleryCatalogPart.cs` by right-clicking on the `App_Code` folder and choosing `Add File`. When the file is created, ensure that the `CentralGalleryCatalogPart` class inherits

Figure 5.17   A custom gallery named Central Gallery with its two web parts is contained within the CatalogZone.

from `CatalogPart`, and give it a friendly and distinct title to display when it appears within the `CatalogZone` so that users will know what it is.

```
public class CentralGalleryCatalogPart : CatalogPart {

    public override string Title {
        get {
            string title = base.Title;
            return string.IsNullOrEmpty(title) ?
                "Central Gallery" : title;
        }
        set {
            base.Title = value;
        }
    }
}
```

Next we'll need to add a property to our catalog part to tell it where the web parts are located. Having this as a configurable property will make it easy to move the application between different environments such as development, testing, and production. It will also make it easier to re-use our catalog so that we could potentially have several catalogs reading from different places on the network. Listing 5.6 shows the `GalleryPath` property marked with the `WebBrowsable` attribute so that an administrator can configure the location from the portal by using the `EditorZone` and the standard `PropertyGridEditorPart`.

Listing 5.6 The GalleryPath property contains the location where web parts are stored for the custom gallery.

```
private static string _galleryPath = "~/WebParts/";
[Personalizable(PersonalizationScope.Shared)]
[WebBrowsable(true)]
public virtual string GalleryPath {
    get {
        return string.IsNullOrEmpty(_galleryPath) ?
            "~/WebParts/" : _galleryPath;
    }
    set {
        if (!value.EndsWith("/"))
            value += "/";

        _galleryPath = value;
    }
}
```

In the code for listing 5.6 we see that the `GalleryPath` property is marked with certain attributes. The `Personalizable` attribute marks the property as shared for personalization; so that whenever the gallery path is modified, all users of the portal will be affected by the changes—not just the current user. By marking the `GalleryPath` property with the `WebBrowsable` attribute we ensure that users will be able to set its value from within the `PropertyGridEditorPart` at runtime.

By this point, we've set the Title for our `CatalogPart` and provided a way for users to set the location path to the place where the parts will be stored. Now we need to think about how to retrieve the web parts and what format they should be stored in.

Adding and retrieving web parts

To store the web parts we'll use the XML web part definitions we've worked with when using the standard import/export functionality in the portal. Our catalog part will have one method that takes the XML for a web part and adds it to the catalog and another method which takes a web part description and returns a web part from the gallery. The method for adding parts to the catalog will be implemented as a static helper method so it can easily be called from within the application.

```
public static void ImportWebPart(string partTitle, string partContent) {

    string path = _galleryPath + partTitle + ".xml" ;
    path = HttpContext.Current.Server.MapPath(path);
    File.WriteAllText(path, partContent);
}
```

As we can see, the `ImportWebPart` method is marked as static, so that calling code does not entail creating an instance of the class to use the `ImportWebPart` method. The `ImportWebPart` method takes a string to serve as the title of the web part which is also the file name that the web part is saved against. Finally, the web part XML definition is saved by using the `WriteAllText` helper method of the `System.IO.File` class.

The method for retrieving a web part is called `GetWebPart` and is a method that must be implemented when inheriting from the abstract `CatalogPart` class. The `GetWebPart` method is responsible for returning a `WebPart` based on a `WebPartDescription` passed to it. The `WebPartDescription` is a class containing information about an item listed in a `CatalogPart` such as its Title, Description, ID, and `CatalogIconImageUrl`, and is used as the standard way to pass information about web parts between the `CatalogZone` and the `CatalogPart` controls. Listing 5.7 shows the code for the two overrides of the `GetWebPart` method.

> **Listing 5.7   The GetWebPart method returns a web part from the gallery's store.**

```
public override WebPart GetWebPart(WebPartDescription description) {
    return GetWebPart( description.Title ) ;
}

protected virtual WebPart GetWebPart( string partTitle ) {
    string path = _galleryPath + part.Title + ".xml";
    path = HttpContext.Current.Server.MapPath(path);
```

```
WebPart wp = null;

using (FileStream fs = File.OpenRead(path)) {
    XmlTextReader reader = new System.Xml.XmlTextReader(fs);
  string errorMessage = "" ;
    wp = WebPartManager.ImportWebPart(reader, out errorMessage);
}

return wp;
}
```

Create XmlTextReader from filestream

Use WebPartManager to create WebPart

When we receive the WebPartDescription, we extract its Title property and call off to a second overload for the GetWebPart method. This method has been created especially for our class, which accepts a path to the file where we have the XML description file stored. Once we have a file path, we need only load the XML file into an XMLTextReader and pass it the WebPartManager class, which knows how to convert the XML into a web part instance.

Naturally, we could implement any logic for creating web part controls within the GetWebPart method based on the WebPartDescription that is passed in. We could fetch the web parts as XML from the filesystem as we have here, or we could fetch the XML from a web service. As a matter of fact, the GetWebPart method could even load assemblies directly using Reflection. There are no limits to what the GetWebPart method can do, as long as it accepts a WebPartDescription instance and returns a WebPart instance. Sometimes the GetWebPart method needs to return a control that does not inherit from the WebPart class. For example, if we wrote a custom gallery that could store any standard ASP.NET controls, it would be up to the GetWebPart method to wrap the server control within a GenericWebPart before returning it.

So far, all is looking good! We've set out to create a catalog part that could be used from within multiple applications and now we are almost finished. We've created the catalog part and provided it with methods that allow it to read web parts in and out of a central location. Additionally, we've provided a property which would allow an administrator to configure the exact location for web parts storage. In the few steps remaining we'll add the few lines of code required to have our catalog part display its web parts in the CatalogZone.

Displaying the web parts

The final method to be implemented when inheriting from the abstract Catalog-Part class is called GetAvailableWebPartDescriptions. This method is responsible for returning a WebPartDescription for each of the web parts within the catalog. To create an instance of the `WebPartDescription` class we can use either of the following two constructors:

```
public WebPartDescription (
    string id,
    string title,
    string description,
    string imageUrl
)
public WebPartDescription (
    WebPart part
)
```

At runtime the `CatalogZone` hosting our web part will use the `WebPartDescriptions` that we return from the `GetAvailableWebPartDescriptions` method to display the web parts contained within the gallery. The `CatalogIconImageUrl`, Description, Title and properties of the `WebPartDescription` class are aligned with properties of the same name on the `IWebPart` interface:

- *CatalogIconImageUrl*—the URL of an image displayed for a web part when that part is displayed in a catalog of web parts.
- *Description*—Descriptive text about a web part displayed for a web part when that part is displayed in a catalog of web parts. This property is also used to display tooltip information about a web part.
- *Title*—the title of a web part control.

Listing 5.8 shows the code required to return the available web part descriptions for our custom gallery.

Listing 5.8   The GetAvailableWebPartDescriptions method returns a collection of the descriptions of web parts available from the custom gallery.

```
public override WebPartDescriptionCollection
GetAvailableWebPartDescriptions() {                          Offer custom
                                                        experience when  part
                                                           is in design mode
    if (base.DesignMode) {
        return CentralGalleryCatalogPart.DesignModeAvailableWebParts;  ◁

}

    List<WebPartDescription> coll = new List<WebPartDescription>();

    string path = HttpContext.Current.Server.MapPath(this.GalleryPath);

                                                              Only load files with a
    foreach (string file in Directory.GetFiles(path)) {       .webpart file extension
        if (file.EndsWith(".WebPart")) {           ◁
            string partTitle = Path.GetFileNameWithoutExtension(file);
            WebPart wp = GetWebPart(partTitle);
            wp.ID = partTitle;
```

```
            coll.Add(new WebPartDescription(wp));
        }
    }
    return new WebPartDescriptionCollection(coll);
}
```

In our implementation of the GetAvailableWebPartDescriptions method we loop through each file within the directory that stores the web parts for our custom gallery and create a WebPartDescription by passing the file name of each file to our helper GetWebPart method. Passing a web part as the constructor argument of the WebPartDescription will ensure that the web parts listed in our custom gallery will have catalog images and tooltips associated with them if they are present in the XML web part definition file.

Adding design-time functionality

At the beginning of the GetAvailableWebPartDescriptions method, you will notice how we first check to see whether we are in design mode, and if so we display some sample web part data so that our control offers a good design-time experience.

To provide the design-time data, some sample WebPartDescriptions are created in a static constructor for our custom catalog part and assigned to a private static property named DesignModeAvailableParts, as seen in listing 5.9.

> **Listing 5.9** From within the static class contstructor we add web part descriptions to display in Visual Studio when the CentralGalleryCatalogPart is displayed in design mode.

```
static CentralGalleryCatalogPart() {
    WebPartDescription[] designParts = new WebPartDescription[3];

    designParts[0] =
        new WebPartDescription("Part1", "WebPart 1", null, null);
    designParts[1] =
        new WebPartDescription("Part2", "WebPart 2", null, null);
    designParts[2] =
        new WebPartDescription("Part3", "WebPart 3", null, null);

    DesignModeAvailableWebParts =
        new WebPartDescriptionCollection(designParts);    ◁─┐ Set value of static
}                                                             DesignModeAvailable-
                                                              WebParts property

private static WebPartDescriptionCollection DesignModeAvailableWebParts;
```

Having this type of design-time experience ensures that our custom catalog part will offer an identical design experience as the existing ASP.NET catalog parts.

The code for the Adventure Works portal can be found in the chapter 5 section of the resources website for this book. That code contains additional web parts that have been added to a new project named `AW.Portal.Web.SharedWebParts`. The code in the Adventure Works portal in the chapter 5 folder already includes new web parts and the new custom gallery that we built in this chapter.

5.7   SUMMARY

Throughout this chapter we've seen how zones are much more than simple rectangles on a web page. In fact, zones can have a dramatic impact on the display of the web parts they contain. In addition to the zones themselves, we saw that custom chrome can be used to add a finer level of control over the display of zones and their web parts.

Like the other web part controls we've seen so far—`WebParts`, Connections, and the `WebPartManger`—zones are one of the fundamental building blocks of the portals we will build. The purpose of this chapter has been to give you an understanding of the purpose of zones and their capabilities. In future chapters we'll apply this core knowledge of web part controls to create more custom functionality. In chapter 7 we'll dive into zones and chrome again to explore adding new verbs to our web zones that provide users with an easier way to edit web parts. We'll also create a `Catalog-Zone` which is implemented as a dialog window and will provide us with an opportunity to mix some client-side scripting with the web part controls.

C H A P T E R   6

Understanding personalization

6.1 INTRODUCTION

The world of website offerings has changed markedly in just a few years. I first visited websites to find the media soundtracks from my favorite shows, such as *The Simpsons*. At that time, most sites were nothing more than a few pages and the page listing media clips required endless scrolling. These pages often had weird background images and bizarre soundtracks. Other pages on those early websites sometimes included a links page—a page with links to all the other sites the owner recommended.

These days, users expect much more from websites and generally require them to be more customizable than their predecessors. Instead of being presented with a simple list of media soundtracks, users can now often personalize a page so that it contains tracks from their favorite artist or music genre. Quite often users can even aggregate their favorite items on a single page through sites that offer more advanced customization services. Sites offering the ability to personalize content become "stickier" as a result, because users stay on the sticky site rather than browsing to other sites for the remainder of the content they want. The benefit for the owners of sticky websites is that their sites serve more ads and thus generate greater revenue.

6.2   DEFINING PERSONALIZATION

There is an intensifying move away from the brochure-style sites of the early days to the portal model where users can add a range of content to pages when and where they like. In the past, every site that provided advanced personalization capabilities had to engineer its own database system to store the customization information from the users of the site and then develop complex code to pull the personalization from the databases and reapply it when a user returned to the website. In ASP.NET 2.0 all the tasks of creating databases and writing custom logic have been completed for us, and these elements exist as a set of services jointly known as Personalization.

Personalization is an application service responsible for saving, retrieving and reapplying data that represents customizations which have been made to controls on a web page. The personalization service knows how to store the customization data for a page and then retrieve it when a user requests the page again. When a page with saved personalization data is re-requested, the personalization service fetches the data so the page can be recreated for the user making the request.

This chapter explains how personalization works. We will see how personalization data is stored, and how the personalization classes within ASP.NET 2.0 removes the complexity of managing user customization. We will explore how the personalization classes allow us to alter their behavior to customize the storing and retrieval of personalization data.

What personalization affects

Everything we've seen in the portal framework so far—WebParts, Zones, and the WebPartManager—sits above personalization and requires personalization to re-create the state of web pages after user customizations have been applied. Without personalization there would be no use having the CatalogZone, and no sooner would we dynamically add to a web page a web part we've taken from another location than it would be forgotten, and the page would revert to its original format. Without personalization, the changes made through parts within the EditorZone would also be forgotten as soon as we navigated away from the page.

What personalization saves

To understand what type of data must be saved as part of the personalization process, consider some of the following changes that can be made by users, and which must be remembered by personalization:

- Using the EditorZone to change the properties of web parts
- Using the CatalogZone to add or remove web parts from the page

- Moving web parts between zones
- Changing connection attributes
- Adding or removing web parts from a page

The data saved for personalization has to be sufficient to completely re-create a web page exactly as the user left it, regardless of which previously mentioned changes have occurred.

Personalization state

Before delving into personalization more deeply, it's worth contrasting it with some of the other state mechanisms that are offered by ASP.NET to see how it differs from other methods of persisting data in ASP applications:

- *ViewState*—ViewState provides a way to store state information for a specific web page that can be persisted across page postbacks but not across separate visits to the web page.

- *Cookies*—Cookies allow us to store user-specific personalization data that can be persisted across visits to the site. One of the limitations of cookies is that they only store a small amount of data. Some browsers only allow up to 4096 bytes of data to be stored within cookies, and also limit the number of cookies a site can store. In addition to these limitations, users can elect to turn cookies off, so they should not be relied upon to store important information.

- *Session*—The Session object allows values to be stored on a per-user basis for the duration of a single visit to a website. When a user revisits the site, a new session is created and all values are re-initialized.

- *Profile*—The ASP.NET profile feature allows data to be stored for individual users and have it persisted across visits to the website. Profile is generally used to store information about a user, such as a birth date or a favorite color. Profile is also used to store complex user data such as shopping cart information and have it persisted between page postbacks or site visits.

- *Personalization*—Personalization data is stored for controls on a web page and is specific to individual users. Personalization data is persisted between visits to a site. Unlike Profile data, personalization data is specific to preferences that have been made to web part controls and is tied to changes that have been made to a specific page.

Personalization differs from the other state mechanisms because

- It is tied to the identity of a user on a per-page basis.
- It is long-lived and therefore persists beyond a single user session.

In addition to storing data based on the identity of a user and a page address, personalization also takes into account a concept known as *scope*. Scope indicates whether a change in personalization data affects only the user who made the change, or whether all users of the portal are affected by the change.

Personalization scope

Within ASP.NET portals there are two scopes: shared scope and per-user scope. Changes made to data while a page is in shared scope mode will be visible to all users within the portal. This means if a web part is moved from one zone into another while the page is in shared scope mode, all users of the portal will experience that change. On the other hand, any changes made to the portal while a page is in per-user scope mode will only be visible to the user making the change. Because of this, the ability to make changes while in shared scope mode is a feature that is normally restricted to those portal users who have administrative privileges. To bring this point home, the next section presents an example of how the personalization service works.

6.3   PERSONALIZATION IN ACTION

To better understand how the personalization service works, let's create a small example that allows us to view the behavior of a web page while making personalization changes to it. To do this we will create a small application that allows us to make changes for different users, pages, and scopes; and in doing so we will see how each of those variables affects the personalization data that is persisted.

Our application will have two web pages and will allow for multiple users to log in and make personalization changes to those pages. As we work through this section, we will see that personalization data is saved on a per-user, and per-page basis. In addition to the per-user changes made, we'll also allow certain users to change the scope of the page into shared scope and make changes that affect all users of the portal. By allowing multiple users to log in we'll be able to make different changes for each user, and see how the page looks differently, depending on which user we login as. Additionally, we will see that any changes made to the page while in shared scope affect the default settings for all users of the page. Figure 6.1 shows the page we'll be creating and explains some of the controls that can be used to interact with the web page.

To get things started, first open Visual Studio 2005 and create a new web project named UnderstandingScope and add a new master page called Site.master to the project. With the master page open add a WebPartManager at the top of the page. Next, drag two WebPartZone controls from the Toolbox onto the page and, to the first zone, add two TextBox controls. The HTML for the zones and web parts should look something like the code in the following snippet.

```
<asp:WebPartZone ID="WebPartZone1" runat="server" >
        <ZoneTemplate>
                <asp:TextBox ID="TextBox1" runat="server" Title="WebPart 1" />
                <asp:TextBox ID="TextBox2" runat="server" Title="WebPart 2" />
        </ZoneTemplate>
</asp:WebPartZone>


<asp:WebPartZone ID="WebPartZone2" runat="server" />
```

The two zones in the preceding snippet are the same two zones shown in figure 6.1, and will be used to allow us to drag the web parts between them whenever the page is in design mode.

Next we'll add the controls to the top of the web page. This allows us to manage the page and view information about the logged-in user. The first control we'll add is a LoginName server control which displays a greeting message to the authenticated user, and will enable us to identify which user is currently logged in. The LoginName control is a simple server control used to display the username of an authenticated user. We can use the FormatString property of the LoginName control to display

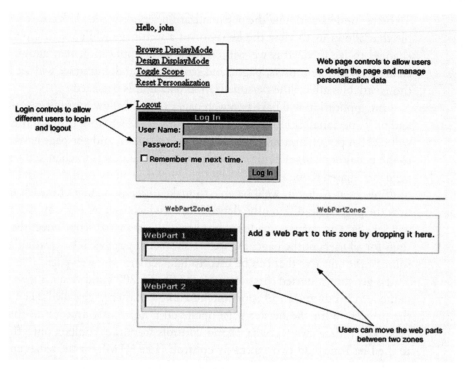

Figure 6.1 A prototype application will allow us to view the behavior of personalization on a per-user, per-page, and per-scope basis.

a message to the currently logged-in user, as displayed in the following snippet of HTML code:

```
<asp:LoginName ID="LoginName1" FormatString="Welcome, {0}" runat="server" />
```

Next, we must establish controls that allow us to change the display mode of the page and to change personalization scope and to reset personalization for the page. For these we will use `LinkButton` controls and write server code to handle their click event as shown in the following:

```
<asp:LinkButton ID="lnkBrowse" runat="server"
        OnClick="lnkBrowse_Click" Text="Browse DisplayMode" />
<asp:LinkButton ID="lnkDesign" runat="server"
        OnClick="lnkDesign_Click" Text="Design DisplayMode" />
<asp:LinkButton ID="lnkToggle" runat="server"
        OnClick="lnkToggle_Click" Text="Toggle Scope" />
<asp:LinkButton ID="lnkReset" runat="server"
OnClick="lnkReset_Click" Text="Reset Personalization" />
```

Finally, a `LoginStatus` control is used to allow authenticated users to log out and a `Login` control allows unauthenticated users to login. The `Login` server control displays the user interface elements necessary to allow a user to enter their authentication credentials. The control then exposes that information as properties we can use to validate them, and accept or deny a login request. When added to the page, the HTML for those controls will look like so:

```
<p>
        <asp:LoginStatus ID="LoginStatus1" runat="server" />

        <asp:Login ID="Login1" runat="server"
            OnAuthenticate="Login1_Authenticate" />
</p>
```

To give the page its required behavior, code must be written that runs when each of the link buttons is clicked. The code for the two buttons responsible for switching the display mode of the page is similar to the code we wrote in chapter 4 when we wrote the `ModeChanger` user control. It simply sets the `DisplayMode` property of the `WebPartManager` for the page to the appropriate value:

```
protected void lnkBrowse_Click(object sender, EventArgs e) {
        WebPartManager1.DisplayMode = WebPartManager.BrowseDisplayMode;
}


protected void lnkDesign_Click(object sender, EventArgs e) {
        WebPartManager1.DisplayMode = WebPartManager.DesignDisplayMode;
}
```

The code that allows us to toggle the personalization scope between per-user scope and shared scope is similarly trivial, because that functionality is also exposed via helper methods which we access from the `WebPartManager`. The `ToggleScope` functionality alternates the personalization scope for the page between shared scope and per-user scope. We use this feature to switch the page into shared scope mode to see how changes made while in that mode affect all users of the portal, and not just the current user.

```
protected void lnkToggle_Click(object sender, EventArgs e) {
        WebPartManager1.Personalization.ToggleScope();
}
```

The Reset Personalization button calls the `ResetPersonalizationState` method of the `WebPartManager`'s personalization property, and causes any personalization changes made to a page by a user for a given scope to be reset.

```
protected void lnkReset_Click(object sender, EventArgs e) {
        WebPartManager1.Personalization.ResetPersonalizationState();
}
```

To process the login request, we handle the Authenticate event of the `Login` control. For our application we can simply accept any username with a password of "password."

```
protected void Login1_Authenticate(object sender, AuthenticateEventArgs e)
{
        if (!string.IsNullOrEmpty(Login1.UserName)
                && Login1.Password == "password") {
                e.Authenticated = true;
        } else {
                e.Authenticated = false;
        }
}
```

The last step we need to take is to configure our web application to use forms authentication rather than Windows authentication. We must also configure the authorization settings for personalization so that authenticated users can switch the personalization scope into shared scope mode. To make these configuration settings we must make changes to the `web.config` file for the application. Listing 6.1 shows the authorization elements that must be added to the web configuration file to allow authenticated users to enter into shared scope within the portal.

Listing 6.1 The portal must be configured to allow users to enter into shared scope mode for personalization.

```
<system.web>
        <authentication mode="Forms" />

        <webParts>
                <personalization>
                        <authorization>
                                <deny verbs="enterSharedScope" users="?" />
```

```
                              <allow verbs="enterSharedScope" users="*" />
                    </authorization>
               </personalization>
          </webParts>
</system.web>
```

In listing 6.2 code is added that runs during the pre-render phase of the page, and ensures that the link buttons are hidden until a user has logged in and then hides the Login control when the user has been authenticated:

Listing 6.2 The OnPreRender method is used to configure the visibility of the controls for the application.

```
protected override void OnPreRender(EventArgs e) {
     base.OnPreRender(e);
     this.lnkToggle.Visible =
          WebPartManager1.Personalization.CanEnterSharedScope;
     this.lnkReset.Visible =
             WebPartManager1.Personalization.CanEnterSharedScope;
     this.LoginStatus1.Visible = Page.User.Identity.IsAuthenticated;
     this.lnkBrowse.Visible = Page.User.Identity.IsAuthenticated;
     this.lnkDesign.Visible = Page.User.Identity.IsAuthenticated;
     this.Login1.Visible = !Page.User.Identity.IsAuthenticated;
}
```

Now that the code for the page is complete, all that remains is to create two content pages by right-clicking on the master page in the Solution Explorer within Visual Studio 2005 and choosing the Add Content Page option twice. This should create two content pages named Default.aspx and Default2.aspx. We can now run the Default.aspx page in a browser and make personalization changes so that we may observe the behavior. With the Default.aspx page displayed, enter the following credentials into the login form:

Username: Jane
Password: password

After logging in, the page shown in figure 6.2 should be displayed with both web parts contained in a single zone.

Notice how the name of the user is now displayed and there is a link that allows us to log out, so that we can log in as another user. While logged in, press the button labeled Design DisplayMode to allow design

Figure 6.2 When a user is authenticated, controls are displayed that allow personalization changes to be made.

changes to be made to the page. Drag WebPart2 into the second zone so that the page now looks like the page shown in figure 6.3.

When I'm learning new concepts, I always like to create small prototypes such as the one we've just created so that I can use it to observe behaviors and understand how things work. I hope this technique will be helpful to you, too. Now that we've created our portal we can run some experiments to help us see how personalization works under different circumstances.

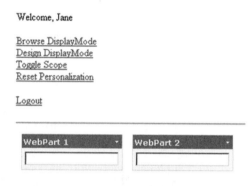

Welcome, Jane

Browse DisplayMode
Design DisplayMode
Toggle Scope
Reset Personalization

Logout

Figure 6.3   The web page after WebPart2 has been moved into the right zone for the user named Jane.

Observing personalization changes

In this section, running some experiments over our prototype will enable us to catch a glimpse of the true nature of personalization so that we will know how to use it, and understand where it might work to best advantage. Once we have the results of these experiments we can drill further into the personalization class. The most important things to observe and understand about personalization are that it is scoped to the

- Current user
- Current page
- Current personalization scope

To see the effect of this scoping with our own eyes we can perform the following experiments:

1. *Check that personalization data is saved on a per-page basis*—To prove that changes made on the Default.aspx page only affect that page, browse to the second page that uses the master page named Default2.aspx. While on the Default2.aspx page, notice that both web parts are still in the first zone.

2. *Check that personalization data is saved on a per-scope basis*—While still logged in as Jane, browse back to the Default.aspx page and click on the link titled Toggle Scope to change the page into shared scope mode. Notice that even though we are logged in as Jane, both web parts are contained within the first zone; this is because the changes made by Jane were made while the page was in per-user scope and therefore are only visible by that user.

3. *Check that shared-scope changes affect all portal users*—While logged in as Jane and in shared scope mode, move WebPart2 into the second zone so that it becomes the default for all users of the portal. Log Jane out by clicking on the

Logout link; and while no users are logged in, notice that `Default.aspx` now shows a web part in each zone as the new default behavior for the page.

4 *Check that resetting personalization returns a page to its default state*—Log in and switch the page into shared scope mode. Click on the Reset Personalization link. This has the effect of resetting the personalization data for the current page, user, and scope. After resetting the personalization data, log out and observe that both web parts are back in the left zone again.

Having run through these small exercises, we've now seen how personalization data is saved for a web page and what factors come into play when a personalized web page is reconstructed. By completing the exercise we witnessed firsthand that personalization data is saved uniquely by user, page, and also by scope.

NOTE The full source code for the `UnderstandingScope` project can be found in the chapter 6 folder of the resources website for this book—http://manning.com/neimke.

Another interesting aspect of personalization shown in the example is that there are methods accessible via the `Personalization` property of the `WebPartManager` that allow us to perform certain personalization duties. For example, when switching the page between per-user scope and shared scope we used a method named `ToggleScope` to do so. We accessed two other personalization members. First was the `CanEnterSharedScope` property, which was used to determine whether or not to expose the `ToggleScope` functionality to the user. The second personalization member was named `ResetPersonalizationState`, which allowed the resetting of the personalization data for the page.

The `Personalization` property of the `WebPartManager` is actually an instance of a `WebPartPersonalization` class associated with the page. It's this class that provides us with most of the logic and is implemented to carry out the low-level personalization operations within our portal. Let's take a look at the `WebPartPersonalization` class in more detail to see what else it has to offer.

WebPartPersonalization class

The `WebPartPersonalization` class contains the logic for personalization operations performed on web part controls within portal applications. Sometimes the `WebPartManager` needs to perform personalization tasks on web controls such as extracting personalization changes from controls and re-applying personalization data to controls that have previously had personalization changes made to them. The `WebPartManager` performs these tasks through the `WebPartPersonalization` class. As we saw in our example, we are also able to access this object from code to perform common personalization operations such as changing the current personalization scope, or resetting the personalization data for a web page. Table 6.1 shows the important public members of the `WebPartPersonalization` class.

Table 6.1 Key Public Members of the WebPartPersonalization Class.

Member Name	Description
CanEnterSharedScope	Indicates whether the current user is allowed to enter into shared personalization scope for the current page.
IsEnabled	Indicates whether or not personalization is enabled for the current user and page and whether it has successfully loaded.
InitialScope	Gets or sets the default personalization scope to use for web pages.
ProviderName	Gets or sets the personalization provider name for use.
Scope	Gets the personalization scope for the current web page.
ResetPersonalizationState	Resets the personalization data for the current page, user, and scope.
ToggleScope	Alternates the personalization scope for the page between shared scope and per-user scope.

We can use these public members to help us perform personalization tasks such as those shown in the example. The following snippet of code highlights how we used the `CanEnterSharedScope` property of the `WebPartPersonalization` class to ensure that the link for toggling the personalization scope was displayed only to users able to view the page in shared-scope mode:

```
this.lnkToggle.Visible =
    WebPartManager1.Personalization.CanEnterSharedScope;
```

In addition to the public members listed in table 6.1, the `WebPartPersonalization` class contains protected members that can be overridden to alter some of the lower-level behavior regarding personalization data extracted from and re-applied to web part controls. Table 6.2 lists the important protected members of the `WebPartPersonalization` class.

Table 6.2 Key Protected Methods of the WebPartPersonalization Class.

Member Name	Description
ApplyPersonalizationState	Applies personalization data to either the WebPartManager for the page or for a specific web part control.
CopyPersonalizationState	Copies the personalization state from one web part to another web part.
ExtractPersonalizationState	Extracts the personalization data from either the WebPartManager for the page or from a specific web part.
Load	Initializes the personalization process by requesting that personalization data be retrieved for the current page, scope, and user from the underlying data store.
Save	Saves the personalization data for the current page, scope, and user to the underlying data store.

Changing the way that personalization data is mapped to web part controls is not a common task; therefore, most of the time we will be able to use the default behavior for these methods. Taking on the job of implementing these methods is quite tricky because of the complex logic required to perform tasks such as

- Versioning data reloaded for a web part control that has had its definition changed since its state was persisted
- Merging data that is being re-loaded with properties a user has changed
- Deciding how to determine when the state for a web part is considered "dirty"

We've seen the effect that scoping has on the personalized view for a user, and we've also learned about the raw interfaces of the WebPartPersonalization class; now it's time to see how and when these are applied during the page lifecycle.

6.4   LIFECYCLE OF PERSONALIZATION DATA

What happens at runtime that allows personalization data to be fetched from a data store and applied to a web page? That's the question we're going to answer now. Understanding the lifecycle of the personalization data will allow us to see when things occur; thus we will know where to write code if we ever need to affect personalization at a really low level—such as to change the data store used to store personalization data. Since this section covers a number of topics and represents the major chunk of this chapter, it may be helpful for you to see what you're in for. Here's the ground we're going to cover:

- Where personalization data is stored
- When personalization data is fetched from storage
- The process that applies the personalization data to the web page
- The process that gathers up modifications to personalization data at the end of the page lifecycle
- When personalization data is persisted back into storage
- How to change the personalization provider of an application

Personalization is actually a two-phase operation. We've seen in the first phase how the WebPartPersonalization class collects and aggregates state data for each web part control on a web page. The second phase occurs when the data collected from the controls on the page is sent to a data store to be persisted. This process can be seen in figure 6.4.

This figure shows that, between visits to a web page, personalization data for web part controls on the page is persisted in a data store. The process of communicating with the data store is handled by a PersonalizationProvider class which defines methods that are required to read and write personalization data to a data store, as described in the section that follows.

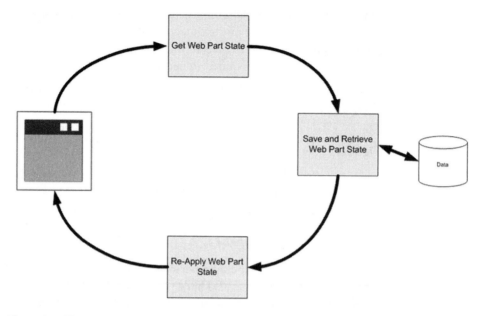

Figure 6.4 The personalization process involves both saving and loading personalization data from a data store.

6.4.1   Storing personalization data

At runtime, the process of saving and restoring personalization data is kicked off by the WebPartManager, as it manages the behavior of the portal during the event lifecycle of the page. The process begins when a user visits a web page within the portal. When this happens, the WebPartManager waits until the InitComplete phase of the page lifecycle, and then uses the WebPartPersonalization class to apply any existing personalization data to controls on the page. To do so, the WebPartPersonalization class requests the personalization data from the PersonalizationProvider.

At the end of the page lifecycle—during the OnPageSaveStateComplete phase—the WebPartManager calls the Save method on the WebPartPersonalization class to save the state of the web part controls on the page. The WebPartPersonalization class gathers the personalization data for each of the web part controls on the page, and then hands it off to the PersonalizationProvider class for saving.

Figure 6.5 provides an overview of the lifecycle of how personalization data is saved and loaded against controls on a web page.

As you can see, the role of the PersonalizationProvider class is limited to data access within the lifecycle of saving and retrieving personalization data.

CHAPTER 6   UNDERSTANDING PERSONALIZATION

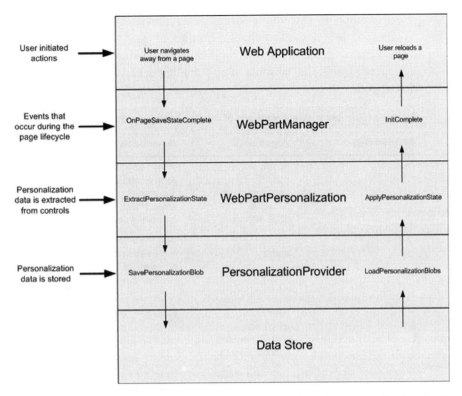

User initiated actions → User navigates away from a page | Web Application | User reloads a page

Events that occur during the page lifecycle → OnPageSaveStateComplete | WebPartManager | InitComplete

Personalization data is extracted from controls → ExtractPersonalizationState | WebPartPersonalization | ApplyPersonalizationState

Personalization data is stored → SavePersonalizationBlob | PersonalizationProvider | LoadPersonalizationBlobs

Data Store

Figure 6.5 The code that performs the job of loading and storing personalization data is separated into several layers making it easier to customize specific functionality within the process.

6.4.2   The PersonalizationProvider class

The `PersonalizationProvider` class is marked as abstract. This means it cannot be instantiated, and has been created solely to define a set of class members that must be implemented by another class which inherits from it. Defining an abstract class for saving and retrieving personalization data is a common extensibility pattern within ASP.NET 2.0, as it allows developers to easily write specific data providers, which act against any type of data store. For example, in one application personalization data might be stored in an SQL Server database, whereas in another application personalization data might be stored in an Oracle database. By inheriting from the `PersonalizationProvider` class, a developer can create a custom `PersonalizationProvider` class and implement the logic required to access data in the data store which the developer will be using. At runtime when data must be saved or loaded, the portal framework makes calls against the base `PersonalizationProvider` class, and is therefore unaware of the exact type of the underlying data store.

In addition to the simple saving and retrieval operations, the Personalization-Provider class also defines a number of query-related methods that must be implemented. Table 6.3 shows the key methods that must be implemented when inheriting from the abstract PersonalizationProvider class and briefly describes their use.

Table 6.3   The key abstract methods of the PersonalizationProvider class.

Method Name	Arguments	Description
FindState	scope query pageIndex pageSize totalRecords	Returns a collection of personalization state data for a given query. The pageIndex and pageSize arguments provide a way to page through large sets of data. This method exists to allow administrative queries to be run against the data store.
GetCountOfState	scope query	Returns a count of the number of rows of personalization data that exist in the data store for a given query. This method exists to allow administrative queries to be run against the data store.
LoadPersonalizationBlobs	webPartManager path userName sharedDataBlob userDataBlob	Loads the raw personalization data from a data store for a given web page.
ResetPersonalizationBlob	webPartManager path userName	Resets the personalization data for a user on a given page. If the userName argument is not specified then it is the shared scope data that is reset.
ResetState	scope paths usernames	Resets the personalization data for users on a list of pages. If no usernames are provided then it is the shared scope data that is reset.
ResetUserState	path userInactiveSinceDate	Resets the personalization data for a given page
SavePersonalizationBlob	webPartManager path userName dataBlob	Saves the raw personalization data to a data store for a given web page

As you can see, the PersonalizationProvider class contains methods for retrieving and saving personalization data, as well as methods for running queries against personalization data that is currently saved.

Configuring a PersonalizationProvider

To allow the portal framework to know which personalization provider class to use, ASP.NET provides us with a personalization element in the web configuration file where we can specify the details of our personalization provider. Listing 6.3 shows the configuration entry that is required to specify values for configuring a personalization provider named `OraclePersonalizationProvider`.

```
<system.web>
    <webParts>
        <personalization
            defaultProvider="OraclePersonalizationProvider">
            <providers>
                <add
                    name="OraclePersonalizationProvider"
                    type="Testing.OraclePersonalizationProvider"
                    connectionStringName="LocalOracleServer"
                    applicationName="/"
                />
            </providers>
        </personalization>
    </webParts>
</system.web>
```

As we can see, the personalization element is configured to use a provider named `OraclePersonalizationProvider`. The settings for the `OraclePersonalizationProvider` are configured in the providers element where we can specify the assembly qualified class name and the connection string to use for our data provider class.

SqlPersonalizationProvider

By default, ASP.NET comes pre-configured with a provider for managing personalization data against an SQL Server store called `SQLPersonalizationProvider`. This class derives from the base `PersonalizationProvider` class and implements each of the methods that are listed in table 6.3 against an SQL Server data store. The `SQLPersonalizationProvider` is pre-configured in the `machine.config` file and so, if we are using SQL Server as our data store for personalization data, no configuration entry is required.

If we need customizations to the way that personalization data is loaded or retrieved from an existing provider, we can simply inherit from the existing provider class and override the appropriate methods to tweak the behavior. Tasks that typically require this type of tweaking include:

- Caching stored data to reduce the load on databases when retrieving personalization data
- Changing the keys against which personalization data is stored
- Encrypting stored data to make it secure when it is in storage

To better understand why we might want to customize the behavior of personalization, let's look at an example. When we created our prototype to observe the behavior of personalization, we saw that personalization data is saved on a per-page basis. Having data saved on a per-page basis is ideal for portals where each page allows many users to personalize the content—such as with SharePoint. However, personalization data keyed off the URL of the page wouldn't necessarily suit applications in which web parts are expected to remain static throughout the site. A blogging application is an example of an application in which changes are typically made for all pages instead of for just a single page.

A typical blogging application might have the following pages:

- The Home page which lists recent blog posts
- A page that displays a summary of historical blog posts
- A page that displays actual blog post content

Now think of the blog owner who takes time to personalize his or her blog using web parts. To do this the owner could browse to the home page and add parts such as a Top Rants web part and a Most Recent Rants web part of the page. After making these modifications the owner would save the changes and switch back into browse mode again.

Unfortunately the changes made by the owner will only be applicable to the home page. When users click an article link in the Top Rants web part, they will be taken to the page that displays blog post content to read the article, but the Top Rants web part will no longer appear.

For small sites such as blogging applications, having navigational consistency is critical for allowing users to find their way around the site. For a site such as this, it just won't do to have key navigational aids, such as the Top Rants web part, appear and disappear at random. Instead, for this blogging application, we need to ensure that any personalization changes made to one page also carry through onto all other public pages, so that all of the navigational aids are consistent for all users of the site.

To change the saving and loading of personalization data so that it is no longer keyed by the URL of the page, we must first create a custom provider which inherits from the base provider class we are using in our portal like so:

```
public class
SingleKeySqlPersonalizationProvider :
  SqlPersonalizationProvider {

}
```

In this code snippet we are creating a class named `SingleKeySqlPersonaliza-tionProvider` which inherits directly from the `SqlPersonalizationProvider` class, and which therefore by default has the same behavior as the `SqlPersonaliza-tionProvider`. The personalization provider uses the `LoadPersonalization-Blobs` method to retrieve personalization data and the `SavePersonalizationBlob` method to store it. If we take a closer look at those methods, we can see that one of the parameters the method uses is the path of the web page. By overriding each of these methods and changing the path to be a single, common path, we can ensure that all personalization data will be keyed for a single location and therefore will be the same for the entire site. Listing 6.4 shows the code required to override these methods and create a single path named `urn:GlobalKey`.

Listing 6.4 Customizing the loading and saving of personalization data so that all data is stored and retrieved for a single key.

```
protected override void LoadPersonalizationBlobs(
      WebPartManager webPartManager,
      string path,
      string userName,
      ref byte[] sharedDataBlob,
      ref byte[] userDataBlob) {          Storing personalization
                                          data against a single,
                                          hard-coded path.
      path = "urn:GlobalKey";   <────
      base.LoadPersonalizationBlobs(
            webPartManager,
            path, userName,
            ref sharedDataBlob,
            ref userDataBlob
            );
}


protected override void SavePersonalizationBlob(
      WebPartManager webPartManager,
      string path,
      string userName,
      byte[] dataBlob) {                  Storing personalization
                                          data against a single,
                                          hard-coded path.
      path = "urn:GlobalKey";   <────
      base.SavePersonalizationBlob(
            webPartManager,
            path,
            userName,
            dataBlob
            );
}
```

In both the load and save methods shown in listing 6.4, we simply change the path to our single, common path and then call through to invoke the base class implementation of the method to save and load the data.

NOTE C# uses the base keyword to call through to methods in an inherited class, whereas VB uses the MyBase keyword.

Finally, we must configure the application to use our custom personalization provider by specifying our custom provider in the personalization section of the web configuration file. Listing 6.5 shows the configuration entry required for the application to use the SingleKeySqlPersonalizationProvider.

Listing 6.5 The portal is configured to use a custom personalization provider that stores all data against a single path key.

```
<system.web>
  <webParts>
    <personalization
      defaultProvider="SingleKeySqlPersonalizationProvider">
      <providers>
        <add connectionStringName="LocalSqlServer"
          name="SingleKeySqlPersonalizationProvider"
          type="WebPartTests.SingleKeySqlPersonalizationProvider" />
      </providers>
    </personalization>
  </webParts>
</system.web>
```

NOTE The full source code for a project named SingleKeyWebsite can be found on the resources website for this book. This project contains a custom SqlPersonalizationProvider which demonstrates how to modify the storing and loading logic of a personalization provider.

Now that we know how to override the loading and storing behavior of the personalization provider class, we can explore how these methods might be used to inject other application logic such as encryption or caching.

6.4.3 Setting up the database

Before we can use the SqlPersonalizationProvider to store personalization data, the tables and other database objects that are used by that class to perform data access must first be created in an SQL Server database. To create these database objects, the ASP.NET team has supplied us with a tool called the ASP.NET SQL Server Setup Tool. This tool can be run against a database to create all the Tables, Views, Stored Procedures, and User Accounts necessary to perform personalization data storage operations in an SQL Server database. The tool is named aspnet_regsql.exe and can be found either in the folder location where you installed the .NET Framework—such as C:\WINDOWS\Microsoft.NET\Framework\<version number>\aspnet_regsql.exe, or you can access the tool directly by running the Visual Studio Command Prompt.

The ASP.NET SQL Server setup tool

The `aspnet_regsql` tool can be run either as a Windows GUI application or as a command-line tool. To run the tool in its GUI mode, simply run the .exe without specifying any command-line arguments, like so:

```
aspnet_regsql.exe
```

When the .exe is running in GUI mode the Windows application displayed in figure 6.6 is displayed. This application allows us to easily configure the commands that need to be run against an SQL Server database to create the ASP.NET application objects in the database.

As you can see, the GUI tool allows us to specify which SQL Server database the application objects will be created in. It also enables us to specify what credentials are needed to allow the tool to connect to the database in the first place. The tool can also be run in console mode by supplying certain command-line arguments when running the application.

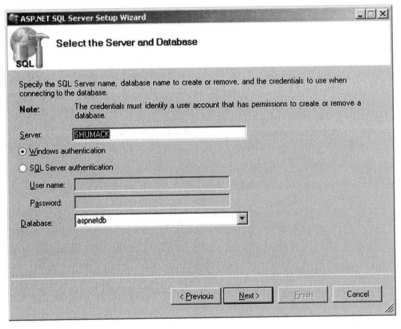

Figure 6.6   The ASP.NET SQL Server Setup Wizard is a GUI version of the aspnet_regsql tool used to create database objects to store personalization data in a SQL Server database.

Running Server Setup in command-line mode

When the tool is run in command-line mode each of the parameters we entered via the user interface of the Windows application must be passed in as command-line arguments. Table 6.4 outlines which command-line arguments are available for use:

Table 6.4   The command-line arguments for the ASP.NET SQL Server Setup Tool.

Argument	Description
-?	Displays Help text for the tool.
-W	Runs the tool in Windowed Mode.
-C	A full connection string, including user credentials, of the database to use when creating the ASP.NET database objects. Alternatively, connection string components can be specified individually by using the -S, -U, -P, and -d arguments.
-S	The name of the server running the SQL Server instance where the database is installed.
-U	The username of a user that has login permissions in the target database. Not required if using the -E option for Windows credentials.
-P	The password of a user that has login permissions in the target database. Not required if using the -E option for Windows credentials.
-E	Authenticates using the Windows credentials of the currently logged-in user.
-d	The name of the database to create or modify. If the database is not specified, the default database name of "aspnetdb" is used.
-sqlexportonly filename	Generates a script containing SQL commands to create the ASP.NET database objects. The specified actions are not performed.
-A (options)	Adds support for one or more ASP.NET features. Each individual ASP.NET feature has a corresponding letter that can be specified after the -A command argument. The letters corresponding to ASP.NET features are: all - All features m - Membership r - Role management p - Profile c - Web parts personalization w - Web events
-R (options)	Removes support for one or more ASP.NET features. Each individual ASP.NET feature has a corresponding letter that can be specified after the -A command argument.
-Q	Runs the tool in quiet mode. When in quiet mode, no confirmation is offered for removal options.

To understand how to use the SQL Server setup tool, take a look at the following commands that use it:

```
aspnet_regsql -A c -E -S . -d MyDatabase
aspnet_regsql -R c -A m -E -S . -d MyDatabase
```

The first command adds the database objects for the personalization feature to a database named MyDatabase. The second command adds the database objects for the membership feature and removes the database objects for the personalization feature to a database named MyDatabase.

Personalization database schema

When the ASP.NET SQL Server setup tool is run, database objects are created for the specified features. For personalization those objects include tables, views, and stored procedures. Table 6.5 lists the database objects created for personalization.

Table 6.5 Database objects that are created in SQL Server to support the personalization feature.

Tables	dbo.aspnet_Applications
	dbo.aspnet_Paths
	dbo.aspnet_PersonalizationAllUsers
	dbo.aspnet_PersonalizationPerUser
	dbo.aspnet_SchemaVersions
	dbo.aspnet_Users
Views	dbo.vw_aspnet_Applications
	dbo.vw_aspnet_Users
	dbo.vw_aspnet_WebPartState_Paths
	dbo.vw_aspnet_WebPartState_Shared
	dbo.vw_aspnet_WebPartState_User
Stored Procedures	dbo.aspnet_AnyDataInTables
	dbo.aspnet_Applications_CreateApplication
	dbo.aspnet_CheckSchemaVersion
	dbo.aspnet_Paths_CreatePath
	dbo.aspnet_Personalization_GetApplicationId
	dbo.aspnet_PersonalizationAdministration_DeleteAllState
	dbo.aspnet_PersonalizationAdministration_FindState
	dbo.aspnet_PersonalizationAdministration_GetCountOfState
	dbo.aspnet_PersonalizationAdministration_ResetSharedState
	dbo.aspnet_PersonalizationAdministration_ResetUserState
	dbo.aspnet_PersonalizationAllUsers_GetPageSettings
	dbo.aspnet_PersonalizationAllUsers_ResetPageSettings
	dbo.aspnet_PersonalizationAllUsers_SetPageSettings
	dbo.aspnet_PersonalizationPerUser_GetPageSettings
	dbo.aspnet_PersonalizationPerUser_ResetPageSettings
	dbo.aspnet_PersonalizationPerUser_SetPageSettings
	dbo.aspnet_RegisterSchemaVersion
	dbo.aspnet_Setup_RemoveAllRoleMembers
	dbo.aspnet_Setup_RestorePermissions
	dbo.aspnet_UnRegisterSchemaVersion
	dbo.aspnet_Users_CreateUser
	dbo.aspnet_Users_DeleteUser

Many of the objects in the table are shared between two or more of the ASP.NET features. For example, the following tables that are created for personalization are shared with other features such as membership and roles, and profile:

- aspnet_Applications
- aspnet_Paths
- aspnet_SchemaVersions
- aspnet_Users

Similarly, many of the Views and Stored Procedures that deal with Applications and User entities are shared by more than one of the ASP.NET application features.

By this point in the chapter, you've steered your way slowly and steadily through a good deal of material. To recap, you've learned about the nature and behavior of personalization. You've seen the lifecycle of personalization data and now understand the mechanics of how the personalization data is stored and retrieved right down to the actual structures within the database. Of course in programming there's always more to learn, and personalization is certainly no exception to that maxim. Throughout the remainder of this chapter you will work through some real-world scenarios for using personalization data so that you can see the complex issues involved when dealing with personalization data and the features that can help you with this.

6.5 WORKING WITH PERSONALIZATION DATA

Suppose you wanted to create a web part to display and maintain the details of employees. The web part could be supported with personalizable, web-browsable properties representing the data of a staff member, thereby allowing us to maintain the data in the standard `PropertyGridEditorPart`. The properties might include data for a `FirstName` and `LastName`. There could be other properties to store data on the address information for an employee such as: Street1, Street2, City, State, and Zip Code. Each of these pieces of data would be represented by a simple string property.

In the world of object-oriented design, it is more likely that we would represent the data for employees using classes or structs. Here we would have an Employee class with a `FirstName`, a `LastName`, and an `Address` property. The `Address` property would itself be a class encapsulating the properties required to store address information. Having complex properties such as this can be problematic when working with personalization data. Having said that it is difficult to use complex data types to store personalization data, I should point out that it is also quite common to want to do it, so we need to find the solution. In the remainder of this section we will see just how this is done.

In the portal framework, personalization data for web parts is saved only when changes to the data occur. Therefore, given a web part with a simple string property, the personalization data for the web part will only be saved when the value of the string is changed. If no changes are made to the value of the property, the personalization data will not be saved. This is actually a good thing because it can mean that unnecessary trips to the database aren't occurring.

For value data types such as numbers, enums, Booleans, or immutable data such as strings, it is easy to check if their values change because you can simply compare the value of the data with an earlier value. However, with reference data types such as an Array, ArrayList, Dictionary, or custom data objects, it is not so simple to determine when data changes occur. This is because the value of complex reference types can change without their reference changing, and the framework therefore cannot tell that a change has occurred.

6.5.1   SetPersonalizationDirty

In all the web parts we've created so far, we've seen that marking web part properties with the `Personalizable` attribute property ensures that values are automatically persisted and re-loaded for us by personalization. This is fine for properties based on value data types and immutable data types, because the portal framework knows how to track changes made to data. It is not sufficient, however, when we have web parts which have reference data types as properties. As a result, objects such as complex business objects or collections cannot be persisted by simply marking those properties with the `Personalizable` attribute.

To assist us with the task of saving complex data, each web part has a method named `SetPersonalizationDirty` that we can use to inform the portal framework that a web part has changes and must have its data saved. To do this we simply call the `SetPersonalizationDirty` method on the `WebPart` to notify the portal framework when a change occurs. Consider the following web part used for managing information about employees. It has a complex property for storing the employee data.

```
public class EmployeeWebPart : WebPart {

    private Employee _employee;

    [Personalizable]
    public Employee Employee {
        get { return _employee; }
        set { _employee = value; }
    }
}
```

A consuming page might expect to make changes to the Employee data and have them saved via personalization simply by making changes to the Employee values as we see with the following snippet of code:

```
EmployeeWebPart.Employee.FirstName = this.FirstNameTextBox.Text;
EmployeeWebPart.Employee.LastName = this.LastNameTextBox.Text;
```

Changes made in this way would not be persisted by personalization, as personalization would not be able to determine that the Employee property had changed, even though its values had. For the data to be saved, we need a way to set the dirty state of the web part whenever the employee data changes. The following snippet of code shows a method that could be exposed by the `EmployeeWebPart` to allow callers to set the `SetPersonalizationDirty` method of the web part whenever employee data is changed:

```
public void SetDirty() {
    this.SetPersonalizationDirty();
}
```

Now when the web page needs to update the employee details, it performs the same operations as before, but can now also call the `SetDirty` method on the web part to ensure that the data is correctly saved by personalization:

```
EmployeeWebPart.Employee.FirstName = this.FirstNameTextBox.Text;
EmployeeWebPart.Employee.LastName = this.LastNameTextBox.Text;
EmployeeWebPart.SetDirty() ;
```

The changes made to the data in the `EmployeeWebPart` will now be saved.

> **NOTE** In the chapter 6 folder of the resources included with this book, there is a project named `PersonalizationInterfaces` which contains the full source code for a web page named `TestSetPersonalization-Dirty.aspx`, which can be used to test the `SetPersonalization-Dirty` behavior.

In this example the calling web page is required to call the `SetDirty` method on the web part to ensure that changes are saved. Failure to implement that method call will result in a loss of data for users who make changes and expect to have them saved. Calling the `SetDirty` method is therefore an unintuitive additional step which is likely to lead to data being lost. A better way would be to include the call to the `Set-PersonalizationDirty` method directly within the `Employee` property of the web part itself, like so:

```
[Personalizable]
public Employee Employee {
    get { return _employee; }
    set {
        SetPersonalizationDirty() ;
        employee = value;
    }
}
```

This way, whenever the Employee data was set, the web part would be flagged as dirty and the personalization data would be saved. Although this change would be useful for calling code because there would no longer be a need remember to call the `Set-Dirty` method, it also would mean that the data for the `EmployeeWebPart` would always be marked as dirty. This is because personalization uses this property setter when it is re-loading personalization data at the beginning of lifecycle of the page. What we really need is a way to have the call to `SetPersonalizationDirty` included in the property setter, but only have it called when the data being set is from some operation other than personalization loading. We can see an example of this in the following code snippet:

```
[Personalizable]
public Employee Employee {
    get { return _employee; }
    set {
        if( !this.IsLoading )
            SetPersonalizationDirty() ;

        employee = value;
    }
}
```

To help solve problems such as this, the portal framework supplies special interfaces that can be implemented to hook into the loading, saving, and state tracking activities performed throughout the lifecycle of a web part. In the next section we'll see how these interfaces are used and look at some scenarios surrounding their use.

6.5.2 Personalization interfaces

As mentioned, the portal framework contains certain interfaces that can be implemented to allow us to extend web part controls with custom logic. These interfaces provide hooks into the lifecycle of saving and loading personalization data and allow us to create custom solutions for loading and storing personalization data as well as tracking activity that occurs throughout the lifecycle. The personalization interfaces are

- IPersonalizable—Provides methods that allow us to take ownership of the loading and storing process of personalization data for an individual web part control.
- IVersioningPersonalizable—Provides a way to manage personalization data for a web part that has now had its definition changed.
- ITrackingPersonalizable—Allows us to write code to perform tasks at various stages during the loading and saving of personalization data.

By implementing these interfaces, developers can control how data is loaded, tracked, and saved by writing code to manage complex personalization. Let's take a deeper look at each of the personalization interfaces to see what they are and how we can use them to assist us when dealing with complex personalization scenarios.

IPersonalizable

Implementing IPersonalizable on a web part control requires that the following property and two methods be implemented:

- IsDirty—This property indicates whether data for the control has changed
- Load—Custom logic for loading the data for the control
- Save—Custom logic for saving the data for the control

Both the `Load` and `Save` methods are passed a `PersonalizationDictionary` object which contains a collection of `PersonalizationEntry` items as shown by the following method signatures:

```
Load(PersonalizationDictionary state)
Save(PersonalizationDictionary state)
```

For example, consider a web part that maintains a list of a user's favorite website links. Such a web part might maintain the list of links in a complex property such as the following property, which uses a generic list of strings to store data:

```
private List<string> _hyperlinks = new List<string>();
[Personalizable]
public List<string> Hyperlinks {
        get { return _hyperlinks; }
        set { _hyperlinks = value; }
}
```

For such a class, this data would not be persisted because the standard personalization behavior for ASP.NET portals does not know how to deal with complex data types such as this. By implementing the `IPersonalizable` interface, custom code such as that shown in listing 6.6 can be written to store any serializable data types in the `PersonalizationDictionary`.

> **Listing 6.6 Implementing the Load and Save methods of the IPersonalizable interface provides a way to write custom logic for handling personalization data.**

```
public new void Load(PersonalizationDictionary state) {

        PersonalizationEntry pe = state["Hyperlinks"]
          as PersonalizationEntry;

        if (pe != null) {
                this.Hyperlinks = (List<string>) pe.Value;     ◁──────┐
        }                                                              │
}                                              The PersonalizationEntry is cast to
                                               the correct data type during loading.

public void Save(PersonalizationDictionary state) {

        PersonalizationEntry entry =
                new PersonalizationEntry(
                  this.Hyperlinks,
                  this.WebPartManager.Personalization.Scope    ◁──────┐
                  );                                                   │
        state["Hyperlinks"] = entry;                  The PersonalizationEntry
}                                                     contains our custom data.
```

We see here that, by writing directly to the `PersonalizationDictionary` we can store any serializable objects by creating our own `PersonalizationEntry` object and assigning our data as the value of it.

NOTE   In the chapter 6 folder of the resources website for this book, there is a project named `PersonalizationInterfaces` which contains the full source code for a web part named `FavouritesWebPart`, which is the full implementation of the above snippet.

PersonalizationEntry

The `PersonalizationEntry` class is a simple data class whose sole purpose is to store the state data for web part data. When personalization data is passed around within the portal framework, it is often passed as `PersonalizationEntry` objects so that methods within the portal have a structured way to work with personalization data. The `PersonalizationEntry` class exposes the following three properties that can be used by code to examine personalization data and to assist with making decisions about its use:

- *IsSensitive*—Indicates whether the personalization data contains sensitive information.
- *Scope*—Gets or sets the personalization scope associated with this piece of personalization data.
- *Value*—Gets or sets the personalization data for the personalization entry.

Having encapsulated data such as this is good, because strongly typed data is less likely to be the cause of coding errors. Visual Studio can check code which accesses the `PersonalizationEntry` class advising of any errors before we deploy our code.

By setting the properties of the `PersonalizationEntry` class, we can be guaranteed that our data will be handled in a consistent manner by other members of the portal framework. For example, by setting the `IsSensitive` property of a `PersonalizationEntry` to true, we can be sure the `WebPartManager` will handle the data in a secure manner when performing export operations on a web part that contains the property associated with it.

IVersioningPersonalizable

The `IVersioningPersonalizable` interface exists for the purpose of allowing us to work with web parts that have had some part of their definition changed and therefore require versioning. In this case, data may be retrieved which is orphaned because the property it represents has been removed or renamed. By implementing the `IVersioningPersonalizable` interface, a developer can map data he saved for a property that has been removed or renamed and map it to a new property. Implementing the `IVersioningPersonalizable` interface requires us to implement a single method named Load which receives a dictionary of any orphaned data after normal personalization loading has taken place. The following snippet shows the signature of the IVersioningPersonalizabel Load method:

```
public new void Load(IDictionary unknownProperties)
```

As an example of when to use this interface, consider a web part with a property that stores a collection of user data such as a list of phone numbers in an ArrayList. At some stage the developer of the web part may decide to use a different data type such as a custom PhoneNumberCollection data type to store the data. In this case, the developer would implement the new data type for the property and then write code in the Load method to map between the two data types for any personalization data which had been saved for the previous data type.

> **NOTE**   In the chapter 6 folder of the resources website for this book there is a project named PersonalizationInterfaces. This project contains the full source code for a web part named VersionedWebPart and includes an implementation of the IVersioningPersonalizable interface.

Unlike the IPersonalizable interface, IVersioningPersonalizable is not an interface that we are likely to implement on a common occurrence. However, when we need to be able to handle version changes to our web parts, the IVersioningPersonalizable interface is exactly the right tool for the job.

ITrackingPersonalizable

The last of the personalization interfaces is named ITrackingPersonalizable and allows a developer to write code that is run before and after personalization data is loaded or saved. A key reason for this is because we may need to ensure that some code within our class does not run during the loading or saving phases of the page. In such a case we can create a special boolean variable to act as a flag which indicates that loading or saving is taking place. We would then set the value of this flag to true in a pre-load event to indicate that loading is taking place, and then reset it to false in a post-load event to indicate that loading has completed. The same sort of semantics would apply for saving. Having set the value of the flag, other code in the class which may get executed from logic in our load or save event handlers can then check the value of the flag and use it to determine whether to execute or not—for example, if the value of the flag were true, a method may choose not to execute any of its logic. The ITrackingPersonalizable interface defines the following four methods and one property that must be implemented by classes of this type:

- TracksChanges—Indicates whether the web part maintains tracking logic of its own changes
- BeginLoad—Runs at the beginning of the load phase of personalization data
- EndLoad—Runs at the end of the load phase of personalization data

- `BeginSave`—Runs at the beginning of the saving phase of personalization data
- `EndSave`—Runs at the end of the saving phase of personalization data

Typically, the `ITrackingPersonalizable` interface is implemented by classes that intend to track their own state changes. To do this a class should implement `ITrackingPersonalizable` and return true from the `TracksChanges` property. For web parts with complex properties such as collections or custom types, understanding the `ITrackingPersonalizable` interface is very important. Without implementing this interface, the web part's property setters will not know whether or not they should call `SetPersonalizationDirty` and the personalization service will not know to save the property values.

That covers the last of the main personalization interfaces and has provided us with a clear understanding of what we have to work with when customizing our portal to handle exceptional circumstances. Having learned about these interfaces and the lifecycle of personalization, we are well equipped to take control of the behavior of personalization. Let's apply some of this knowledge to the Adventure Works portal to see how we go about implementing this knowledge in the real world.

6.6 PERSONALIZATION OF THE ADVENTURE WORKS PORTAL

This morning an e-mail arrived from the manager of the HR department asking for a few small changes and additions to the HR portal. The first change they requested is for a simple way to allow certain users to make changes to the portal that will be seen by all users. For example, the web part displaying the greeting message should not be customizable for each person, but should instead be customized once for all users to see.

The next change they requested is for a web part that allows users to keep track of personal notes; this would be like sticky notes for the portal. The idea is that users can create notes to store messages such as notes about tasks needing to be done. Because these messages could contain sensitive information, the manager of the HR department has requested that all data contained within the messages be stored in a secure manner so that it cannot be read or even tampered with.

> **NOTE** If you don't have a copy of the project from chapter 5, you can grab from the chapter 5 folder which is located in the resources website for this book.

OK, time to roll up our sleeves and get started!

6.6.1 Allowing users to change personalization scope

The first change request we're going to tackle is to provide administrative users with a way to switch the portal into shared scope mode at runtime. Figure 6.7 shows the area of the page to which we'll add new functionality.

Figure 6.7
The Adventure Works portal provides administrative users with the ability to easily toggle the personalization scope between shared scope and per-user scope.

As we see from the image, there will be a message displayed just below the page header which shows the user what the current scope of the page is and provides a link allowing him to toggle the scope.

Adding PageTasks

To get things started we will create a panel underneath the page header to display the controls for managing the scope of the page. It is likely as time goes by that other page related tasks will also go into this area, so we'll refer to it by the generic sounding name of the PageTasks. Other tasks we might add to this panel could include the following:

- A link that offers quick access to the web part catalog
- Tools for managing content versions for content on the web page
- A link that allows a user to manage the portal

We'll see some of these functional items added to the portal as we progress through the next three chapters and start to add more application-specific functionality to our portal.

At this stage we want to display the PageTasks only to users who have permissions to view the portal in shared scope mode. Therefore, we'll create a Placeholder to contain the user interface elements for the PageTasks controls and set its visibility to hidden by default. We can then write logic that will display the Placeholder only for users who have permission to manage personalization scope. To add the Placeholder and the PageTasks controls, open the master page for the portal and add the HTML shown in listing 6.7 just below the header section:

Listing 6.7 The markup code that creates the PageTasks panel including controls for toggling the personalization scope

```
<asp:PlaceHolder ID="pnlPageTasks" runat="server" Visible="false">
    <div id="pagetasks">

        <asp:Label ID="lblCurrentScope" runat="server"      ⟵  A Label displays
            Text="" Font-Bold="true" />               the current scope

        <asp:Image runat="server" ID="imgToggle"               An Image
            ImageUrl="App_Themes/Images/allusr.GIF"            displays an
                                                               icon which
            ImageAlign="AbsMiddle" BorderStyle="None" />  ⟵   represents the
                                                               target state
```

```
            <asp:HyperLink id="lnkToggle" runat="server"
                Text="Show Shared View" />  ◁
    </div>
</asp:PlaceHolder>
```

> A HyperLink allows the user to toggle the personalization scope

The HTML for the PageTasks controls provides a Label that will be used to display the current personalization scope to the user, as well as an Image and a HyperLink to allow the user to toggle the personalization scope. There are a couple things worth noticing here. The HTML DIV element that contains the PageTasks controls is given an ID so that we can refer to it both with client-side JavaScript and CSS. By writing CSS code and placing it in the default.css file for the current theme, we can provide the PageTasks panel with a suitable look and feel. In this case we will simply give it a light-grey background and a solid border at the bottom so that it looks like its own distinct section on the page. Open the default.css file and add the following CSS definition for the PageTasks panel:

```
#pagetasks
{
    background-color: #eeeeee;
    color: #333333;
    text-align: left ;
    border-bottom: 1px solid #cccccc;
}
```

The beauty of having the style definition in the themes folder is that whenever we want to create a new theme, we can also create a look and feel for our PageTasks panel suitable to the surrounding feel of the page. The same can be said of the image we are using alongside the link for toggling the scope. As you can see, this Image control loads its content from an images folder underneath the App_Themes folder. At runtime this image points to the images folder for the current theme of the application—in our case that will be the images folder underneath the folder named Blue in the App_Themes folder.

Now that we have the visual elements in place for the PageTasks controls, we can write the logic that first determines whether they are visible for the current user. Then we can write the logic for toggling the scope of the page.

The best place for the logic that chooses whether the PageTasks panel is displayed is in the PreRender phase for the page. The reason for putting the logic here is that we want it to run as late as possible to ensure it only runs once—and we therefore incur the cost of running the code just once. If we put the code for manipulating the PageTasks controls too early in the page's lifecycle, we run the risk of it running twice. This is because when the ToggleScope method is called, a Server.Transfer is invoked, which means the page will run through its initialize and loading events twice. The code displayed in listing 6.8 shows the logic required to manage the controls in the PageTasks panel.

```
protected override void OnPreRender(EventArgs e) {
    base.OnPreRender(e);

    this.pnlPageTasks.Visible =
        _wpm.Personalization.CanEnterSharedScope;

    if( this.pnlPageTasks.Visible ) {

            string path = this.Request.Url.AbsolutePath;

        if (_wpm.Personalization.Scope == PersonalizationScope.User) {
            lblCurrentScope.Text = "Current Page Scope: Per-User";
            imgToggle.ImageUrl = "~/App_Themes/Images/allusr.GIF";
            lnkToggle.Text = "Show Shared View";
            lnkToggle.NavigateUrl = path + "?view=shared";
        } else {
            lblCurrentScope.Text = "Current Page Scope: Shared View";
            imgToggle.ImageUrl = "~/App_Themes/Images/perusr.GIF";
            lnkToggle.Text = "Show Per-User View";
            lnkToggle.NavigateUrl = path;
        }
    }
}
```

Ascertain whether the user can view the PageTasks panel

Display controls to toggle into shared scope mode

Display controls to toggle into per-user scope mode

Notice how we first check to see whether the user can enter shared scope mode and we set the visibility of the PageTasks panel based on that. We then configure the display text, image URL, and the hyperlink based on the current personalization scope of the page. If the current scope is per-user, the controls are configured to allow the page to be toggled into shared scope mode and vice versa.

The logic for toggling the personalization scope is based off of a querystring argument named "view." If the view querystring argument is present and its value is shared, the page should be displayed in shared scope mode, or else it should be displayed in per-user mode. The code that performs this check is placed in the OnInit phase of the page so that it is run as early as possible. Listing 6.9 shows the logic for managing the current personalization scope of the page:

Listing 6.9   The OnInit method is used to ascertain whether the user has requested a scope change.

```
protected override void OnInit(EventArgs e) {
    base.OnInit(e);

    bool requiresToggle = false;

    _wpm = WebPartManager.GetCurrentWebPartManager(this.Page);
```

```
if (Request.QueryString["view"] != null) {          ◁─┐ Ascertain if the user requested
    string view = Request.QueryString["view"];        │ to display shared scope
    if (view == "shared" &&
            _wpm.Personalization.Scope != PersonalizationScope.Shared) {
        requiresToggle = true;
    }
} else if (_wpm.Personalization.Scope == PersonalizationScope.Shared) {
    requiresToggle = true;  ◁─┐ Decide if we should switch
}                             │ into per-user scope

if (requiresToggle) {
    _wpm.Personalization.ToggleScope();  ◁─┐ ToggleScope
}                                          │ if required
}
```

In the OnInit method we check to see whether the view argument is present within the querystring for the page and, if so, we check the current scope of the page to see whether we need to toggle the scope. Likewise, if the view argument is not present within the querystring then the page should be in per-user scope, so we must check that as well.

When the portal is run, the `PageTasks` panel will be displayed for users who have been configured to see it from within the authorization section of the web configuration file. The following snippet of code from the web configuration file shows how to add the shared scope capability for users of the portal:

```
<webParts enableExport="true">
    <personalization>
        <authorization>
            <deny verbs="enterSharedScope" users="?" />
            <allow verbs="enterSharedScope" users="*" />
        </authorization>
    </personalization>
</webParts>
```

In this snippet we see that only authenticated users have been allowed to enter into shared scope mode for the portal.

6.6.2 Adding a Notes web part

The second feature we've been asked to add is a web part that allows users to add arbitrary chunks of text to a page and which encrypts the contents of the web part when it is saved to the data store. Figure 6.8 shows that one of the portal users has used this web part to keep track of some outstanding HR tasks she needs to follow up on.

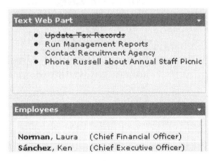

Figure 6.8 The Text Web Part allows users to enter text and have it saved securely in an encrypted format.

In this image the user has added some HTML content to the body of the web part to display a list of tasks as a bulleted list. By default the web part displays its content in a read-only format within a label control, but will also allow a user to switch into an edit mode. When the web part is in edit mode the content will be displayed within a TextBox, allowing the user to make changes to the text. To get things started we'll create a web part and add a property to contain the content and a property that lets us know whether or not we are currently in edit mode. Create a class file named TaskNotes.cs and add the code from listing 6.10 to it.

Listing 6.10 The TaskNotes web part implements the IPersonalizable interface and therefore does not mark its personalizable Message property with the Personalizable attribute.

```
public class TaskNotes : WebPart, IPersonalizable {

    private string _message;
    public string Message {
        get { return _message; }
        set { _message = value; }
    }

    public bool IsEditing {
        get {
            return Convert.ToBoolean(this.ViewState["IsEditing"]);
        }
        set { this.ViewState["IsEditing"] = value; }
    }
}
```

Store in ViewState to persist across page postbacks

Notice that the property for the web part is not marked with the Personalizable attribute; this is because we'll be implementing the IPersonalizable interface and therefore taking control over the loading, saving, and state tracking of the web part. Writing this logic ourselves allows us to insert our encryption and decryption logic.

Implementing IPersonalizable

As we saw earlier in the chapter, implementing IPersonalizable means writing Load method and Save method and exposing a property which indicates whether or not the control is "dirty." The logic for each of these is actually quite simple as we are simply writing or reading values directly from the PersonalizationEntry-Collection. Listing 6.11 shows the code we will use to implement the IPersonalizable interface.

```
private bool _isDirty = false;
public bool IsDirty {
    get { return _isDirty; }
}


public new virtual void Load(PersonalizationDictionary state) {

    PersonalizationEntry pe = state["Message"] as PersonalizationEntry;

    if (pe != null) {                                    Decrypt the
        try {                                            personaliztion
                                                         data when loading
            string data = pe.Value.ToString() ;
            string message = EncryptionHelpers.DecryptData(data);   ◁
            this.Message = message;
        } catch (CryptographicException ex) {
            this.Message = ex.Message;
        }
    }
}

public void Save(PersonalizationDictionary state) {

    if (this.WebPartManager != null) {           Encrypt user entered
                                                 data when saving

        string data = EncryptionHelpers.EncryptData(_message);   ◁

        PersonalizationEntry entry =
            new PersonalizationEntry(data, PersonalizationScope.User);
        state["Message"] = entry;   ◁  Write encrypted data
    }                                  into the state bag
}
```

The logic here is identical to the logic we saw earlier in the chapter when we took our
first look at the IPersonalizable interface, except the data we are saving is passed
off to a couple of methods that help us with encryption before saving and after loading has occurred.

Encrypting Message Content

The .NET Framework provides us with some useful classes for performing crypto-
graphic services for making data secure such as encryption and hashing operations.
These classes can be found in the System.Security.Cryptography namespace
and make the job of encrypting and decrypting data a relatively simple task. For our
purposes we will choose an encryption provider that implements the logic of the Triple

Data Encryption Standard (`TripleDES`) algorithm to encrypt and decrypt our web part data.

To use the `TripleDES` encryption provider that ships with the .NET Framework we create an instance of the `TripleDESCryptoServiceProvider` class which exposes the necessary encryption and decryption services for us to use:

```
private static TripleDESCryptoServiceProvider _crypto =
    new TripleDESCryptoServiceProvider();
```

Now that we have an instance of the `TripleDES` crypto provider, we can use it to work with our data. First, we'll want to have it encrypt data that has been entered by the user. To do this, we can create a helper method which takes the plain-text data the user has entered and encrypts it. Listing 6.12 shows the helper method we will use to encrypt user-entered data.

Listing 6.12   Encrypting the message data is handled by the TripleDES-CryptoServiceProvider and returned as an encrypted string.

```
public static string EncryptData(string data) {

    string encryptedData = "";

    if (!string.IsNullOrEmpty(data)) {

        byte[] receivedBytes = Encoding.Unicode.GetBytes(data);
        byte[] encryptedBytes =
        _crypto.CreateEncryptor().TransformFinalBlock(     ◁── An encryptor is
                receivedBytes,                                  used to encrypt
                0,                                              data
                receivedBytes.GetLength(0)
                );

        encryptedData = Convert.ToBase64String(encryptedBytes);
    }
    return encryptedData;
}
```

As we can see, the text passed into the `EncryptData` helper method is converted into a byte array, which is then encrypted by the encryptor that is created by the `TripleDES` crypto provider. Finally the byte array is converted to a string and returned to the calling code. Similarly, the code for decrypting encrypted text converts the string to a byte array which can be used by a decryptor to decrypt the bytes and then return a decrypted string to the calling code. The helper method shown in listing 6.13 shows how this is done.

```
public static string DecryptData(string encryptedData) {

    string decryptedData = "";

    if (!string.IsNullOrEmpty(encryptedData)) {
        byte[] base64 = Convert.FromBase64String(encryptedData);
        byte[] bytes = _crypto.CreateDecryptor().TransformFinalBlock(
            base64,
            0,
            base64.GetLength(0)
            );

        decryptedData = Encoding.Unicode.GetString(bytes);
    }

    return decryptedData;
}
```

A decryptor is used to decrypt the encrypted bytes

Both of these helper functions are implemented as static methods so that they can be easily used by calling code without having to first create an instance of a class. This is possible because we do not need to keep hold of any state outside of the two helper methods.

Now that our data is being saved and loaded in a secure format, all that remains is to create the logic within the web part that allows users to switch it into an editing mode so that they can change the content for the web part.

Managing WebPart behavior

We have a number of options at our disposal to allow the user to switch the web part into edit mode so that the content can be updated. One way might be to display some custom controls on the chrome of the web part—such as a button—to allow the user to toggle in between an editing and a viewing state. For our web part, we will simply use verbs to allow the user to invoke the necessary actions, because using a verb is probably a slightly simpler task than adding a button and handling its click event. The snippet shown in listing 6.14 shows the code required to add the necessary custom verbs to our web part that will allow management over the content.

```
public override WebPartVerbCollection Verbs {
    get {
        List<WebPartVerb> verbs = new List<WebPartVerb>();
        EditNoteVerb verb = null;
```

```
            WebPartManager wpm =                                    Display a verb
            WebPartManager.GetCurrentWebPartManager(this.Page);     based on
                                                                    the current
            if (this.IsEditing) {                            <──── editing state
                verb = new EditNoteVerb("Save Note", SaveNoteHandler);
            } else {
                verb = new EditNoteVerb("Edit Note", EditNoteHandler);
            }

            if (verb != null) {
                verbs.Add(verb);
            }

            return new WebPartVerbCollection(verbs); ;
        }
    }
```

When the web part is in an editing mode, a Save Note verb is displayed that allows any changes to be saved, and switches the mode back into a viewing state. When we are in viewing mode for the page, a save verb will be added that allows the user to edit the content. The following code shows the logic for the methods that handle the verb operations:

```
void EditNoteHandler(object sender, WebPartEventArgs e) {
    this.IsEditing = true;
}

void SaveNoteHandler(object sender, WebPartEventArgs e) {

    this.Message = this._tb.Text;
    this._isDirty = true;
    this.IsEditing = false;

}
```

As we can see, the code for saving the changes for the web part is quite simple. First, the new message text is set based on the input by the user. Next, we set the isDirty flag to indicate that the web part has changes. This is very important, and failure to do so will result in our changes going unsaved. This is because the portal framework uses the IsDirty property of the IPersonalizable interface to know whether or not to call our Save method. Finally, the IsEditing flag is set to false so that the rendering logic can know to display the message contents in a Label rather than a TextBox.

The code for the Adventure Works portal can be found in the chapter 6 folder of the resources that come with this book. The code in that folder contains the Task-Notes web part and the PageTasks panel that have been integrated into the portal.

6.7 SUMMARY

This chapter has been a necessarily long discussion on the topic of personalization because of the significant role that personalization plays within the portal. It is also the last of the chapters which I refer to as "building block" chapters. The building block chapters have covered the core ASP.NET objects used to create portal applications and include:

- Web parts
- Zones
- Connections
- WebPartManager
- Personalization

By using and customizing the behavior of these core portal objects we can create truly unique and compelling portals that rival modern portals such as SharePoint and http://Live.com. In the remaining chapters we take the lessons learned in the building block chapters and use that knowledge to give the Adventure Works portal a facelift. After surgery, the portal will sport features that cannot be implemented straight out of the box. In performing the surgery, we learn the important lessons of planning and implementing custom application features in our application.

Extending the portal framework

In chapters 7 through 10 you will master the art of portals and learn how to mix the things you've learned so far into a recipe that will help you to produce portals that are not only highly customized but that users will enjoy using. We'll do this by looking at some of the common customizations that are applied to modern portals to see how to apply them to our own portal.

C H A P T E R   7

Creating an enhanced editing experience

7.1 INTRODUCTION

Managing a portal is a bit like owning a B & B. In both cases we want our clients to have a unique experience and for their stay at the site to be as long and useful as possible. But with B & Bs and portals, there's a catch to capturing customers. What attracts users to your portal may not be the underlying wizardry you're so proud of; after all, not everyone likes ginger in their blueberry muffins. Most portal visitors aren't dazzled by the "coolness" of zones, personalization, web parts, or even the web part manager. Users either take those elements for granted or don't even see them. On the other hand, they do care about and notice the ability to personalize a substantial amount of content and see the same content when they revisit the website.

What else do users feel strongly about? Ease of use is certainly important. This means that use of features should be intuitive and easy. Consider the way that we've been editing the web part values throughout this book. How many actions has the user just performed to personalize that web part?

- One: Select the edit item in the dropdown list.
- Two: Open the verbs menu for the web part.
- Three: Select the edit verb.
- Four: Save changes.

Four clicks. That's not too bad, right? Well, it's important to remember that all of these clicks add up and to the visitor of our site, they all count. To stay on top of the usability issue, we need to pay attention to things such as mouse clicks and to keep them to a minimum. For example, in the preceding example, could you include logic within the web part itself to determine whether the current user has editing rights and if so, add an edit button to the web part? When the user clicked on the edit button we could handle the logic for switching the page into edit mode automatically; then the user would only need a single click to perform editing. Changes such as this might seem small, but to the users this can mean the difference between a good portal and one which is perceived as being difficult to use.

Throughout this chapter we will use some elbow grease to polish the Adventure Works application and make it shine when it comes to providing the user with a great editing experience. Not only will we see how to reduce the complexity of our design by removing mouse-clicks but we will also see how to beef-up the power behind the EditorZone itself to allow users to perform complex operations within it. In fact, that's exactly where we are going to start, by taking the FavoritesWebPart that we saw in chapter 6 in the discussion of the IPersonalizable interface, and providing users with a rich user interface to manage the hyperlink data.

7.2 SUPPLYING CUSTOM EDITING CONTROLS

In chapter 6 we discussed a web part named FavoritesWebPart which allowed users to add the URLs to their favorite websites and have them remembered.

NOTE The FavoritesWebPart discussed here is included in the sample project named PersonalizationInterfaces that can be found in the chapter 6 section of the resources website for this book.

To allow the user to add hyperlinks, the page that hosted the FavoritesWebPart had a textbox and a button that allowed the user to submit hyperlink data to the web part. When the user pressed the button on the page, data was taken from the textbox and passed to a method named AddHyperlink that was exposed on the web part. Figure 7.1 shows a picture of the page in which you can see the textbox, the "Add Hyperlink" button, and the web part which displays the data for two existing hyperlinks.

While the favorites web part is undoubtedly useful, it also has some drawbacks. For example, how do users remove hyperlinks when they no longer hold the esteemed status of "favorite"? Another drawback is that the user can enter only a URL

Figure 7.1   The FavoritesWebPart that we created in chapter 6 displays a listing of the users' favorite hyperlinks.

for the hyperlink; this would make it extremely difficult to read and understand links that contained large amounts of data appended to the URL. Finally, and probably the most limiting drawback, is that to be of any use at all, the web part relies upon the page to provide the controls and code that allows the user to enter the hyperlinks in the first place. Having a web part that relies upon functionality provided by the web page is not good because the web part is no longer portable and cannot be arbitrarily added to any page by a user.

> **NOTE**   The relationship between any two objects is referred to as their "coupling." Objects that are highly reliant upon one another are referred to as being tightly coupled while objects that are free-standing are referred to as loosely coupled. Wherever possible we want our web parts to be loosely coupled so that they are not dependant upon other objects and can therefore be used in a wider range of applications.

There are many things that we can do to improve the FavoritesWebPart and in the process we'll also make it easier for users to work with. One option is to allow users to enter additional data about each hyperlink—such as a display title and a description. The extra information can then be used to improve the appearance of the hyperlink when it is displayed in a web page.

In the next section we'll take the FavoritesWebPart and make several improvements to it. First we'll give it a rich data type that will allow it to store the title, hyperlink, and a description. Then we'll really whip it into shape by creating a custom editor control to make it easy for users to work with the web part and add new favorites.

7.2.1   Improving the FavoritesWebPart

As mentioned, we are looking for ways to improve the usability of our portal, and we've started by taking a look at how users maintain and edit web parts within the portal. We're now going to take the FavoritesWebPart and make a number of improvements to it. Throughout the course of these improvements we'll learn some important lessons about how to work with web parts that have complex data for their properties, and we'll see how to work with the EditorZone by adding our own custom editor parts to it.

The FavoritesWebPart in the PersonalizationInterfaces sample used a simple string data type to store its hyperlinks data. In order for us to be able to store extra information about each hyperlink we need to create a complex data type that contains properties to store the data for us. To do this we can create a data class and add a property for each additional piece of information that we wish to store. Listing 7.1 shows the code for a class named HyperlinkData that can store additional information about our hyperlinks.

Listing 7.1   The custom HyperlinkData class is created to store additional information about each favorite.

```
[Serializable]
public class HyperlinkData {

        public HyperlinkData(string displayName, string
        description,
          string url) {
                this._displayName = displayName;
                this._description = description;
                this._url = url;
        }

        private string _displayName;
        public string DisplayName {
                get { return _displayName; }
                set { _displayName = value; }
        }


        private string _description;
        public string Description {
                get { return _description; }
                set { _description = value; }
        }


        private string _url;
        public string URL {
                get { return _url; }
                set { _url = value; }
        }
}
```

As we can see, the HyperlinkData class is very simple and has a public property for each piece of data that we need to keep track of. The DisplayName property will be used as the value to display when we render the hyperlink and the Description property will be used to display additional information alongside of the hyperlink in the page. Figure 7.2 shows us what the FavoritesWebPart will look like when it is displayed in a browser.

In Figure 7.2 we can see that a `FavoritesWeb-Part` is displayed that contains three hyperlinks and each hyperlink displays its description text alongside the link. Additionally, the display text is shown to the user instead of the raw URL of the hyperlink. Now that we have the data type that will store the information for our web part sorted out, we need to provide the user with a way to enter the data required to create hyperlinks. Having seen the `PropertyGridEditorPart` in earlier chapters, you might be thinking that the portal framework will automatically provide us with a form for entering new hyperlinks. If so, think again because we'll see in just a moment that the `PropertyGridEditorPart` doesn't know how to present an editing interface for web parts that expose complex data types as their property data.

Figure 7.2 The new FavoritesWebPart uses the additional information contained within the HyperlinkData class to provide a richer display for the user.

Coping with complex data

As I just mentioned, when we first think about how the user will manage the hyperlink data within the `FavoritesWebPart` we would probably envisage the data automatically appearing within the standard `PropertyGridEditorPart` as we discussed in chapter 5 when we learned about the `EditorZone` and its editor parts. From that chapter you will remember that personalization properties can be added to the `PropertyGridEditorPart` simply by marking them with the `WebBrowsable` attribute as shown in the following code snippet. Figure 7.3 shows how a custom property named "data" appears when displayed in the `PropertyGridEditorPart`.

The following snippet of code shows how the `WebBrowsable` attribute is applied to the property to ensure that it appears within the editor part:

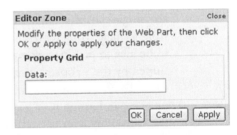

Figure 7.3 The PropertyGridEditor part can automatically create editing elements for simple data types such as enums, strings, dates, and integers.

```
[Personalizable]
[WebBrowsable()]
public string Data {
        get { return _data; }
        set { _data = value; }
}
```

The standard `PropertyGridEditorPart` serves us well for simple types such as strings, integers, booleans, and dates, but cannot do so for properties that are complex types. As an example, by default the property in the following listing, which is a custom data type, will not appear within the `PropertyGridEditorPart`:

```
[Personalizable]
[WebBrowsable()]
public MyNumberType NumberData {
        get { return _numberData; }
        set { _numberData = value; }
```

In this snippet the `NumberData` property is not one of the simple data types that I just mentioned but is instead a custom data type named `MyNumberType`.

The reason that complex types are not displayed within the `PropertyGridEditorPart` is that this `EditorPart` only displays a single editing element for each property marked with the `WebBrowsable` attribute. Representing a complex type as a single field would require the class being edited to know how to convert itself to and from a single field representation. For example, given a single textbox to enter all of the data for our `HyperlinkData` class, there would have to be some agreed standard about how to enter it in a single field and the user would need to know how to do that. Perhaps the data for each property would be delimited by a known character as shown in the following snippet where the data for a hyperlink is delimited by two dollar symbols ($$):

```
Microsoft$$http://microsoft.com$$The Microsoft website$$5
```

In this example, the user has entered data for the `DisplayName`, URL, Description, and `DisplayOrder` properties with the delimiting character separating each one.

The TypeConverter class

It turns out, that the .NET Framework does provide us with a useful way to represent any single class as a single string and have that class know how to convert itself to and from a single string representation. Having this capability provides us with the means to be able to provide a complex data type to store our favorites data and have it consumed by the `PropertyGridEditorPart` as a string so that changes can be made to it. To do this we can create a special type of class that is known as a `TypeConverter` and assign it to a class that will use it. The `TypeConverter` class provides the special logic for converting a class from one type into another type—in our case this means converting our favorites data to and from a string representation.

The chapter 7 folder of the resources that came with this book contains a project named `TypeConverterExample`. The `TypeConverterExample` project contains the source code for a web part named `ConvertibleWebPart` which provides a full implementation of a web part that uses a `TypeConverter` to display its complex data within the `PropertyGridEditorPart`. Figure 7.4 shows the `ConvertibleWebPart` displayed on a page and shows that its `NumberData` property (which is a complex data type) is represented within the `PropertyGridEditorPart`.

TypeConverters are widely used within the .NET Framework as a way to access values on underlying objects. This is actually one of the ways that server controls which have properties that are complex types can be represented and managed within the Visual Studio property grid. Figure 7.5 shows the `ConvertibleWebPart` displayed in the Visual Studio designer and shows that the complex `NumberData` property on the `ConvertibleWebPart` can also be managed within that environment.

In figure 7.5 we can see a web part titled "My Web Part" shown within the Visual Studio environment at design-time. Notice the `NumberData` property that is shown in the property window and see that it is able to be managed as string data. Under the covers it is a `TypeConverter` that provides the means for the `NumberData` type to convert to and from a string in this way.

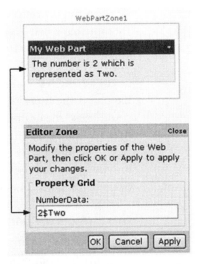

Figure 7.4   A TypeConverter can be used to convert a complex type into a string representation and made available to the standard PropertyGridEditorPart.

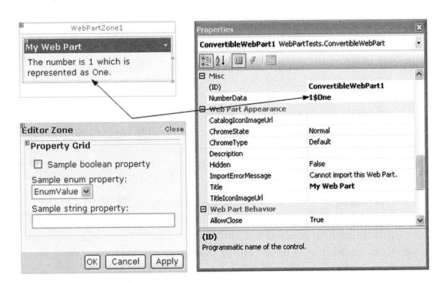

Figure 7.5   TypeConverters are also used by the Visual Studio design environment to represent complex types in the property grid.

While it might seem fine that we now have a way of providing the user with the ability to manage their hyperlink data via a `TypeConverter`, it's still far from ideal. To begin with, the user is now required to know what delimiter we are using to separate out the property values and they also need to know in which order those properties are to be entered within the string. To top it off, there's no validation. What would happen if the user entered a number in the place where a boolean was expected? It could cause the entire web part to fail and die. The user needs an intuitive interface that allows him to enter hyperlink data in a manner that is appropriate for that data type. The user also needs data validation and advanced user interface features, such as providing custom user interface elements that allow him to change the display order of the hyperlinks. The portal framework satisfies these user needs.

Custom editor parts

The portal framework provides us with a way to associate any custom user interface elements with our web parts to allow users to manage the web parts in totally custom ways. To handle this function, the web part class contains a method named `Create-EditorParts` that can be used to return custom user interfaces for managing complex data types within the `EditorZone`.

In this next section we will create a custom editor part that will allow users to manage all of the data contained within the `Hyper-linkData` data type and then we'll associate it with the `FavoritesWebPart` so that our custom editor part is displayed whenever the user edits `FavoritesWebPart` web part. Figure 7.6 displays the editor parts as they will be displayed within an `EditorZone` at runtime.

We can see from figure 7.6 that our custom editor part will allow users to manage the properties of the `HyperlinkData` data type and click the OK or Apply buttons provided by the `EditorZone` to create new links. Also notice that the textbox for entering the description is displayed in multi-line mode to make the job of entering large descriptions easier. Now contrast the image shown in figure 7.6 with the one shown in figure 7.4 and you will immediately see the usability gains that we get by providing a custom editor part to manage the hyperlink data.

Figure 7.6 The portal framework allows us to associate custom controls with web parts to provide a custom editing experience for complex data types.

Creating a favorites editor part

To create a an editor part that can be loaded into the `EditorZone` we are required to create a class that inherits from the same base class as each of the existing ASP.NET editor parts—the `EditorPart` class. The following snippet of code shows the beginnings of our custom editor class which is named `FavoritesEditorPart`.

```
public class FavoritesEditorPart : EditorPart {

    TextBox txtDisplayName, txtDescription, txtUrl;

    FavoritesWebPart FavoritePart {
        get { return (FavoritesWebPart)this.WebPartToEdit; }
    }
}
```

In this code snippet we can see that the `FavoritesEditorPart` has three textboxes which are declared as private fields within the class. The reason for scoping those fields at class level is so that the textboxes will be available to be referenced both when we are creating the controls for our user interface, and again when we are responding to a user-invoked action to save the data that is contained within those fields. I've also added a convenience property named `FavoritePart` to encapsulate the logic for accessing the underlying `FavoritesWebPart` that is being edited.

The `EditorPart` class is an abstract class and contains two methods named `ApplyChanges` and `SyncChanges` that we must implement. With the `Apply-Changes` method we write the logic to save changes that the user has made in our custom editor part with the underlying web part that is being edited. The `ApplyChanges` method is called internally by the portal framework when the user presses the OK or Apply buttons on the `EditorZone`, so it's important that we write saving logic here to give users an experience that is similar with other editor parts that they use.

Handling changes and updates

The `SyncChanges` method allows us to write code to synchronize the user interface elements of our custom editor part with values in the underlying web part being edited. In the case of the `FavoritesEditorPart` there is no need to include any logic within the `SyncChanges` because there is no way that the editor part can get out of sync with the underlying web part that is being edited. Listing 7.2 shows the code that is required for our implementation of the `ApplyChanges` and `SyncChanges` methods.

Listing 7.2 The ApplyChanges method of an EditorPart is used to synchronize data with the web part that is being edited.

```
public override bool ApplyChanges() {

        string displayName = this.txtDisplayName.Text;
        string description = this.txtDescription.Text;
        string url = this.txtUrl.Text;

        if (!string.IsNullOrEmpty(displayName) &&
            !string.IsNullOrEmpty(url)) {
```

```
            HyperlinkData hyperlink =
                    new HyperlinkData(displayName, description, url);   ◁┐
                                                                          Create an instance of the
            this.txtDisplayName.Text = "";                                HyperlinkData class
            this.txtDescription.Text = "";
            this.txtUrl.Text = "";

            FavoritePart.AddHyperlink(hyperlink);   ◁┐ Call the AddHyperlink
        }                                              method to save the
                                                       hyperlink data
        return true;
    }


public override void SyncChanges() {
        return;
    }
```

As mentioned earlier, the ApplyChanges method will get called automatically by the EditorZone whenever the user clicks either of the OK or Apply buttons on the EditorZone user interface. Notice that the ApplyChanges method returns a boolean result to the caller. This allows the editor part to inform the EditorZone if errors have occurred during the save operation so that the EditorZone can know whether it should do things such as close the zone after the OK button has been clicked by a user. In this case where the user clicks the OK button and false is returned from an editor part, the EditorZone does not close itself but instead stays open so that the user can correct his data.

In our ApplyChanges method we grab the values from the textboxes and validate that they contain both a display name and a URL. If the data is sufficient then a new instance of the HyperlinkData class is created to contain the data that the user has entered and is passed to a method on the FavoriteWebPart called AddHyperlink, which adds the link to its current collection of links. The AddHyperlink method is shown here:

```
public void AddHyperlink(HyperlinkData hyperlink) {
        this.SetPersonalizationDirty();
        _sorted = false;
        this.Hyperlinks.Add(hyperlink);
        CreateChildControls();
    }
```

Whenever the FavoriteWebPart class adds a new hyperlink it must also set its personalization state to dirty so that the portal framework knows that the web part has changes when it is saving personalization data at the end of the page's lifecycle. The FavoriteWebPart also makes a call to CreateChildControls so that its user interface will be redrawn with the new hyperlink added to it.

Associating the editor part with a web part

Now we've created our editor part and we have just one more thing to do before we can run it and see it working. The final task that we have remaining is to associate our new editor part with the `FavoritesWebPart` so that it will be automatically displayed whenever the `FavoritesEditorPart` is being edited. Each web part exposes a method named `CreateEditorParts` which is used to return a collection of `EditorPart` instances to use as custom editors for the web part. This is how we will associate the `FavoritesEditorPart` with the `FavoritesWebPart`—by overriding that method and having it return an instance of our custom editor part.

The following code snippet shows how to return our editor part from the `CreateEditorParts` method:

```
public override EditorPartCollection CreateEditorParts() {

    FavoritesEditorPart editorPart = new FavoritesEditorPart();
    editorPart.ID = this.ID + "_addLinkPart";
    editorPart.Title = "Add New Link";


    EditorPartCollection parts =
            new EditorPartCollection(new EditorPart[] { editorPart });

    return parts;
}
```

Although we've only returned a single editor part, you can see that the method actually returns a collection of editor parts so it is possible to return more than one. One other task that we might perform from within the `CreateEditorParts` method is to store a reference to the editor part instances in a local variable. Doing so would allow the web part to directly call `SyncChanges` on any editor parts that it knew about when changes occur. To understand when this scenario arises, consider a web part that not only allowed for changes to be made within editor parts, but which also exposes some user interface elements on the web part itself that allow certain changes to be made. In this case, when a user made changes to the web part via the controls on the web part interface, the web part could cycle through its custom editor parts and call `SyncChanges` on each of them to be sure that they refreshed themselves.

The last thing that we need to look at for this example is how the `FavoritesWebPart` uses the `HyperlinkData` data type to store its hyperlinks. We are also going to sort the hyperlinks before we display them so that they are displayed in alphabetical order in the page—which will make it easier to locate a hyperlink as the lists grow larger. Just like the collections that we saw in chapter 1 when we created the `AdventureWorks` data layer, our web part will use generics to store the hyperlinks as a generic list. The following code snippet shows the property that the web part uses to store the hyperlink data:

```
private List<HyperlinkData> _hyperlinks = new List<HyperlinkData>();
[DesignerSerializationVisibility(DesignerSerializationVisibility.Content)]
public List<HyperlinkData> Hyperlinks {
      get { return _hyperlinks; }
      set {
            _hyperlinks = value;
      }
}
```

Notice too, that the Hyperlinks property is marked with a special attribute named DesignerSerializationVisibility. This attribute is useful for letting the Visual Studio form designer know what data needs to be persisted at design-time to provide a good design experience for developers. In this case we are stating that the HyperlinkData should be persisted, but not the generic class that gets dynamically created. If we fail to specify this setting, Visual Studio will attempt to persist the generic type but will fail and cause the web part to show up with errors in the Visual Studio design surface. Figure 7.7 shows how the

Error Creating Control - FavouritesWebPart1

Cannot create an object of type 'System.Collections.Generic.List`1 [[WebPartTests.HyperlinkData, App_Code.- eusufuy, Version=0.0.0.0, Culture=neutral, PublicKeyToken=null]]' from its string representation '(Collection)' for the 'Hyperlinks' property.

Figure 7.7 When a custom server control exposes a collection type, custom attributes must be used to inform the designer how to handle serialization at design time. Failure to supply this information to the designer will result in an error being displayed at design time but not at runtime.

FavoritesWebPart appears at design time if we fail to mark the Hyperlinks property with the correct DesignerSerializationVisibility attribute value.

Even though the web part in the figure displays an error at design time it will work just fine at runtime when the generic collection type can be serialized. So while this error can be safely ignored, it doesn't make the design-time experience of our web part very good at all.

The task of sorting the hyperlink data also turns out to be quite a simple job because the generic List<T> data type already contains a sort method that can be called. We call this method just before rendering the hyperlinks, as listing 7.3 shows us.

Listing 7.3 The controls for displaying our Favorites links are added in the CreateChildControls method of our web part.

```
protected override void CreateChildControls() {

      this.Controls.Clear();
                                                    Sort the hyperlinks
                                                       by display name
      if (!_sorted) {
            this.Hyperlinks.Sort(new HyperlinkComparer());   ◁┘
            _sorted = true;
      }
```

CHAPTER 7 CREATING AN ENHANCED EDITING EXPERIENCE

```
foreach (HyperlinkData linkData in this.Hyperlinks) {

    if (this.HasDescriptions &&  ◄────┐  Check if we need to
        !string.IsNullOrEmpty(linkData.Description)) {   display a description

        this.Controls.Add(new LiteralControl("<p>"));
        DisplayHyperlink(linkData);
        DisplayDescription(linkData);
        this.Controls.Add(new LiteralControl("</p>"));

    } else {
        DisplayHyperlink(linkData);
    }
}
}
```

The Sort method takes an optional argument that is an IComparer and which provides us with a simple way to sort custom data types in any manner we choose. The code for the HyperlinkComparer is shown in the following code snippet:

```
internal class HyperlinkComparer : IComparer<HyperlinkData> {
    public int Compare(HyperlinkData x, HyperlinkData y) {
        return x.DisplayName.CompareTo(y.DisplayName);
    }
}
```

As you can see, this class implements the IComparer<T> interface and uses the Compare method of that interface to supply its own logic for comparing two HyperlinkData objects. In this case we are simply comparing the values of the display names of each item.

NOTE   The code for the completed FavoritesWebPart and the Favorites-EditorPart are included in the code for the AdventureWorks portal in the chapter 7 section of the resources website for this book.

If you feel you've just moved through a substantial chunk of material, you're right. This section had to be long to include some important lessons that will help us whenever we need to create web parts that provide an editing experience with a high degree of usability. Let's take a minute to recap. We learned how to work with complex data types. When working with complex data types we saw that custom editor parts can be created to manage the editing of rich data and how editor parts synchronize their data with the underlying web parts that they represent. As a bonus we caught a glimpse how the .NET Framework uses TypeConverters to convert objects from one type to another.

7.3 IMPROVING USABILITY

The act of clicking a computer mouse can be tedious. I've come to this realization because when I have to click on a website more than I think necessary, I become unsatisfied and sometimes even agitated. Sites that require unnecessary clicks and mouse moves quickly disappear from my favorites list and probably disappear from yours too.

A quick search on the internet reveals an abundance of links that point to articles on this very topic. In fact, experts earn good money in checking the usability of high-exposure websites. When you stop and think about what happens when a user clicks on a link, you understand exactly why it can be so annoying. When the user clicks a link, a request is sent off to the web server for a new page to be created and sent back to the browser. This process is referred to as "round-tripping" or a "postback"—which is the term that we've been using in this book when a page round-trips to itself. Part of the problem with a round-trip is that all the HTML must be sent from the web server to the browser, and this takes time. Surfing around the internet today, we can see that many pages take several seconds to load; it's this time that is the cause of the angst that is associated with mouse clicks.

Because mouse clicks can cause long waits for users, it's important to pay attention to this issue and to constantly strive to remove clicks whenever possible. In the next section we'll find some of the redundant mouse clicks in our portal and remove them by finding smarter ways to present user interface options to our users.

7.3.1 Reducing mouse clicks

Now that we have a good understanding of the cost that is associated with mouse clicks, let's make some adjustments to the AdventureWorks portal to reduce the clicks required to perform common editing tasks. There are a couple of things that we'll do. First we'll automatically add an edit verb to each web part that will be displayed to users that are authorized to perform edits on the page. Providing the edit verb will allow users to place a web part into edit mode with just a single click compared with the two clicks that are currently required. Figure 7.8 shows how our web parts will appear to our portal users at all times after we've added our new edit verb.

> **NOTE** If you don't have a copy of the project from Chapter 6 you can grab it from the Chapter 6 section of the resources website for this book.

Enabling single-click editing

At the beginning of this chapter we looked at how many mouse clicks are required to edit the properties of a web part and we saw that four clicks are required. Remember that the first step in the process was to place the page into edit mode. We did this because, by default, the edit verb is only displayed when the the page is in edit mode and we need to use the edit verb to edit a web part. Placing the page in edit mode requires a postback which, as we've been discussing, can be the source of angst for our users.

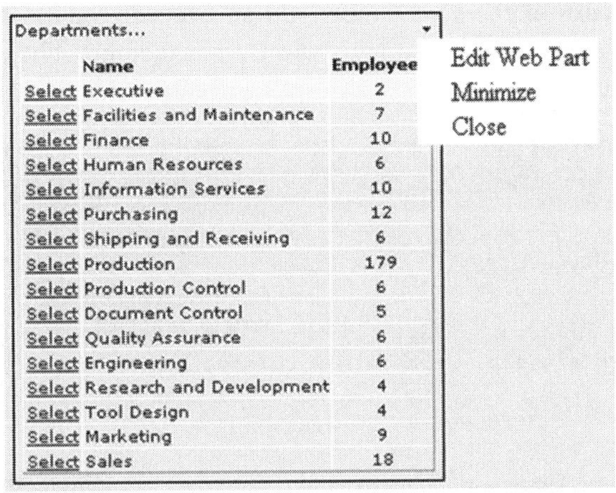

Figure 7.8
The edit verb that is shown here is a custom verb that replaces the standard edit verb and is always available to authenticated users even when the current page is not in edit mode.

We'll now learn how to ensure that an edit verb is always available to our users so that web parts can be edited with just a single click, thereby removing the initial postback to the server. The steps involved with enabling single-click editing are

- Ensure that the in-built edit verb is not rendered.
- Add our own edit verb to each web part on the page.
- Write code that runs when the user clicks the edit verb to place the page in edit mode and select the web part for editing.

When we were working with web parts in chapter 2 we saw that there are zone verbs—such as edit, connect, close and delete—that get added to all web parts by the zone that contains them. We also saw that custom verbs can be added to individual web parts by overriding the Verbs property of the web part and returning instances of the WebPartVerb class. Because we want our new edit verb to be present on all web parts, it is more analogous with the zone verbs than the custom verbs that are added individually on each web part. For this reason it makes sense to add our verb at the zone level rather than adding it for every web part. By adding the verb individually on each part we would run the risk of missing some web parts and then our behavior would be inconsistent.

The WebPartZone class contains a method named OnCreateVerbs that we can override to create verbs and have them added to all web parts that are contained by the zone. So we'll use this method to hide the in-built edit verb and replace it with our own. To be able to write code in the OnCreateVerbs method we must create a custom WebPartZone class and then use it in the portal. The following snippet of code shows how to create a custom WebPartZone class:

```
public class PortalWebPartZone : WebPartZone {

}
```

Now that we've got a custom zone, we simply add an override for the OnCreate-Verbs method and implement our own logic within that method. The code in listing 7.4 shows what our implementation of the OnCreateVerbs method looks like.

Listing 7.4 By overriding the OnCreateVerbs method of the zone the existing edit verb is hidden and a custom edit verb added.

```
protected override void OnCreateVerbs(WebPartVerbsEventArgs e) {
        base.OnCreateVerbs(e);

        this.EditVerb.Visible = false;  ◁────┘  Force the standard edit
                                                 verb to be hidden
        Collection<WebPartVerb> verbs = new Collection<WebPartVerb>();

        HttpContext ctx = HttpContext.Current;

        if (ctx.Request.IsAuthenticated) {           Display the edit
                                                     verb if the user is
                WebPartVerb editVerb = new WebPartVerb(  ◁┘  authenticated
                        "editVerb",
                        new WebPartEventHandler(HandleEditClick)
                        );

                verbs.Add(editVerb);               Display the appropriate
                                                       text for the verb
                if (this.WebPartManager.Personalization.Scope == ◁┘
                        PersonalizationScope.Shared) {
                        editVerb.Text = "Edit Shared Web Part";
                } else {
                        editVerb.Text = "Edit Web Part";
                }
        }
        e.Verbs = new WebPartVerbCollection(verbs);
}
```

The first thing that we do in the OnCreateVerbs method is to hide the in-built edit verb so that it isn't displayed to the user. After we've hidden the existing edit verb we then go about adding our new verb. It's worth noting that in our implementation we simply check if the user is authenticated before adding the new verb but we could base our logic on some other check, such as whether the user is in a certain role group. The last thing that we do before we set the Verbs property of the EventArgs that are passed to us is to change the text to provide the user with a visual cue of whether they are about to edit the shared view or the per-user view of the web part. The code that runs when the user clicks the edit verb can be seen in the following code snippet:

```
void HandleEditClick(object sender, WebPartEventArgs e) {

        WebPart wp = e.WebPart;

        if (wp != this.WebPartManager.SelectedWebPart) {
                this.WebPartManager.DisplayMode =
                WebPartManager.EditDisplayMode;
                this.WebPartManager.BeginWebPartEditing(wp);
        }
}
```

In this method we first check that the web part is not already being edited and then we switch the page into edit mode. With the mode set to edit, we can commence editing on the web part by calling the BeginWebPartEditing method on the current web part manager instance for the page.

Using the custom EditorZone

Now that we've created our custom WebPartZone class we must register the namespace of the class with the web page so that it can be used. After registering the namespace we can convert the control declarations for the existing web part zones over to use our new class. The following snippet of code shows the register declaration that makes our new class available to the page, and then shows the server tags that should be used for the web part zones on the page:

```
<%@ Register Namespace="AW.Portal.Web" TagPrefix="portal" %>


<portal:PortalWebPartZone ID="LeftZone" runat="server">
...
</portal:PortalWebPartZone>
```

Aftrer changing the code in the Default.aspx page so that our new web part zone class is used we should run the page and check that everything is working well and that everything compiles.

Having confirmed that everything is running, you might notice that after changing the class that is used for the web part zones, all the styles have disappeared from the web parts and their associated menus. This occurs because, when we changed the tag for our web part zones from asp:WebPartZone to portal:PortWebPart-Zone, the styles that we've already defined in the Theme folder no longer match the new control tag. To get the styles re-applied we can simply open the theme file and change the themed control to match our new tag as shown in listing 7.5. Note that the register declaration is also added to the theme file in the same way that it was added in the page.

```asp
<%@ Register Namespace="AW.Portal.Web" TagPrefix="portal" %>

<portal:PortalWebPartZone runat="server" BorderColor="#CCCCCC" Font-
Names="Verdana" Padding="6">
        <PartChromeStyle BackColor="#EFF3FB" BorderColor="#D1DDF1" Font-
        Names="Verdana" ForeColor="#333333" />
        <SelectedPartChromeStyle BorderStyle="Dashed" BorderWidth="4"
        BorderColor="#da8b32" />                          ⟵  Display a dashed border
        <MenuLabelHoverStyle ForeColor="#D1DDF1" />            for selected web parts
        <MenuLabelStyle ForeColor="White" />
        <MenuVerbHoverStyle BackColor="#EFF3FB" BorderColor="#CCCCCC"
        BorderStyle="Solid"
        BorderWidth="1px" ForeColor="#333333" />
        <HeaderStyle Font-Size="0.9em" ForeColor="#CCCCCC"
        HorizontalAlign="Center" />
        <MenuVerbStyle BorderColor="#507CD1" BorderStyle="Solid"
        BorderWidth="1px"
        ForeColor="White" />
        <PartStyle Font-Size="1em" ForeColor="#333333" />
        <TitleBarVerbStyle Font-Underline="False" ForeColor="White" />
        <MenuPopupStyle BackColor="#507CD1" BorderColor="#CCCCCC"
        BorderWidth="1px"
        Font-Names="Verdana" Font-Size="0.8em" />
        <PartTitleStyle BackColor="#507CD1" Font-Bold="True" Font-
        Size="1em" ForeColor="White" />
</portal:PortalWebPartZone>
```

Notice that the themed control now matches the control that we are using on the Default.aspx page in the Adventure Works portal. I also added a style for the SelectedPartChromeStyle to add a dashed border to a web part when it is selected. This is a visual feature that I like to add in my own portals as it makes it very obvious what web part is being edited. This feature is not so important when there are only a small number of web parts on a page but as the number of web parts on the page grows, remembering which web part is being edited can get difficult. Figure 7.9 shows how web parts appear when in edit mode based on the new theme style.

That's it! With single-click editing in place we can feel confident that we've done our small bit to reduce the internet's unnecessary clicks.

Another unnecessary evil in web applications is pages that require the user to scroll up and down or from side to side in order to view content. I'm sure that you're aware of this one too. The root of this evil is content that is either really wide or extra long, or worse still—both! You often see this in reporting applications and it means that you have to constantly scroll backwards and forwards or up and down to read all of the content.

This type of problem can easily manifest itself in our portals with the EditorZone control. Think about it for a moment. Here you have a control that will often display

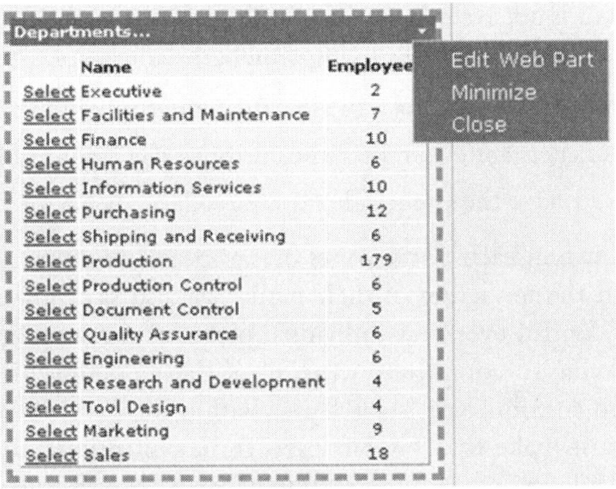

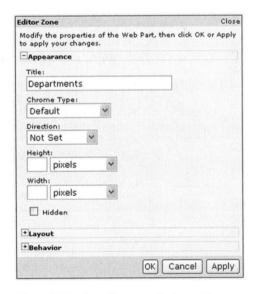

Figure 7.9
Adding a dashed border helps users understand which web part is being edited.

the four standard editor parts but, as we've seen, can easily contain more than that. At a screen resolution of 1200 x 800 pixels, a standard screen has only enough real estate to display about two parts at a time, and the `BehaviorEditorPart` alone takes up an entire screen. This means that if a user is making many edits, he or she is probably scrolling a good deal and re-positioning the mouse cursor. This can also lead to poor user acceptance of a portal application. How do you solve this problem?

7.3.2   Creating a collapsible EditorZone

The way that the Sharepoint team solved the problem of having an `EditorZone` that caused the page to scroll vertically was by allowing users to expand and collapse each editor part. When the `EditorZone` is initially displayed in Sharepoint, only the first part is shown in an expanded state. In this next section we'll change the `EditorZone` in the Adventure Works portal so that its editor zone also has expand/collapse functionality. Figure 7.10 shows how the `EditorZone` will appear when complete.

In figure 7.10 we see that the `EditorZone` contains three editor parts: the `AppearanceEditorPart`, `LayoutEditorPart`, and `BehaviorEditorPart`. Although the zone contains these three parts, the screen real estate

Figure 7.10   An editor zone that provides expandable/collapsible editor parts allows users to better manage screen real estate.

that is taken up by the zone is not excessive because both the layout part and the behavior part are collapsed. The steps that we'll take to implement the collapsible editor zone are

- Create custom `EditorPartChrome` to alter the rendering of the editor parts.
- Create a custom `EditorZone` to return the custom `EditorPartChrome`.
- Add JavaScript to manage the client-side expand/collapse behavior.

Back in chapter 5 we saw that each of the zones uses a special class that is referred to as "chrome" to perform the rendering of their parts. We also saw how the chrome gave us a finer level of control over how individual pieces of the parts are rendered, thus saving us from having to completely write all of the rendering logic for parts when we simply need to customize an isolated area within the part. So it is with the adjustments that we must make to allow our parts to be collapsible. To do this we only need to alter the rendering of the outer section of the part so that we can add the plus or minus graphic and insert some JavaScript to control the expandable behavior of the part. We certainly wouldn't want to render all of the controls within the body of each part simply to insert those small features.

Creating the EditorZone

To customize the rendering of the outer area of parts including their title descriptions, use the `RenderEditorPart` method of the `EditorPartChrome` class. Overriding the `RenderEditorPart` method will require us to create a custom `Editor-PartChrome` class. Naturally enough, to have an editor zone that knows enough to use the custom chrome that we'll create, we will also have to create a custom `EditorZone` class and specify the chrome type to use in its `CreateEditorPartChrome` method. Listing 7.6 shows the code for a custom `EditorZone` class named `Collapsible-EditorZone` that uses a class named `CollapsibleEditorPartChrome`.

> **Listing 7.6   Our `CollapsibleEditorZone` uses custom chrome for rendering the editor parts**

```
public class CollapsibleEditorZone : EditorZone {

    public CollapsibleEditorZone() { }
                                              Determines whether editor
                                              parts are already added
    bool editorPartsAdded = false;
    public bool EditorPartsAdded {
            get { return this.editorPartsAdded; }
            set { editorPartsAdded = value; }
    }


    protected override EditorPartChrome CreateEditorPartChrome() {
            return new CollapsibleEditorPartChrome(this);
    }                                          Replaces standard
}                                              EditorPartChrome with custom chrome
```

I've added a property named `EditorPartsAdded` to the editor zone to keep track of when the first editor part has been added. We need to know this so that we can display the first part in an expanded state, but each additional part that is added will be displayed as initially collapsed. At runtime an instance of the editor part chrome class is instantiated as each editor part is added and that's why we must store this state in the editor zone and not in the chrome class.

That's all the code that is required for our `EditorZone` class, although, remember that the server control tags in the master page must be changed to refer to the new class as will any theme tags that exist for the editor zone—much the same set of tasks that we ran through when we implemented our custom `WebPartZone` in the previous section.

Now that we've created the custom editor zone and specified the type of chrome to be used, we must create the chrome class and write the custom rendering logic for the title of the editor parts.

Adding our own chrome

To create our custom `EditorPartChrome` class we create a class that inherits from the `EditorPartChrome` class as shown in this snippet of code:

```
public class CollapsibleEditorPartChrome : EditorPartChrome {

    public CollapsibleEditorPartChrome(EditorZoneBase zone)
        : base(zone) { }

}
```

The `EditorPartChrome` class has two main methods for rendering editor parts named `RenderEditorPart` and `RenderPartContents` and, as mentioned, we must override the `RenderEditorPart` method to customize the rendering of the title area of each part. Figure 7.11 illustrates the user interface area that we'll be rendering in the `RenderEditorPart` method.

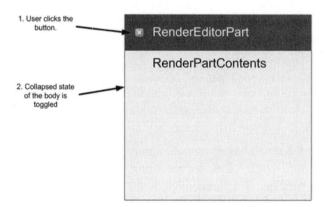

Figure 7.11
EditorPartChrome provides the methods necessary to custom render the header and body of each individual editor part. Here we customize the rendering of the header to add a button for collapsing or expanding the state of the part.

The figure shows a darker section on the editor part that must be recreated when we override the RenderEditorPart method so that we can add a button to manage the collapsing behavior of the body of the part. In the RenderEditorPart method we'll re-draw the head section of the part and add our button, and we'll also wrap the body section in an HTML DIV element and give it a known ID so that we can toggle its visibility at runtime; Listing 7.7 shows the code required to do this.

> **Listing 7.7   The RenderEditorPart method allows us to customize the rendering of the outer area of each editor part including its header and footer sections.**

```
public override void RenderEditorPart(HtmlTextWriter writer,
  EditorPart editorPart) {

        if ((chromeType == PartChromeType.TitleAndBorder)
                || (chromeType == PartChromeType.TitleOnly)) {

                this.RenderTitle(writer, editorPart);      ◁⎤ Displays head
        }                                                    ⎦ section of part

        if (editorPart.ChromeState != PartChromeState.Minimized) {
                Style style2 = this.Zone.PartStyle;
                if (!style2.IsEmpty) {
                        style2.AddAttributesToRender(writer, this.Zone);
                }
                                              ⎤ Explicit ID makes identification
                writer.AddAttribute(  ◁──────⎦ of body easy
                        "id",
                        "EditorPartBody_" + editorPart.ClientID
                        );
                                                        ⎤ Hides body if parts
                if (this.EditorZone.EditorPartsAdded) { ◁⎦ are already added
                        writer.AddStyleAttribute("display", "none");
                }

                writer.RenderBeginTag(HtmlTextWriterTag.Div);
                this.RenderPartContents(writer, editorPart);   ◁⎤ Displays
                writer.RenderEndTag();                           ⎦ body

                this.EditorZone.EditorPartsAdded = true;   ◁⎤ Advises zone
        }                                                    ⎪ that parts have
}                                                            ⎦ been added
```

The first step is to call out to a helper method named RenderTitle that we'll see in just moment. We'll put all of the logic for rendering the head section of the part into the RenderTitle method. The remainder of the RenderEditorPart method copies the style attributes that have been declared by the page author and then prepares a DIV element to wrap the body of the editor part within it. You can see that we've added an ID attribute to the DIV so that we know exactly what it will be at runtime when we need to reference the DIV to toggle its display. We see this in the following line of code:

```
writer.AddAttribute("id", "EditorPartBody_" + editorPart.ClientID);
```

The last things we do in the `RenderEditorPart` method are to check whether this is the first editor part being added by querying our `EditorPartsAdded` property of the `EditorZone`, and then conditionally hide or show the body based on that. A call to `RenderPartContents` is made so that the body of the editor part can be created. Then we explicitly set the `EditorPartsAdded` property to true so that on the next time through the editor part can be hidden.

Implementing the client-side behaviors

When the body of the editor part is hidden, we'll display a plus image in the head section to indicate that the body can be expanded. When the body is visible we will show a minus image, which indicates that the body can be hidden. So at runtime, in addition to toggling the expanded state of the editor part, we must also take care to swap the images at the same time. Performing these actions in the browser requires us to write a small piece of JavaScript code that can access the HTML image and DIV elements and change their state. We then tie the JavaScript code to an action that is performed by a user so that it runs whenever the user clicks on the button in the head of the editor part. The JavaScript code is shown in listing 7.8:

Listing 7.8   JavaScript function runs in the broswer and toggles the visibility of the editor part.

```
function ToggleEditorDisplay( divClientID,
imgClientUrl,
  expandImageUrl, minimizeImageUrl ) {

        var el = document.getElementById(divClientID) ;
        if( el.style.display=='none' ) {
                el.style.display='';
                document.images[imgClientUrl].src= minimizeImageUrl;
        } else {
                el.style.display='none';
                document.images[imgClientUrl].src= expandImageUrl;
        }
}
```

As you can see, the JavaScript method is named `ToggleEditorDisplay`, and we must pass it certain arguments so that it knows which HTML elements to perform its actions upon. In this case, we pass it the ID of the DIV whose visibility we want to toggle and also the ID of the image to swap. Finally, we pass in the paths of the images to display based upon the current visibility state of the body of the editor part.

In the `RenderTitle` method we need to create the HTML for the head section of the editor part and when we add the button that allows the user to toggle the visibility of the border, we add JavaScript to invoke the `ToggleEditorDisplay` method in the browser. Listing 7.9 shows the code that is required to display the head section of each editor part.

Listing 7.9 The RenderTitle helper method displays the header area of each editor part and adds the clilckable elements and JavaScript that hides and shows the part in the browser.

```
protected virtual void RenderTitle(HtmlTextWriter writer,
  EditorPart editorPart) {

        HttpContext ctx = HttpContext.Current;                    Explicit ID used
        string imageID = string.Format(                           identifies the
          "EditorPartImage_{0}",editorPart.ClientID);             body area
        string expandImageUrl = "Images/Expand.gif";
        string minimizeImageUrl = "Images/Minimize.gif";          Creates
                                                                  Javascript to
        string js = string.Format(                                handle user clicks
                "ToggleEditorDisplay(
                  'EditorPartBody_{0}', '{1}', '{2}','{3}')",
                editorPart.ClientID,
                imageID,
                expandImageUrl,
                minimizeImageUrl
                );

        Style style2 = this.Zone.PartTitleStyle;
        if (!style2.IsEmpty) {
                style2.AddAttributesToRender(writer, this.Zone);
        }

        writer.RenderBeginTag(HtmlTextWriterTag.Div);
                                                              Adds the onclick
        writer.AddAttribute("onclick", js);                  handler to the image
        writer.AddStyleAttribute(HtmlTextWriterStyle.Cursor, "hand");
        writer.AddAttribute(
          "src",
          this.EditorZone.EditorPartsAdded ?
            expandImageUrl : minimizeImageUrl);
        writer.AddAttribute("id", imageID);
        writer.RenderBeginTag(HtmlTextWriterTag.Img);
        writer.RenderEndTag();

        writer.Write(editorPart.Title);
        writer.RenderEndTag();
}
```

The first half of our `RenderTitle` method is responsible for generating the piece of JavaScript that is attached to the image and will invoke the client-side `ToggleEditorDisplay` JavaScript function. You can see that each argument that must be passed to that function is prepared and the formatted into runnable piece of JavaScript code. This JavaScript code is then assigned to the onclick attribute of the image as can be seen in this section of code:

```
writer.AddAttribute("onclick", js);
writer.AddStyleAttribute(HtmlTextWriterStyle.Cursor, "hand");
writer.AddAttribute(
  "src",
  this.EditorZone.EditorPartsAdded ?
    expandImageUrl : minimizeImageUrl);
writer.AddAttribute("id", imageID);
writer.RenderBeginTag(HtmlTextWriterTag.Img);
```

The only code that remains to be written after the image has been created is the code that displays the title of the editor part.

That's all the work needed to create the custom chrome class and ensure that the editor zone in the portal contains collapsible editor part items. Even though implementing this change required writing only about 100 lines of code, the usability impact of it on the portal will be great. No longer will users be required to constantly scroll up and down the page in order to make changes to web parts in the editor and have them saved.

You can see how the new `EditorZone` works by opening the Adventure Works portal from the chapter 7 folder of the resources that come with this book and running the application. When you start the application, each web part will have a verb titled "Edit Web Part" that you can click to display the editor zone. By displaying the editor zone, you'll see that you can in fact display or hide each individual editor part within that zone. With the new editor zone displayed, I'd like to draw attention to the buttons that appear at the top and bottom of this control that allow users to save or apply their changes or to cancel the editing process for a web part. Figure 7.12 contains arrows that show where the buttons are on the editor zone that allow users to perform the save, apply, or cancel actions.

By clicking these buttons, a user is able to end the editing process for a web part, but the page itself remains in edit mode. Try it out. Place a web part in edit mode and use the editor zone to make some changes. Once you've made the changes, click OK and you'll see that although the editor zone closes and the changes are reflected in the web part, the page is still in edit mode.

7.3.3   A finishing touch

Generally when users finish editing a web part, they either want to completely step out of the editing process or they want to begin editing a different web part—in which case they click the edit verb for the new part that they want to edit. Now that we've implemented single-click editing on each of the web parts, it makes sense to have the

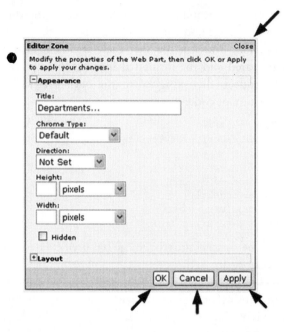

Figure 7.12
The buttons used to save changes or cancel the editing process.

page automatically revert to display mode when the user finishes editing a web part. When the page reverts automatically to display mode, the user is no longer required to switch modes manually and therefore we eliminate an extra mouse operation.

The editor zone handles the click events of these buttons by implementing the `IPostbackEventHandler` interface and having code in the `RaisePostBackEvent` method that checks an event argument that caused the postback to see which button was clicked. For example, when a user clicks on the Close verb in the head of the editor zone, the event argument that is passed to the `RaisePostBackEvent` is a string with the value of `headerClose`. By overriding the `RaisePostBackEvent` method of the `EditorZone` class we can actually intercept the code and write custom code to handle the behavior of the portal whenever a user clicks on any of these buttons.

For the example, we want to automatically revert the page to display mode whenever the close or cancel buttons are clicked and we want to do the same when the OK button is clicked, but first we need to save any changes in each of the editor parts. The code in listing 7.10 shows how to override the `RaisePostBackEvent` method of our custom editor zone to automatically place the page in browse mode when the user finishes editing a web part.

Listing 7.10 Overriding the RaisePostBackEvent method of the EditorZone allows us to customize the behavior in response to users invoking close, cancel, or save operations.

```
protected override void RaisePostBackEvent(string eventArgument) {
        WebPartManager wpm =
            WebPartManager.GetCurrentWebPartManager(this.Page);
```

CHAPTER 7   CREATING AN ENHANCED EDITING EXPERIENCE

```
        if (eventArgument == "headerClose" || eventArgument == "cancel") {
                wpm.DisplayMode = WebPartManager.BrowseDisplayMode;
        } else if (eventArgument == "ok") {
                ApplyAndSyncChanges();
                wpm.DisplayMode = WebPartManager.BrowseDisplayMode;
        } else {
                base.RaisePostBackEvent(eventArgument);      <─┐ Ignore all other
        }                                                       │ event argument
}                                                               │ data.


void ApplyAndSyncChanges() {
        foreach (EditorPart part in this.EditorParts) {
                part.ApplyChanges();
                part.SyncChanges();
        }
}
```

As shown in the code listing, we check the event argument that is passed into the
RaisePostBackEvent handler so that we can handle those events with our own
logic. The first set of event arguments that we check for are the headerClose and
cancel strings that are received whenever the user clicks the close button at the top
of the editor zone or the cancel button that appears in the footer. When we find
either of these arguments, we simply set the current display mode to browse mode,
which forces editing to cease. When the user has clicked the OK button, we receive
the "ok" argument and we handle that with slightly different logic. In this case we
first save any data changes that have been made in the editor parts by enumerating
each part and calling the ApplyChanges and SyncChanges on them to ensure that
each of the parts saves their changes. After the data has been saved, we set the current
display mode to browse to cease editing.

For all other event arguments that are passed in to the RaisePostBackEvent
method—such as the "apply" string that is passed in when the user clicks on the
Apply button—we simply relegate the handling to the base EditorZone class to
supply the logic for us.

Our portal is starting to take shape now that we've started fine-tuning some of its
moving parts. The changes that we made to enhance the editing experience will mean
that our users can manage their web parts in the timeliest manner. Figure 7.13 shows
what our portal looks like after the changes made during this chapter.

Notice how the dashed border around the Departments web part makes it easy to
spot which web part is being edited. Note too how our collapsible EditorZone fits
neatly within the bounds of the page. These are some of the small things that we've
done to make the portal a picture of usability!

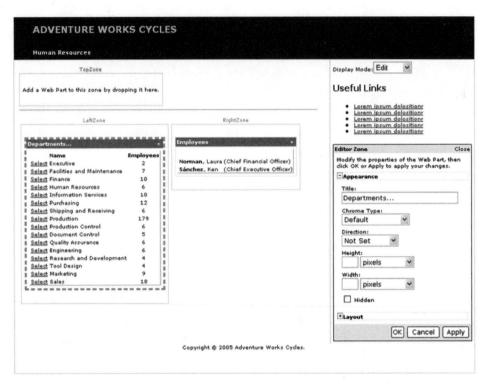

Figure 7.13   The Adventure Works portal in its current state displayed with the Departments web part being edited.

7.4   SUMMARY

In this chapter we plunged deeper into ASP.NET and the portal framework so that we could learn how to do things that are non-standard—such as creating a collapsible `EditorZone` and adding single-click editing capabilities to our web parts. Having now seen some of the more obscure extensibility points within the framework that can be used to customize our solutions - such as chrome—we are well on the way to being free to implement the fullest solutions that we can create.

In chapter 8 we will use the same fine-toothed comb that we used in this chapter and apply it to other areas of the portal.

C H A P T E R   8

Useful portal customizations

8.1   INTRODUCTION

In the world of applications development, we walk a fine line between the desire to implement cool new features and the need to supply applications that are easy to use. I know from my own experiences with Rapid Application Development (RAD), it can be easy to lose sight of the big picture when tempted by the dizzying array of cool new features and options at our disposal. Because of this, projects often veer off course when a developer pipes up with an idea like, "Let's just add one of these clever gadgets to the application." By the time the application is deployed, so many "little gadgets" have been randomly added that the application is downright unwieldy. Almost as common—and equally as difficult to use—is the application with few or no features at all. With this type of application, users lack the tools and features they require to interact with the application and therefore invent their own methods of performing common tasks.

Sitting smartly between the applications with no features and the applications with poorly planned features are the applications that have been carefully planned from the start and which provide the right balance between features and usability. You know the feel of these applications—you can jump right into them and begin working with very little guidance, because their features are intuitive. The fact that these applications tend to be popular indicates that users—even expert technical users—appreciate a well-designed application! This chapter examines the Adventure Works portal and explains what features are needed to make the portal simple and enjoyable to use.

The features we'll be adding to the portal are common to many popular web portals, and are therefore likely to be requested by our customers when we are building portals for them. The features I've selected for us to add are

- A toolbar displaying common portal management tasks
- An approval step to the editing process
- A separate area for the tool zones to eliminate their encroaching on the main layout area of the page
- A `CatalogZone` dialog window

The underlying intent in adding these features is improving the user experience because, in most cases, we are improving how we expose existing features to the user. Take the toolbar as an example. Adding this toolbar provides a common area for accessing features that allow a user to perform common functions, such as changing personalization scope, switching the page mode, and viewing and approving versions of personalization data. Without this common toolbar, each of those major functions would be placed randomly on the page, and it would require the close attention of the user to locate and identify them. Additionally, as new functions are added to the toolbar, they will be more obvious to the user because of their very position in the toolbar.

Now you understand how adding these four new features will improve usability. But there is another, different reason for adding them. Adding the features gives you an opportunity to learn skills critical to performing a wide range of portal customizations. For example, when you create the `CatalogZone` dialog window, you learn some important lessons about how to use client-side JavaScript to communicate between two browser windows.

Let's proceed now with adding the features. By the end of this chapter, our portal will be almost complete and ready for deployment into the production environment. There, our users will test out the portal and either pat us on the back or pepper us with potshots.

8.2 MAKING COMMON TASKS ACCESSIBLE

Before beginning the process of adding new features to our portal, let's look back a bit. Figure 8.1 shows the display mode dropdown list we built way back in chapter 4 to change the mode of the page.

In chapter 7 we improved the usability of the application by removing the edit mode option from the list and adding it directly to each web part as a verb, so that users could edit web parts with a single click. Giving users the ability to edit web parts with a single click is a much more natural action for editing web parts than having to first select Edit from a general list of options.

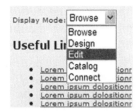

Figure 8.1   The display mode dropdown list enables the user to change the mode of the page.

In fact, editing web parts is actually a common task, so we need to ensure that our users are always able to find the mechanism for performing that task. Another common task within the portal is toggling the personalization scope of the page between individualized user scope and shared user scope. Until now we have not provided our users with any way to change the personalization scope—instead it has been hard-coded in the load method of our pages—so we need to enable users to perform this operation. As we look at editing and personalization, we realize there are a number of tasks our users perform regularly, and it's by making these tasks easy to locate and use that we'll be able to impress those users and make them happy to use the application.

8.2.1   Identifying common tasks

When trying to identify common tasks, it is important to realize that our users will often simply browse through the pages of our portal, quite content to read the text on the pages or to view the information exposed by web parts on the page. But at other times they will enter the portal to manage it by adding new content or changing the web parts that are displayed on a given page. Each of the tasks users perform within the application is known as a scenario, and it's the complete list of scenarios that determines the total feature set of an application.

When creating an application and determining which tasks are most common, it is useful to create personas for fictitious users of your application and then write paragraphs describing the tasks they perform. Some of the scenarios we might see for the Adventure Works portal would include

- *Mike designs the home page*—Mike needs to rearrange the positioning of web parts on the portal's home page, so he uses the Design button in the Common Tasks area to place the page into design mode and then drags various parts to their intended location.

- *Betsey adds some shared content*—Betsey wants to add a news item to the home page. To do this she clicks on the Shared button in the Common Tasks area to place the page into shared personalization scope and then clicks the Add Content button from the Common Tasks area to display the catalog zone. When the catalog zone is visible, Betsey can select a news web part and add it to the page. Once the news web part is displayed on the page, she can add the content of the news item.

- *Mitch approves content changes*—When Mitch visits the home page of the portal, he can see by an alert on the Common Tasks area that the page has content requiring approval. After viewing the changes, Mitch uses the Approve Content button on the Common Tasks area to save the changes and make them visible to all portal users.

Having these scenarios defined allows us to easily identify the most common tasks performed and ensures that they are easily accessed from a prominent location on the screen. By reading the scenarios, you can clearly understand that common tasks for our portal include designing the page, changing the scope of the page, and adding new web parts to a page. Therefore, we need to ensure that users can complete these tasks with a minimum of fuss.

8.2.2 Creating a common tasks MenuBar

Now that we have identified the common tasks, we need a way to expose them from a highly prominent place in our application so that they are easily accessible to our users. In Windows programs such as MS Word, Internet Explorer, and the Windows File Explorer, common tasks are positioned on a menu at the top of the screen so that they can always be accessed by a single click. Placing the important tasks in such a prominent position has another advantage— it makes it easier to introduce new common tasks to users without causing confusion. In this next section we'll add a menu bar to our portal to display common tasks to users. When this work is completed the home portal page will look like the image shown in figure 8.2.

Looking at figure 8.2, we can see that each common task—Show Per-User View, Add Web Parts, and Design—is now prominently displayed to users and is available to them through a single click. The Common Tasks area displays the current personalization scope of the page clearly so that there is no confusion about what the current scope is. This is important, because it can be very frustrating for the user who makes many personalization changes to a portal and then finds that he's done so in the wrong scope and that the wrong group of users is now seeing the content changes.

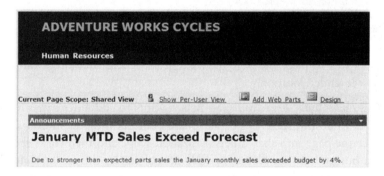

Figure 8.2   A common area at the top of the page displays links with which the user can perform common tasks.

We're not going to cover all the code required for each of the common task buttons because we've already seen most of it before—such as how to toggle display modes and how to change the personalization scope of the page. The main point of this exercise has been to highlight the importance of aggregating these important operations into a single menu area.

At this point, I'd like to highlight an interesting point. Each of the links on the Common Tasks is able to change its display based on certain criteria. For example, when the current personalization scope of the page is Shared, the text of the link button that allows the user to change the scope displays the following text: Show Per-User View. When the current scope is Per-User, however, the text displays the words: Show Shared View. Likewise, the button for adding web parts is visible only when the display mode is not currently catalog mode, and the design button is visible only when the display mode is not currently design mode. All the code required to set the values for these buttons and to set their visibility is added to the pre-rendering phase of the page, as can be seen in listing 8.1.

Listing 8.1 Conditionally setting the visibility of Common Task buttons

```
protected override void OnPreRender(EventArgs e) {
    base.OnPreRender(e);                          Change the personalization
                                                  scope text and icon based
    if (this.Visible) {                              on the current scope

        if (_wpm.Personalization.Scope == PersonalizationScope.User) {  ◁─┐
            lblCurrentScope.Text = "Current Page Scope: Per-User";
            imgToggle.ImageUrl = "~/Images/allusr.GIF";
            lnkToggle.Text = "Show Shared View";
        } else {
            lblCurrentScope.Text = "Current Page Scope: Shared View";
            imgToggle.ImageUrl = "~/Images/perusr.GIF";
            lnkToggle.Text = "Show Per-User View";
        }                                          Hide the "Display Catalog" link
                                                   if the catalog is already visible
        this.pnlCatalogMode.Visible =
            _wpm.DisplayMode != WebPartManager.CatalogDisplayMode;  ◁─┘

        this.LinkButton2.Text =
            (_wpm.DisplayMode == WebPartManager.DesignDisplayMode) ?  ◁─┐
                "Browse" : "Design";                    Toggle the text of the
    }                                                  display mode button based
}                                                      on the current display mode
}
```

The code in listing 8.1 shows us that each item on the Common Tasks area changes, based on the current state of the page. For example, we see that three controls— lblCurrentScope, imgToggle, and lnkToggle—each have a different display based on the current personalization scope of the page.

The Common Tasks area has been implemented as a user control so that its logic is encapsulated within a single component, rather than being included within the page. Having the logic for the Common Tasks area encapsulated in this manner increases the maintainability of our application, because we end up with smaller, more specific controls rather than a single monolithic chunk of logic embedded within each page. To include the Common Tasks area in a page, we simply add the following, single line of markup to the page:

```
<uc:PageTasks ID="PageTasks1" runat="server" />
```

This reduces the amount of code required in the page which contains it and therefore helps to increase the maintainability of the application overall.

> **NOTE** You can find the user control for the Common Tasks area in the Adventure Works portal application in the chapter 8 section of the resources website for this book.

In addition to the maintainability aspect of our enhancement, the users of our application will also be thanking us because they will now know that the Common Tasks area of the page is where they will always find their most-used task items, as opposed to having to hunt around on the page to find them.

In this section we have again seen important usability improvements made by simply grouping important functions in a common area, so that everyday functions become easier for our users to find and use. Additionally, because many of the popular, modern portals already employ this tactic, now our portal not only acts like a portal but it is also starting to look more and more like a portal.

While we are focused on how our own portal is implementing many features that are found in everyday portals, it's worth looking at another portal feature which has emerged in recent times. The feature gaining favor in portals has existed for many years in systems (CMS), and that is the ability for users to make edits to content but not have those changes appear on the publicly visible version of the site until they have gained approval via a moderation system. Web applications that use web parts extensively can be considered content management systems because of the way they allow the content that is visible on the web page to be changed at runtime. For this reason it has become popular to embed the same moderation functionality in CMS-style applications into portal-style applications too. This helps to ensure that the people who are most responsible for the content on display are able to approve any changes, while allowing people who create content to make edits.

8.3 VERSIONED PERSONALIZATION DATA

To add editing approval capabilities to our own portal we must find a way to create two versions of each page: one version would contain the approved content that is publicly visible, while the other version would contain changes awaiting approval. Figure 8.3 shows the editing process in our portal as it currently stands when a user designs or edits the web parts.

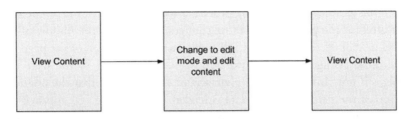

**Figure 8.3   Portal users can switch a page into edit mode to change the proper-
ties of web parts.**

Figure 8.3 shows that users are able to view web pages and change them into edit
mode to make changes to the personalization data. When the edits have been made,
the user can then save the page to update the content. This is in effect the same action
we've been taking throughout this book whenever we've edited a web part and clicked
Save to have those changes persisted.

To provide a way for the changes to be subjected to a moderation process, we
need a way of creating a second version of the page and using that version to store
updates while keeping the approved copy of content in the main page. Figure 8.4
shows us what this would look like.

The user first makes changes to the personalization content by switching a page
into edit mode; this is indicated by the box in the top right corner of figure 8.4.

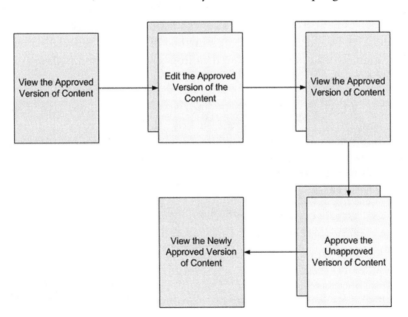

**Figure 8.4   By adding an approval process, changes to web parts will not be visible
to all portal users until they are approved by a moderator.**

When the user begins the editing process, a second version of the personalization data is created for the page to store those changes. The box in the middle of the top row shows us that when the user saves his edits, a second version of the page is created to store those changes. In the third box we see the version of the page that has the changes is not visible to ordinary viewers of the page, and that the original approved version of the personalization data is loaded into the page. To approve the pending changes a moderator can request that the unapproved version of personalization data again be loaded into the page so that they can view the edits made to the page and optionally accept or decline those changes. The final box in the figure shows that after the moderator has approved the changes, only one version of the data exists and that version is visible to all visitors to the portal.

8.3.1 Creating a revision of data

To provide a system that allows for content moderation, the trick is to create a second version of the personalization data—although if you think back to chapter 6 you will remember that we have already seen a sneaky way to do this! In that chapter we saw that by adding some custom code to the loading and saving of personalization blobs, we could save all the personalization data against a single page key. To create a revision version we can write code similar to that shown in chapter 6, so that based on a known condition in our page, we can change the personalization key to reflect the second version of the page. For example, rather than saving data against the page key of urn:global we could instead add some identifier to that key to indicate a revision such as urn:global|revision. In listing 8.2 we see the code that is added to the LoadPersonalizationBlobs method of a custom personalization provider, to conditionally load personalization data from either the main path or from a revision of the data.

> **Listing 8.2   Conditionally changing the path used by the personalization provider gives us the effect of having multiple copies of personalization data per page.**

```
protected override void LoadPersonalizationBlobs(
    WebPartManager wpm,
    string path,
    string userName,
    ref byte[] sharedDataBlob,
    ref byte[] userDataBlob) {

    PersonalizationStateQuery query = new PersonalizationStateQuery();
    query.PathToMatch = path + "|revision";

    bool pageHasRevisionData =                    <───  Create a query to check for
        GetCountOfState(PersonalizationScope.Shared, query) > 0;   existing personalization data

    bool isRevisionPage = ((PortalWebPartManager)wpm).IsRevisionPage;
    ((PortalWebPartManager)wpm).HasUnapprovedChanges
```

```
                = pageHasRevisionData;
                                                              │ Change the path to load
    if (isRevisionPage && pageHasRevisionData) {     ◁───┘ from the revised copy
        path += "|revision";
    }

    base.LoadPersonalizationBlobs(
        wpm,
        path,
        userName,
        ref sharedDataBlob,
        ref userDataBlob
    );
}
```

Quite a lot is happening in listing 8.2, so let's take some time to walk through the code. We should first check to see whether or not a revision version of the page exists. We do this by creating a `PersonalizationStateQuery` object and setting its `PathToMatch` property to the path we want to check. For our purposes we will be storing the unapproved content version in a path which has the text "|revision" added to the path, so that's the value we use for the `PathToMatch` property. After initializing the query, we pass it to the `GetCountOfState` method—which is a method of the personalization provider—and it will return a count of the state items which exist in the data store for the query.

NOTE   We'll take a closer look at the `PersonalizationStateQuery` class in chapter 9 when we look at different ways to manage our portal.

After using the count of state items to ascertain that revision data does indeed exist for the page we are on, we then check with the `WebPartManager` instance for the page to see whether or not the user has requested the revision page. If the answer to both of these questions is "Yes," we alter the path to the revision key so that the revision data is loaded by the call to `LoadPersonalizationBlobs`. Note that the `IsRevisionPage` property on the `WebPartManager` is a custom property, and this explains why we must cast the `WebPartManager` instance to a `PortalWebPart-Manager` before we can gain access to it. The following snippet of code shows the logic for the `IsRevisionPage` property which has been added to the `PortalWeb-PartManager`:

```
public bool IsRevisionPage {
    get {
        return Page.Request.Params["view"] == "edit";
    }
}
```

The code here is simply checking to see whether an item named "view" exists in the Params collection of the Request; and if so, whether its value is set to "edit." Typically this value might come from a `querystring` value.

Notice that the code in listing 8.1 will return the approved version of the page if no revision data is present in the data store, even if the `IsRevisionPage` returns true. This ensures that the first time a user attempts to edit a page, he will be loading the current version of the page and not an empty version of personalization data. This is important because the approved version may already contain personalization changes.

8.3.2 Approving a revision

Now that we are able to load revision data, we must also find a way to ensure it is correctly saved. When performing the save, we need to include logic, such as a check to determine whether the save operation is due to a user who is editing content or whether the save is the result of a moderator approving the content. We determine whether or not the user is committing changes by checking a custom property of the `PortalWebPartManager` called `CommittingChanges`; this property is set from the user interface layer when an administrator performs a commit operation. The code for the `CommittingChanges` property is shown in listing 8. 3.

Listing 8.3 Adding a CommitChanges method to our WebPartManager allows us to flag that personalization data has changes.

```
private bool _committingChanges = false;
public bool CommittingChanges {
    get { return _committingChanges; }
    set { _committingChanges = value; }
}


public void CommitChanges() {
    this.CommittingChanges = true;
    SetPersonalizationDirty();
}
```

At runtime, when an administrator performs a commit operation to accept content changes—typically by pressing a button on the user interface layer—the code that handles that operation simply calls `CommitChanges` on the `PortalWebPartManager` and the `PortalWebPartManager` then takes responsibility for setting the `CommittingChanges` flag to true. It is crucial to notice in listing 8.2 that, in addition to setting the `CommittingChanges` flag to true, the `CommitChanges` method also calls `SetPersonalizationDirty` on the personalization provider to ensure that a save of personalization data is performed at the end of the page's lifecycle.

Listing 8.4 shows the code within our custom personalization provider which ensures that the personalization data is saved correctly, regardless of whether the user is editing or approving content updates.

Listing 8.4 Customizing the saving logic within our personalization provider allows us to route data to the correct path based upon the action that is being committed.

```
protected override void SavePersonalizationBlob(
    WebPartManager wpm,
    string path,
    string userName,
    byte[] dataBlob) {

    bool isRevisionPage =                                   Check to see
        ((PortalWebPartManager)wpm).IsRevisionPage;         whether the
                                                            user is commit-
                                                            ting changes
    if (((PortalWebPartManager)wpm).CommittingChanges) {

        base.SavePersonalizationBlob(
            wpm, path, userName, dataBlob);
                                            Reset the second
        ResetPersonalizationBlob(          version of the content
            wpm, path + "|revision", null);
                                            Otherwise, simply decide
    } else if (isRevisionPage) {            whether this is a revision copy

        base.SavePersonalizationBlob(
            wpm,
            path + "|revision",
            userName,
            dataBlob);

    } else {
        base.SavePersonalizationBlob(
            wpm,
            path,
            userName,
            dataBlob);
    }
}
```

Notice there are three logic branches in the save method. The first branch checks the custom `CommittingChanges` property of our `PortalWebPartManager` to see if the user is committing changes; and if so, the content is saved against the public version of personalization data and the revision copy is cleared out.

If the user is not committing changes, we check to see whether we are currently on the revision page or not to determine against which path the data is saved.

8.3.3   Allowing a user to commit changes

You've now seen all the code required to save and fetch revisions of personalization data. So now all we need to do is to create some user interface elements to allow users to kick off versioning operations. The Common Tasks area we created earlier in this chapter will be the ideal place to surface these operations. Since it's likely that users will be performing these versioning tasks regularly, we want to have this functionality clearly displayed. Figures 8.5 and 8.6 show the new items on the menu bar for managing content revisions.

In figure 8.5 a Revise Content button has been added that the user can click to enter into a state where he may create new versions of the content. When the user clicks on the Revise Content button the view='edit' querystring parameter is added to the URL of the page; this is how we determine that the page is in revision mode. When the page is in revision mode, the toolbar changes to the one shown in figure 8.6 and the text of the Revise Content button changes to End Revising Content. In addition, an Approve Content Changes button is visible so that the user can accept version changes made to the page.

Because the appearance of the buttons we are adding to the Common Tasks menu changes based on the state of the page, we must add some code to the `PreRender` event just as we did in listing 8.1 when we changed the display of certain buttons based on specific criteria. The following snippet shows the code that must be added to the `PreRender` event to manage the state of the Revise Content buttons:

```
this.lnkCreateRevision.Text =
    _wpm.IsRevisionPage ?
        "End Revising Content" : "Revise Content";

this.pnlApprove.Visible =
    _wpm.HasUnapprovedChanges && _wpm.IsRevisionPage;
```

Here we see how the text of the revision button is toggled between Revise Content and End Revising Content, based on whether the page is currently being viewed in its revised state. The second part of the code snippet responsible for setting the visibility of the Approve Content Changes button simply checks the two custom properties we

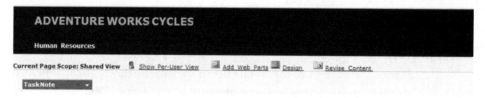

Figure 8.5   Actions displayed in Common Tasks area when the page is in its normal mode.

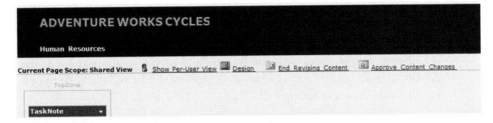

Figure 8.6 Actions displayed in Common Tasks area when the page is in revision mode.

added to the `WebPartManager` to see whether the page has changes, and whether we are on the revision version of the page before displaying the Approve Content Changes button.

The code which handles the click events of those buttons is also quite simple, as we see in listing 8.5.

Listing 8.5 The code for performing revision tasks is quite simple at the page level.

```
protected void lnkCreateRevision_Click(object sender, EventArgs e) {

    string url = Page.Request.Path;
    if (!_wpm.IsRevisionPage) { url += "?view=edit"; }
        Response.Redirect(url);
}

protected void lnkApproveChanges_Click(object sender, EventArgs e) {
    _wpm.CommitChanges();
}
```

Clicking on the Create Revision button simply toggles the page between edit and normal views by either appending or removing the querystring parameter, which is what we can see in the first method shown in listing 8.5. The code for approving the convent revision is even more straightforward as we simply call through to our custom `CommitChanges` method on the `WebPartManager`, and the remainder of the work will be handled by the saving logic that we wrote in our personalization provider in listing 8.3.

Before our solution is complete, we must add code to the load method of the page. This will set the display mode of the page to catalog mode if the user is viewing the revision page; and is similar to code that we've written many times before, as seen in the following snippet:

```
if (_wpm.IsRevisionPage) {
    _wpm.DisplayMode = WebPartManager.CatalogDisplayMode;
}
```

Setting the display mode to catalog mode will ensure that parts can be moved and edited, and that the catalog will be visible so that parts can be added to the page. Lastly, we need to add the configuration entries which will ensure that our new personalization provider with the loading and saving customizations is used instead of the default `SqlPersonalizationProvider`. The following snippet is the same as the code shown in listing 6.3:

```
<personalization defaultProvider="SqlBlogPersonalizationProvider">
    <providers>
      <add connectionStringName="LocalSqlServer"
           applicationName="/"
        name="SqlBlogPersonalizationProvider"
        type="AW.Portal.Web.VersionedPersonalizationProvider" />
    </providers>
</personalization>
```

With these changes in place, our portal is now ready for users to begin making changes to the content that will be hidden from public view until they are approved. The only code needing to be created is the logic that ensures the Approve Content button is only visible to users within specific access rights—presumably users with content management rights. In order to keep this simple, I haven't added that code to our portal solution.

When you run the page and click on the Approve Content Changes button, you will see that the Common Tasks area looks as it did in figure 8.6 and that the catalog zone is displayed. While the page is in revise mode, make some changes to the content—such as adding or removing web parts or moving them around—and then click on End Revising Content to see that the changes are not visible in normal viewing mode. Place the page into revise mode again so you can approve the changes, and after doing so click on the End Revising Content button once again and you will see that the changes are now visible to all portal users.

I mentioned before that when our page is placed into revise mode, the catalog is displayed to allow new web parts to be added. When the `CatalogZone` is displayed you can see that it appears on the right side of the page, just underneath the Useful Links list as shown in figure 8.7.

Having the tool zones appear within the structural area of the page is not bad for sites with a design such as ours, which is mainly rectangular with a fair amount of free space.

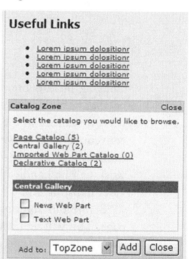

Figure 8.7 Editors and Catalogs are displayed in task zones that are within the content area of the page.

Figure 8.8 Some web page designs are not conducive to accommodating the large rectangular areas required by Task Zones.

But what if the website you are building doesn't have a rectangular design? For example, you might be building a web page designed by graphic artists who object to throwing a large rectangular object into their intricate patterns. Figure 8.8 shows an example of a design from the popular CSS design site—http://www.CssZenGarden.com—which is based on rounded shapes.

Where would you put a large rectangular catalog or editor zone within the content area of such a page? The answer may be to place the tool zones outside the structure housing the main website content altogether.

8.4   CREATING AN AREA FOR TOOL ZONES

In most common portal applications, tool zones are not embedded within the main structure of the page but are instead contained within areas that are dynamically displayed when the user chooses to use them. This is because when web pages are designed, the main layout areas of the page are meant to house only the primary content of the page—the section that is visible all the time. Designing pages in this manner ensures that the page can contain the maximum amount of content without appearing cramped.

One of the tactics for displaying tool zones outside the main content area of the page is to show them within their own window hovering above the main page; this is how the http://my.msn.com site displays the controls for editing web parts. Another very common way to display tool zones is to contain them in a dynamic panel sitting

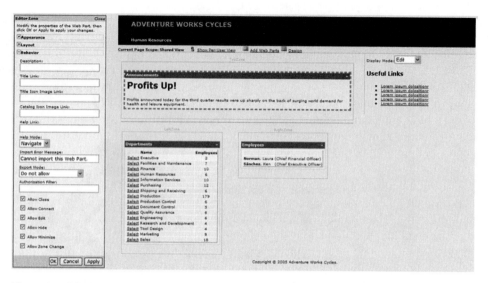

Figure 8.9   Moving the area for displaying Task Zones to outside the main content area means that the zones no longer interfere with the main layout area of the page.

beside the main content area of the page. This is how the http://Live.com and http://Google.com/ig web portals display their catalogs. For our portal we will employ the same tactic as the http://Live.com and http://Google.com/ig portals by creating a dynamic panel which collapses and expands within the page to contain each of the tool zones. Figure 8.9 shows how our page will appear when the editor zone is displayed.

Notice how the area that contains the editor zone extends for the full length of the page, and is no longer restricted by the structure of the area with the content section. By having the editor zone displayed at full length, we ensure that the maximum amount of page area is available to display a tool zone—which ultimately leads to less scrolling by our users. The tool panel we create for our portal will contain the `Editor`, `Catalog`, and `ConnectionsZone`; and when visible will appear on the left side of the page.

8.4.1   Moving our task zones

Because our task zones are currently displayed within the content area of the page, we will need to create a new area to contain them and then move these zones into that area. Presently we have the rectangular regions that make up the layout for our website and these regions are contained both within the master page for the site and also in the `Default.aspx` page itself. The regions in the master page contain the outer elements that define the header row, the footer row, and the middle content section. Figure 8.10 shows the layout of the regions providing the main content areas for our portal.

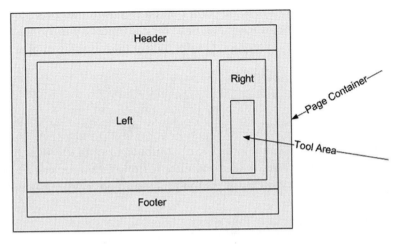

Figure 8.10   Presently the area for tools is heavily embedded within the rectangular regions that make up the layout of the page.

The regions for the Page Container, Header, Footer, and the area surrounding the Left and Right content panels in the middle are contained within the master page; while the Left, Content, Right, and Tool Area panels are contained within the `Default.aspx` page. Our plan is to move the tool zone elements to a separate region outside the Page Container so that the tools do not interfere with our page's structure. To do this we can move the HTML elements that make up the Tool Area region into the master page outside of the Page Container. The illustration in figure 8.11 allows us to see the overall effect that this move will have on our page's structure.

Before we move the `EditorZone`, `CatalogZone`, and `ConnectionsZone` from the `Default.aspx` page, we must add an HTML DIV element in the master page to

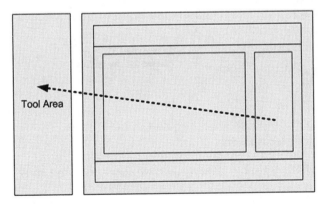

Figure 8.11   Our task is simply to move that rectangular area outside of the main layout region.

house those server controls. To do this, create a DIV with the ID of "toolpanel" and place it between the WebPartManager and the container DIV in the master page. The code for the DIV should now look like the code in the following snippet:

```
<div runat="server" id="toolpanel">

    ... ToolZone server controls go here

</div>
```

When we added the runat='server' attribute to the DIV, the DIV became a server control; and so we could manipulate it from within server-side code. That's how we will affect the visibility of the toolpanel based on the current display mode of the page.

8.4.2 Displaying the TaskZone area

Now that we've moved the tool zones into their own region, we can work on creating the logic to ensure that this region is not displayed until the user requests that a tool zone be visible. The HTML DIV element we've used to contain the tool zones is what is known as a block element. Block elements are HTML elements which, by default, take up 100% of the width of the allocated space. In our case this means that the toolpanel DIV element will span the entire width of the top section of the screen when it is visible, which will force the DIV element for the container to sit underneath it. This is not what we want. To display the toolpanel beside the container we will need to use some CSS code to set the width and other layout information for both the toolpanel and container DIV elements. The code in listing 8.6 shows the CSS code and server-side code responsible for selecting the right CSS class to apply to each panel based on the current display mode of the page.

Listing 8.6 CSS styles are used to control the placement and visibility of the tool zone and the main layout region.

```
.lzv { float: left ; width: 20% ; }          Create the CSS
.lz { display: none ; }                       classes for the panels

.rzv { width: 100% ; }
.rz { float: right; width: 77% ; }
```

```
private void ToggleEditorZone() {

    WebPartDisplayMode mode = this.WebPartManager1.DisplayMode;

    bool displaySidePanel = (                          Check whether to
          (mode == WebPartManager.EditDisplayMode &&    display the side panel
        this.WebPartManager1.SelectedWebPart != null)
```

```
            (mode == WebPartManager.CatalogDisplayMode)

            (mode == WebPartManager.ConnectDisplayMode)
        );
```

Set the CSS attributes on the panels accordingly

```
    if (displaySidePanel) {    ←─────┘
        this.container.Attributes.Add("class", "rz");
        this.toolpanel.Attributes.Add("class", "lzv");
    } else {
        this.container.Attributes.Add("class", "rzv");
        this.toolpanel.Attributes.Add("class", "lz");
    }
}
```

The CSS classes manage the visibility of the panels when they are in their maximized state and in their minimized state. For example, when the toolpanel is visible, it is assigned the lzv (Left Zone Visible) class, which gives it a width of 20% and floats the DIV to the left of screen. At the same time, the container panel is given the rz class, which floats it to the right and gives it a width of 77%. When the toolpanel is hidden, its display is set to none and the container panel is given a width of 100%. All of this gives us exactly the effect that we want.

The server-side code simply checks the current display mode for the page and then toggles the class attributes for the panels accordingly.

Run the application and observe the behavior of the page when the toolpanel is visible, and also when it is closed. Notice when the toolpanel is hidden, the container panel expands to fill the entire page; and when the toolpanel is visible, the container panel contracts so that the tools are displayed on the left side of the page.

The features we've discussed so far in this chapter are all tools that customers are likely to expect when you are creating portals for them. The reason that customers will expect them is because they are fairly standard across major portals today.

Another portal feature we haven't touched upon yet is the topic of tool zones displayed within their own dialog windows; that is, they pop up over the main content of the page and are displayed within their own window. You can see examples of this when you edit web parts on the http://my.msn.com portal. This feature is also included in the 2006 version of SharePoint, where Microsoft has implemented a pop-up version of the web parts gallery. Due to the popularity of these portals it is highly likely that customers will also want to see the tool zones appearing within pop-up dialogs too. Therefore, in the next section we will learn how to implement such a feature.

8.5   *ADDING A CATALOGZONE DIALOG*

Using dialog windows to contain tool zones is an advanced topic because it requires inter-window communication between the window containing the main page and the dialog window. In this section we will create a dialog window that displays catalogs which allow a user to add web parts to a specific zone. The steps involved in creating the catalog dialog are

- Create the catalog dialog page.
- Populate catalogs.
- Display the catalog dialog.
- Communicate between the dialog and the page.
- Dynamically load the assembly and add it as a web part.

For our example we'll create a pop-up catalog that behaves in the same way as the gallery featured in the next version of SharePoint. This means each zone on the page will contain a link that allows users to launch the catalog dialog. It also means that any web parts the user selects within the catalog dialog will be added to the zone the dialog was launched from. Figure 8.12 shows how the catalog dialog will appear when displayed in a browser.

Figure 8.12 shows the catalog dialog displayed in its own window with three gallery tabs visible: Text, Miscellaneous, and Site. When the user clicks on any of these tabs, a list of web parts for that category is displayed underneath the tabs. When the user clicks on a web part, it is added to the zone that launched the catalog dialog window.

The data for the categories and web parts contained within them will come from an XML configuration file that allows us to group web parts and, importantly, to specify the fully qualified class name of each web part. The XML file is named `CatalogData.xml` and contains the entries shown in listing 8.7.

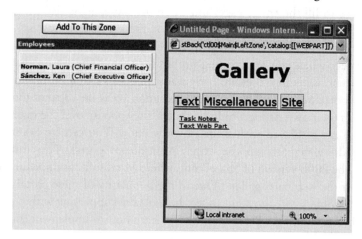

Figure 8.12 When the Add To This Zone button is clicked, a pop-up catalog dialog is used to present the user with a list of web parts that can be added.

```xml
<?xml version="1.0" encoding="utf-8" ?>
<catalogs>
  <catalog displayName="Text">
    <webpart displayName="Task Notes"
        typeName="AW.Portal.Web.SharedWebParts.TaskNotes" />
    <webpart displayName="Text Web Part"
        typeName="AW.Portal.Web.SharedWebParts.TextWebPart" />
  </catalog>
  <catalog displayName="Miscellaneous">
    <webpart displayName="News Web Part"
        typeName="AW.Portal.Web.SharedWebParts.NewsWebPart" />
  </catalog>
  <catalog displayName="Site">
    <webpart displayName="Favourites"
        typeName="AW.Portal.Web.FavoritesWebPart" />
  </catalog>
</catalogs>
```

The `CatalogData` XML file specifies a collection of catalogs with a given display name, and also specifies that each catalog contains a collection of web parts. At run-time we'll display each of the catalogs as a tab; and when the user clicks on a tab, the web parts for that catalog will be displayed as links which the user can select to add that web part to a zone.

To get started with the development of this feature, let's add a new web form named `CatalogDialog.aspx` that will act as the catalog dialog to the project.

8.5.1 Displaying catalogs

In figure 8.12, the button that launches the catalog dialog is displayed at the top of the zone. This button is rendered in the `Header` of each zone, launches the dialog, and passes the dialog window the parameters that can be used to identify which zone launched the catalog dialog.

The easiest way to display the button at the head of each zone is to override the `RenderHeader` method of our custom web part zones. Listing 8.8 shows us how to render the button from within the `RenderHeader` method.

Listing 8.8 The render logic for the zones is changed to include the button that is used to launch the pop-up catalog dialog.

```
protected override bool HasHeader {
    get { return true; }
}

protected override void RenderHeader(HtmlTextWriter writer) {

    HtmlInputButton b = new HtmlInputButton();
```

```
    b.ID = "mybutton1";
    b.Value = "Add To This Zone";

    ClientScriptManager cs = this.Page.ClientScript;
    string postbackReference = cs.GetPostBackEventReference(
        this,
        "catalog:[[WEBPART]]"
        );

    b.Attributes.Add(
        "onclick",
        string.Format(
            "DisplayDialog(\"CatalogDialog.aspx?postbackReference=
        ➥{0}\")",
            postbackReference
            )
        );
    b.RenderControl(writer);
    writer.WriteBreak();

}
```

For the code in the `RenderHeader` method to run, we must first override the `Has-Header` property of the `WebPartZone` control and ensure that it returns true. When a user clicks on the Add to Zone button, a client-side JavaScript function named `DisplayDialog` is called; and the URL of the catalog dialog page is passed as an argument with a postback reference embedded within the querystring of the URL. Notice that the `postbackReference` value is obtained by calling a method named `GetPostBackEventReference` from the `ClientScriptManager` on the page. Calling this method will return a string that can be invoked from within the browser to force a postback to occur. In the code in listing 8.8 the returned string will look like the following snippet:

```
__doPostBack('ctl00$Main$LeftZone', 'catalog:[[WEBPART]]')
```

When this string is executed in the browser, the control that appears as the first argument of the `__doPostBack` method will receive the postback notification on the server and the second argument will be passed as the postback arguments. The client-side JavaScript method named `DisplayDialog` that is launched when the user clicks the button is shown in listing 8.9.

Listing 8.9   JavaScript is used to invoke the pop-up catalog dialog from within the client's browser.

```
function DisplayDialog(url) {
    var opts =
        "width=300,height=250,resizable=yes,status=no,scrollbars=yes" ;
```

```
    var hwnd = window.open( url, "winname", opts ) ;
    if( (document.window != null ) && (!hwnd.opener) )
        hwnd.opener = document.window ;
}
```

This JavaScript function simply uses the `window.open` function to launch a new window with the dimensions and options specified. In our case, we are specifying that the window should be 300 pixels wide and 250 pixels high, that it should be resizable, and that the scrollbars should be present if necessary. The URL of the `CatalogDialog` is passed in with the `postbackReference` embedded within the URL as we specified in our server-side code.

8.5.2 Displaying web parts

The catalog will be displayed using a Repeater and displaying each catalog using a `LinkButton` server control. When the user clicks on one of these `LinkButtons`, a postback will occur, and we will use the link that was clicked to set the selected catalog. At this time we'll use the selected catalog to retrieve a listing of web parts from our `CatalogDialog` XML data file. Listing 8.10 shows the Repeater that is used to display web parts and the server-side code we use to populate the Repeater with web parts for a selected category.

Listing 8.10   Web parts are easily displayed by binding XML nodes to a Repeater server control.

```
<asp:Repeater ID="rptWebParts" runat="server"
    OnItemDataBound="rptWebParts_ItemDataBound">

    <ItemTemplate>
        <a href="#" id="clickme" runat="server">
            <asp:Label ID="Label2"
                runat="Server"
                Text='<%# XPath("./@displayName") %>'    ◁┐ Data binding
                />                                          │ expression to
        </a><br />                                          │ display web
    </ItemTemplate>                                         │ part name

</asp:Repeater>




void BindWebParts() {

    XmlNodeList nodes = null ;

    if (string.IsNullOrEmpty(this.SelectedCatalog)) {
        nodes = _doc.DocumentElement.ChildNodes[0].ChildNodes;
    } else {
```

```
XmlNode node =
    _doc.DocumentElement.SelectSingleNode(          ◁┐ Find the selected
        "//catalog[@displayName='" +                  │ category node
        this.SelectedCatalog + "']"
        );

    if (node != null)                    │ Assign its child nodes
        nodes = node.ChildNodes;       ◁┘ to a local variable
}

this.rptWebParts.DataSource = nodes;     ◁┐ Bind to the
this.rptWebParts.DataBind();               │ data repeater

}
```

In the `BindWebParts` method we use an XPATH data binding expression to find which list of web part nodes to select, and we can then bind the resulting `Xml-NodeList` returned from that query directly to the `rtpWebParts` Repeater control. Something interesting to notice about the binding code in the Repeater control is the use of the XPath statement. In listing 8.10 we're using the ASP.NET XPath statement to evaluate an XPATH expression during the binding operation. This allows us to apply the `displayName` of each web part node to the `Text` property of a `Label` control.

Although the Label that displays the `displayName` of each web part is contained within a hyperlink, we can see that the `href` attribute for the hyperlink is set to #. Instead of setting a URL for the hyperlink in the mark-up code, we will set it from server-side code so that we can format a JavaScript function call and assign it to the `onclick` attribute of the hyperlink instead. Listing 8.11 shows code that will run during the `ItemDataBound` event of the `Repeater` control and dynamically set the JavaScript behavior for the anchor based on the value of the `typeName` attribute for each web part node in the list.

> **Listing 8.11** As the XML nodes are bound to the repeater, JavaScript is inserted to the hyperlink that allows our users to select the web part add it to their page.

```
protected void  rptWebParts_ItemDataBound(
    object sender, RepeaterItemEventArgs e)
{

    XmlNode node = (XmlNode) e.Item.DataItem;
    string typeName = node.Attributes["typeName"].Value;

    HtmlAnchor btn = (HtmlAnchor)e.Item.FindControl("clickme");
    btn.Attributes.Add(
        "onclick",
        "CloseCatalogDialog(\"" +
            this.hdnPostBackReference.Value + "\", \"" +
```

```
                    typeName + "\")"
        );
}
```

The code in listing 8.11 gets a handle to the underlying `XmlNode` being bound to each row of data by using the `DataItem` property of the Item being bound. The `DataItem` property we access from the `RepeaterItemEventArgs` is an instance of the data item being bound to the row, and we can simply cast it directly to the type of data being bound. In this case, because we initially bound our Repeater to an `XmlNodeList`, we can be sure each item in that list will be an `XmlNode`. Once we have a reference to the `XmlNode`, we simply grab the `typeName` from the node and use it to add a client-side JavaScript function named `CloseCatalogDialog` to the hyperlink.

We are almost there. All that remains is for us to create the `CloseCatalogDialog` JavaScript function which will receive the information from the pop-up dialog and to pass that information back to the server so the portal framework can add the web part to the page.

8.5.3   Communicating between web pages

The `CloseCatalogDialog` function is a client-side JavaScript function that accepts two arguments. The first argument accepted by the function is the original `postbackReference` string that was passed into the catalog dialog window by the button in the header of the zone to which we are adding web parts. The second argument of the `CloseCatalogDialog` function is the value that appeared in the `typeName` attribute for the web part in our `CatalogDialog` XML data file. Listing 8.12 shows the `CloseCatalogDialog` function.

> **Listing 8.12   JavaScript is used to communicate the web part selection from within the dialog back to the calling page.**

```
function CloseCatalogDialog(postbackReference, returnValue) {

    if( window.opener ) {
        window.opener.DoCatalogPostBack(postbackReference, returnValue) ;
        window.opener.focus() ;
    }

    self.close() ;
}
```

The `CloseCatalogDialog` function simply checks the `window.opener` property to see whether the window that opened the catalog dialog is still open and, if so, it calls another function named `DoCatalogPostBack` within that window. The `DoCatalogPostBack` function is the piece of code which will force the postback to occur in our original window. After calling `DoCatalogPostBack` the `CloseCatalogDialog` function simply closes the catalog dialog window by calling `self.close()`, which causes the window to close. The following code snippet shows the logic within the `DoCatalogPostBack` function:

```
function DoCatalogPostBack(postbackReference, returnValue) {
    eval(postbackReference.replace("[[WEBPART]]", returnValue));
}
```

Here you can see that the string [[WEBPART]] is replaced by the `typeName` of the web part that was clicked on. The [[WEBPART]] text in our original `postbackReference` string was simply a marker that would be easy to find and replace, so that's what we are doing here. After the replacing, the `postbackReference` string will look something like this:

```
__doPostBack('ctl00$Main$LeftZone', 'catalog:TYPENAME OF SELECTED WEB PART')
```

This string is passed to the JavaScript `eval` method, which essentially forces execution of the string to occur; and when the string is executed, the client-side ASP.NET JavaScript function named `__doPostBack` is fired. The `__doPostBack` function is the piece of code sitting behind all server controls that causes a postback and is responsible for telling ASP.NET which control caused the postback and also sending along any event arguments. As we can see in our example, a control named `ctl00$Main$LeftZone` was the zone that initiated the postback, and the event argument starts with the characters `catalog:` and ends with the type name of the web part to add.

Because ASP.NET knows which control caused the postback to occur, it will send this event information to the method on the control which implements the `IPostBackEventHandler` interface. This method is named `RaisePostBackEvent` and the string it takes as its argument is the same string that was passed as the second argument of the client-side `__doPostBack` function. Listing 8.13 shows the code for the `RaisePostBackEvent` event handler that is coded within our custom web part zone, and which receives the notification of the web part being added from the catalog dialog window.

Listing 8.13 We determine which web part the user is adding by inspecting the postback event arguments and then use the WebPartManager to add that web part to our list of parts for the zone.

```
protected override void RaisePostBackEvent(string eventArgument) {

    WebPartManager wpm =
WebPartManager.GetCurrentWebPartManager(this.Page);

    if (eventArgument.StartsWith("catalog:")) {

        try {
            string[] argParts =
                eventArgument.Split(
```

```
        new char[] { ':' },
        StringSplitOptions.RemoveEmptyEntries
        );
      Type t = BuildManager.GetType(
        argParts[argParts.Length - 1],
        true,
        true
        );
      WebPart wp1 = (WebPart)Activator.CreateInstance(t);

      wpm.AddWebPart(wp1, this, this.WebParts.Count);
    } catch (Exception ex) {
        Console.WriteLine(ex.Message);
    }
  } else {
    base.RaisePostBackEvent(eventArgument);
  }
}
```

In the `RaisePostBackEvent` method we check that the `eventArgument` string starts with our prefix of "catalog:". If it does, we know that the string following those characters will be the name of a class we can create an instance of, and then add to this zone.

The code for creating the web part control is quite obscure, but we are using the `BuildManager` class to create a `Type` instance from the string which we then pass to the `Activator` class and create an actual class instance. Once we have an instance of the class, it is simply passed to the `AddWebPart` method of the `WebPartManager` so that the web part can be added to the zone.

Phew! That was a pretty intense session, so congratulations for making it through. The catalog dialog example is definitely an advanced sample, but I'm sure you'll agree that the lessons learned were well worth the added complexity. When you look back at the beginning of the example, you can begin to appreciate the power of the `Get-PostBackEventReference` method that provided us our `postbackReference`. Having the `postbackReference` string allows us to easily implement client-side solutions that don't require constant and immediate server postbacks to perform complex tasks. This is true even when those tasks are performed within other windows, and can occur at any time. Keep this lesson in mind when you are asked to display `CatalogZone` or `EditorZone` controls within pop-up dialog windows.

8.6   SUMMARY

The point of this chapter has been to show how features common to modern portals are implemented. Looking back over chapters 1 through 7, you can now understand that the first six chapters were designed to provide a basic understanding of the main building blocks of portals and how they interact with one another. Chapters 7 and 8 showed you how to apply the theories from the first part of the book to real world solutions. It is the hands-on experience gained in these last two chapters that will be invaluable when you are asked to create portals of your own.

Clients who ask you to build a web portal will expect to see not only the common portal building blocks—such as having web parts and zones—but the look-and-feel of prominent portals on the Internet. Because of these client expectations, learning these advanced techniques and understanding how to implement common portal behaviors will add some much needed value to your toolbox of development tricks.

C H A P T E R   9

Portal management

9.1   INTRODUCTION

It seems like ages since we started our journey into the world of web parts and portals and we've covered a lot of ground along the way. Having taken on the challenge of creating a web portal for the Adventure Works business, we set about liaising with the end-users of the portal so that we could understand their requirements and ensure that we were building suitable features for them. Well, the good news is that our work is almost complete and soon it will be time to deploy the code onto the company's web server so the HR employees can begin using their new portal application. Before we can deploy our portal though, we need to start the planning that will help us to decide how the portal will be deployed. In addition, we need to work out how to support the portal after it has been deployed.

By the end of this chapter, we will not only have deployed our portal, but we will also have set a strategy for effective management of the portal when it is no longer under our control. Having this strategy in place frees us to be creative in chapter 10, when we look at the newer areas of portal development that are emerging.

When we build software applications, we always go through the well-known Software Development Lifecycle (SDLC) process. The SDLC defines the steps and processes that we must pass through to create quality software applications. This is essentially a linear progression from planning stages though to development, finishing with the testing and deployment stages. Because of the linear nature of the SDLC, it is also commonly referred to as the "lifecycle" of application development.

While the majority of the tasks we've embarked upon so far have been associated with the development stage of the lifecycle, we must now turn our attention to the last two phases of the SDLC lifecycle—testing and deployment.

So what exactly will happen when our application leaves the development environment, and what can we do to ensure that we are able to manage and provide support for the portal when it leaves our hands? This chapter answers those questions.

9.2 PREPARING FOR DEPLOYMENT

Picture this situation: we've finished developing our portal application, so we deploy the application files onto the company's servers and release it to the users in the HR department. For the first week everything goes according to plan and, aside from a few requests for enhanced functionality, there have been no major hiccups and the application is running smoothly. However, in the second week, we start getting phone calls from the users complaining that, at times, our application seems to run slowly and sometimes stops working altogether.

This is the worrisome scenario we face every time we deploy our applications into a production environment. How will we diagnose our application to track down an obscure and hard to locate bug? You might think we could simply run the code in our development environment and observe the bug there by using debugging techniques, but remember that this particular bug took a week to begin showing its beady eyes. In reality there's no guarantee that the bugs that affect our applications in one environment will be reproducible in another environment, because many factors often differ between environments. For example, we typically develop our applications on a machine running a desktop operating system such as Windows XP; but when deployed, these same applications run on a machine running a server operating system such as Windows 2003 Server. In reality, there are hundreds of factors that vary between our development environment and the environments that we deploy our code in.

Of course when our portal is in the development phase of the SDLC lifecycle, it is easy to diagnose the cause of errors occurring in the application, because the code is running on our development machine. In addition, we can use the debugging tools in Visual Studio 2005 to connect to the running application and step through the execution of a page to locate errors and attain the information necessary to help us track down the cause of problems. We saw how to attach the Visual Studio debugger to a web page and view the state of variables in chapter 2. Recall that we used the debugger when we attached it to a web page to look at the state of a `GenericWebPart` at runtime. However, as mentioned, things are not so simple when our applications are beyond reach.

Let's now take a step into the world of application monitoring where we can find out what tools are at our disposal for diagnosing and tracking down errors when our applications are deployed. On this trek, we'll see two things. First, we use code instrumentation to diagnose existing problems. And second, there are ways to monitor the health of the applications so that we might even detect errors before they actually occur.

9.2.1 Code instrumentation

To assist in the task of tracking down bugs in applications, we can add code that will log information about our application when it is running. This practice of adding logging information is known as *instrumenting* our code. We'll now take a look at the `Trace` class in the .NET Framework which can be used to display diagnostic information about the state of our code at runtime. We'll also see how ASP.NET provides built-in support for optionally displaying this diagnostic information at the bottom of each page. Displaying tracing information within a page provides a simple, interactive debugging experience when we are looking for problems in our code at runtime.

The whole point of instrumenting code is to get help diagnosing problems when they arise in our applications. When we add instrumentation it is for the purpose of understanding what's happening in our code in a quantitative way, without having to run it on our own machine. By instrumenting our code and logging the results to an output file or database, we can then analyze the data to diagnose the cause of problems and then work out how to take corrective action.

ASP.NET provides us with the `Trace` class for instrumenting our code using trace statements. `Trace` class also allows the output of those statements to be written to a specific target location such as a log file, the Windows Event Log, or even to simply be displayed at the bottom of the screen. In the following snippet of code, trace statements are used to send messages to the default tracing output location to record when code enters and leaves the `AddHyperlink` method in our `FavoritesWebPart`:

```
public void AddHyperlink(HyperlinkData hyperlink) {

    HttpContext ctx = HttpContext.Current;
    ctx.Trace.Write("Entering AddHyperlink: " + hyperlink.URL);

    ... method code here

    ctx.Trace.Write("Exiting AddHyperlink");
}
```

The `Trace` can be accessed directly from code within our page, but for code contained within controls such as our `FavoritesWebPart` we must first get a handle to an instance of the current page context and access the `Trace` instance directly from the context object. The `Trace` class writes the output of our trace statements into objects known as *listeners*, which take the output and write it to a specific output device. Once we have tracing statements in our code, we can configure our pages to have these statements appear at the bottom of the page at runtime. This is useful for accessing important debug information quickly and is accomplished simply by setting the trace directive of the page to true as shown in the following snippet:

```
<%@ Page Trace="true" %>
```

Now when we run a page and add a hyperlink to our `FavoritesWebPart`, our tracing statements will appear at the bottom of the page as shown in figure 9.1.

In figure 9.1 we see that the tracing output is now being added to the bottom of our page, and that our tracing statements appear within the Trace Information section of that output. By reading this information we can confirm that code entered and exited the `AddHyperlink` correctly, and we can also see the text of the hyperlink that is being added. The From First and From Last columns, appearing in the tracing output can be used to determine how long it takes each section of code within the page's lifecycle to execute. The From First column tells us the time in seconds since the first trace message was output, and the From Last column tells us how many seconds have elapsed since the last trace message was output. By reading the output we can locate code that is slow running and then use our own development environment to look for ways to improve the performance of that particular piece of code.

Another useful member of the `Trace` class is the `Warn` method, which is similar to the `Write` method except that its output is displayed in the Trace Information section in red text. It is customary to use the `Warn` method to write tracing output for extreme conditions that our code encounters such as displaying the text of exceptions that are being handled.

Trace Information

Category	Message	From First(s)	From Last(s)
aspx.page	Begin PreInit		
aspx.page	End PreInit	0.000414298465307742	0.000414
aspx.page	Begin Init	0.000487771490510665	0.000073
aspx.page	End Init	0.00861338522074733	0.008126
aspx.page	Begin InitComplete	0.00871619158300846	0.000103
aspx.page	End InitComplete	0.0208641042367116	0.012148
aspx.page	Begin LoadState	0.0209669105989728	0.000103
aspx.page	End LoadState	0.0243947205580598	0.003428
aspx.page	Begin ProcessPostData	0.0244712665995259	0.000077
aspx.page	End ProcessPostData	0.0301032673147006	0.005632
aspx.page	Begin PreLoad	0.0301848419282339	0.000082
aspx.page	End PreLoad	0.0302971467043996	0.000112
aspx.page	Begin Load	0.0303591657598941	0.000062
aspx.page	End Load	0.0305100229219077	0.000151
aspx.page	Begin ProcessPostData Second Try	0.0305790261052732	0.000069
aspx.page	End ProcessPostData Second Try	0.0306449562723754	0.000066
aspx.page	Begin Raise ChangedEvents	0.0307030642162621	0.000058
aspx.page	End Raise ChangedEvents	0.0307815658135322	0.000079
aspx.page	Begin Raise PostBackEvent	0.0308407912178783	0.000059
	Entering AddHyperlink: http://Microsoft.com	0.0309656674242117	0.000125
	Exiting AddHyperlink	0.0311251849047854	0.000160

Figure 9.1   With page tracing turned on, tracing statements appear in the trace information section at the bottom of the web page.

For example, in our data access layer code we typically handle exceptions using try...catch code blocks, such as the one shown in the following snippet of code:

```
try {
    ... attempt an operation here
} catch( Exception ex ) {
    ... catch any exceptions here
} finally {
    ... perform clean-up tasks here
}
```

Using a try...catch...finally block ensures that any exceptions that might occur are trapped, and therefore do not cause the execution of our page to fail. Catching exception information also helps us to ensure that sensitive information such as a connection string is not displayed on the page to our users. For example, if there were a problem with one of the stored procedures that we wrote for our portal, we wouldn't want users to see that information displayed on the web page, but we would need to write it out in a tracing statement so we could know to fix the problem. To do this we can add a `Trace.Warn` call to the catch block to display details about the exception as shown in listing 9.1:

Listing 9.1 Using Trace.Warn will cause statements to appear in red text within the tracing output, and is the standard to use when instrumenting exceptions.

```
try {

    ... method code here

} catch (Exception ex) {

    HttpContext ctx = HttpContext.Current;
    ctx.Trace.Warn(ex.ToString());

}finally {
    ... perform clean-up tasks here
}
```

Now when an exception is thrown we will be able to view a detailed message about the cause of the exception in our tracing output. For example, we might forget to correctly configure our `AdventureWorks` connection string in the configuration file. If so, when we deploy the application, our web parts will appear on the pages, but they will not display any content. When we view the `Trace` output for the page, the exact nature of the problem will be revealed to us as shown in figure 9.2.

Now when we run the page with tracing turned on, we can clearly see that the reason our web parts are not displaying any content is because we haven't added a connection string configuration setting named `AdventureWorksConnectionString` to our web configuration file.

Trace Information		
CategoryMessage	**From First(s)**	**From Last(s)**
aspx.pageBegin PreInit		
aspx.pageEnd PreInit	0.00346943536119814	0.003469
aspx.pageBegin Init	0.0035138544144577	0.000044
aspx.pageEnd Init	0.046584970994917	0.043071
aspx.pageBegin InitComplete	0.0466576059247754	0.000073
aspx.pageEnd InitComplete	0.0495051745403396	0.002848
aspx.pageBegin PreLoad	0.0495420507354985	0.000037
aspx.pageEnd PreLoad	0.0495738983585903	0.000032
aspx.pageBegin Load	0.0496001586793852	0.000026
aspx.pageEnd Load	0.0497038031369909	0.000104
aspx.pageBegin LoadComplete	0.0497325777438194	0.000029
aspx.pageEnd LoadComplete	0.0641679319578326	0.014435
aspx.pageBegin PreRender	0.0642349795853942	0.000067
System.Configuration.ConfigurationErrorsException: You must have a Connection String configuration setting named AdventureWorksConnectionString at AW.Portal.Data.DataLayer.get_ConnectionString() in C:\Projects\WebPartBook\Chapter9 \AdventureWorksSolution\AW.Portal.Data\DataLayer.cs:line 20 at AW.Portal.Data.DataLayer.GetDataItems[T](String commandText, String[] parameterNames, Object[] parameterValues) in C:\Projects\WebPartBook\Chapter9 \AdventureWorksSolution\AW.Portal.Data\DataLayer.cs:line 124	0.0798836164931576	0.015649

Figure 9.2   This trace output contains the text for two configuration exceptions, which is the result of tracing code contained within the core ASP.NET code.

Seeing tracing in action here makes it clear how useful it is as a tool for detecting the source of problems in our applications. As for prescriptive guidance about where to place tracing statements within an application's code, the obvious place is to find the strategic locations most likely to cause problems at runtime, and target them so we can work out how to diagnose those errors when they occur. At a minimum, I would suggest instrumenting the following code:

- Exception handling blocks
- Calls to external systems which may be expensive, so that we can monitor how long those operations are taking
- Calls to complex business logic operations to help detect erroneous logic

There are many additional topics about managing tracing within our applications worthy of investigation. One such topic is configuring listeners so that the output of tracing statements is directed to areas other than the bottom of the page—such as the Event Log or into a database. As such I highly recommend reading up on ASP.NET Tracing to learn more about options that exist to help with diagnosing problems in web applications.

9.2.2   Health monitoring

Tracing is certainly useful when diagnosing issues that already exist within our application, but ideally we'd like to be a little more pro-active. We'd like to monitor the application in order to detect certain types of issues before they actually become problems. This activity is known as Health Monitoring and involves keeping track of performance counters in code, and viewing these vital statistics periodically to keep an eye peeled for signs that errors are occurring.

Typical use

ASP.NET 2.0 contains an event-based health monitoring system known simply as Health Monitoring that we can tap into to keep track of the health of our applications. We can use the Health Monitoring system to monitor the health of our applications and send notifications as thresholds when certain types of events are raised. For example, periodically the ASP.NET process will be forced to recycle, which will trigger an application restart. Most of the time, these restarts are expected. Here's an example: an administrator changes a web configuration file and thereby restarts the application. However, there are other times when application restarts are symptomatic of an application experiencing extreme difficulty. In this case, we want to receive notifications about the events. For instance, large numbers of application restarts are a typical symptom that a denial-of-service attack is taking place. Using the Health Monitoring service we could configure our application to listen for application restarts, and configure a rule that would cause a notification to be sent after a certain threshold is breached within a given time.

Monitoring system is highly configurable, and therefore allows us to choose which logging provider to use as the output of the notification alert. Table 9.1 displays a list of the standard logging providers configured to work with ASP.NET applications, and details where they target their output:

Table 9.1 Standard logging providers that are provided for the Health and Monitoring service in ASP.NET.

Provider Class	Implements an event provider that ...
System.Web.Management.EventLogWebEvent-Provider	Logs ASP.NET health-monitoring events into the Windows Application Event Log
System.Web.Management.SimpleMailWeb-EventProvider	Sends e-mail for event notifications
System.Web.Management.SqlWebEventProvider	Saves event notifications to an SQL database
System.Web.Management.TraceWebEvent-Provider	Sends ASP.NET health-monitoring events as trace messages
System.Web.Management.WmiWebEvent-Provider	Maps ASP.NET health-monitoring events to Windows Management Instrumentation (WMI) events

In addition to the standard logging providers listed in table 9.1, we can also create our own custom providers. Even more, we can extend and customize the Health Monitoring system at a very granular level. In the next section we'll take a look at the two most common areas of extensibility with the Health Monitoring system: Custom Providers and Custom Events. While learning about these topics we'll also take the opportunity to learn how to configure the Health Monitoring system for our application.

Custom providers

The main reason for creating a custom logging provider is to handle situations when there are specific requirements for how notifications should be delivered. We've seen that, for common notification sinks such as the Windows Event Log, Email, or a SQL Server database, there are already pre-built providers available, but there will also be times when we need to target other types of notification consumers—such as a mobile phone device. When we are targeting a mobile device, we could create a logging provider that would receive notifications of critical behavior and have it send alerts to the cell phone of an application administrator to advise him that things are not quite right. When we need to target a notification consumer that is not supported by the standard logging providers listed in table 9.1, we need to write our own provider and add to it the logic for dispatching the notifications to the device we are targeting.

We create a custom logging provider by creating a class that derives from the `WebEventProvider` class and overriding the `ProcessMessage` method. We place our custom logic for dispatching the event notification in the `ProcessMessage` method. It is this method that will be called by ASP.NET whenever an event that is mapped to our provider is fired. This method receives an argument named `raisedEvent`, which contains information about the Health Monitoring event that occurred. This information includes the event type, event code, and a message describing the event. Once we have created a custom logging provider, we can configure it for use via the provider's element of the `healthMonitoring` section of the web configuration file, as seen in the following code snippet:

```
<healthMonitoring enabled="true">
    <providers>
        <add name="MySmsProvider"
type="SmsWebEventProvider,SmsWebEventProvider" />
    </providers>
</healthMonitoring>
```

In this snippet we are telling the Health Monitoring system that a custom event provider named `MySmsProvider` is available for use within the application.

Events

Notifications are dispatched to the logging providers through events. For example, when an ASP.NET application is restarted, an application restart event is raised by ASP.NET and handled by whatever logging provider is configured to handle events of that kind. If the `SqlWebEventProvider` was configured as the current provider for application restart events, an entry would be written into an SQL Server database each time the restart count reached a threshold that we had configured for the application.

The Health Monitoring system is composed of a large hierarchy of standard events that are raised by ASP.NET as it goes about the job of processing web requests. These events are broken down into the following categories: Request, Error, Audit, and Miscellaneous. In addition to the standard Health Monitoring events, we can also create custom events to notify the Health Monitoring service of things that we want to keep an eye on in our applications. You configure which events should be handled within the application through the eventMappings element of the healthMonitoring section of the web configuration file, as seen in the following code snippet:

```
<healthMonitoring enabled="true">
    <eventMappings>
        <add name="WebServiceCallEvent"
            type="ExternalCallWebEvent, ExternalCallWebEvent" />
    </eventMappings>
</healthMonitoring>
```

In this snippet we are registering a custom event named WebServiceCallEvent with the Health Monitoring system. Note that the type of class configured for this event is a custom class named ExternalCallWebEvent. Listing 9.2 shows the code for the ExternalCallWebEventClass:

Listing 9.2   By creating and raising custom events, we can get fine-grained control over our health monitoring activities.

```
public class ExternalCallWebEvent : WebBaseEvent {

    public ExternalCallWebEvent (string message,
        object eventSource, int eventCode) :
        base(message, eventSource, eventCode) { }
}
```

The WebBaseEvent class that the ExternalCallWebEvent inherits from is the base class for all Health Monitoring events. We use this custom event by creating an instance of the ExternalCallWebEvent class whenever we detect certain conditions in our application and then calling the Raise method of the WebBaseEvent class. The following snippet shows how to raise an ExternalCallWebEvent event in code:

```
ExternalCallWebEvent e = new ExternalCallWebEvent(
    "Some notification message here",
    this,
    WebEventCodes.WebExtendedBase + 1
    );

e.Raise();
```

Judging from the name of the class, you can imagine that we might typically raise this particular custom event in response to an abnormal condition relating to making a call to another website. The example of Health Monitoring included in the Adventure Works sample for chapter 9 is based on a web part called OPMLWebPart. Figure 9.3 shows a picture of how the OPMLWebPart appears when displayed in a browser at runtime.

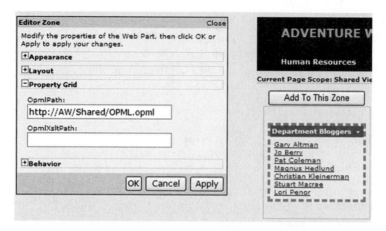

Figure 9.3   The OPMLWebPart reads an OPML file from an external website. Calls to external resources are ideal candidates for health monitoring.

The OPMLWebPart allows a user to configure a URL to third-party site and have an OPML formatted XML file returned from it. Making a call to another website is certainly something we'd want to keep our eye on. Imagine the case when the third-party site takes a long time to respond to our requests, or worse still, stops responding altogether. In such a case we'd want to be notified so that we could take corrective action before our users start reporting errors from our application. Within the code for the OPMLWebPart, health monitoring code records the time it takes to receive a response from the third-party site, and if it is longer than two seconds, the web part starts raising ExternalCallWebEvent health events. This code can be seen in listing 9.3.

Listing 9.3   By monitoring the time it takes to load the OPML file we can raise an alert when it starts taking excessive time to access the external resource.

```
XmlDocument tmp = new XmlDocument();
Stopwatch watch = new Stopwatch();

watch.Start();
tmp.Load(this.OpmlPath);
watch.Stop();

                                              Check time elapsed for
if (watch.ElapsedMilliseconds >= 2000) {  ⟵  making external call
    ExternalCallWebEvent e = new ExternalCallWebEvent(
        string.Format(
            "The call to {0} took {1} milliseconds to complete.",
            this.OpmlPath,
            watch.ElapsedMilliseconds
        ),
        this,
```

```
        WebEventCodes.WebExtendedBase + 1
        );
                                      Raise custom health
    e.Raise();    ←┘   monitoring event

}

return tmp.OuterXml;
```

In the code we create an instance of the `Stopwatch` class to keep track of how long it takes to load the XML from an external site. If that time exceeds 2000 milliseconds, we format a health monitoring event and raise it from within the system. The `Stopwatch` is a special diagnostic class that can be used to perform very accurate timings from within code, and is designed to be used especially for measuring elapsed times.

For our custom event to be logged, it must first be sent to a provider—which in our case will be the `MySmsProvider` configured earlier. To do this we configure the Health Monitoring service to handle our `WebServiceCallEvent`, and tell it which provider to use as the sink for those events. The following snippet shows how to connect our custom event to the SMS provider:

```
<healthMonitoring enabled="true">
    <rules>
        <add name="My SMS Rule"
            eventName="WebServiceCallEvent"
            provider="MySmsProvider"
            />
    </rules>
</healthMonitoring>
```

The rule we have configured here connects our custom `WebServiceCallEvent` to the `SMSProvider` so that whenever the `WebServiceCallEvent` is raised within our application, it will be sent to the SMS provider and our administrators will be alerted that something is wrong and the application requires their attention.

Health Monitoring is a substantial topic and this section has only scratched the surface. I highly recommend spending some time to research Health Monitoring and other techniques for keeping tabs on applications. Just remember that when an application is in a production environment and it starts to misbehave, you will be grateful that you took the time to instrument your code appropriately.

Of course, no matter how hard we try to detect errors ahead of time there will still be problems. We need to have a way to manage those sticky situations, so that the user is not stopped in his tracks with no options for recovery. After all, who wants to take the managing director's midnight phone call when he's grumbling about a broken web page? In the next section we will look at various strategies for assisting users when all is not going according to plan and errors arise.

9.3 RECOVERING FROM ERRORS GRACEFULLY

Earlier in this chapter we learned that we could instrument our code to help detect the root cause of problems, and saw how to use Health Monitoring as an early warning system to alert us when our application's health is waning. With all of these safety measures in place, we can now deploy our application, comfortable in the knowledge that we can detect errors before our users do, right? Well, unfortunately this is not the case, and in reality even the best applications succumb to errors at times. What we need is a way to handle errors when they occur at runtime and provide a way for our application to handle these errors gracefully, so that users are not left looking at an ASP.NET Error page such as the one shown in figure 9.4.

This is typical of what users see when something goes wrong with an ASP.NET page and an unhandled exception occurs. Displaying such a page to users is disconcerting

Figure 9.4 The dreaded ASP.NET error page will be displayed by default whenever an unhandled exception gets thrown.

because the page shows code, detailed error messages, and other technical information that users would simply not understand. Showing this level of technical information could be even worse if it were viewed by a visitor with mischievous intentions—such as a hacker. A hacker viewing technical details shown in figure 9.4 might gain valuable insight into database connection strings and other information that could then be used to hack the website. Having said all that, the ability to view such detailed information about errors is very useful when we are developing the application, as it helps us find errors and apply fixes faster. So we need to have the ability to flip a switch and have this page displayed in the development environment, but to display a custom error page when the application is deployed into other environments. Thankfully, ASP.NET provides us with this ability.

9.3.1 Providing a custom error page

To display a custom error page whenever unhandled errors occur, we can simply use the configuration settings of our application to tell ASP.NET which page to redirect to when errors occur. We do this by using the `customErrors` configuration element in the web configuration file. The following snippet shows an example of the `customErrors` element being set so that `ErrorPage.aspx` will be displayed whenever an unhandled error occurs within the application.

```
<?xml version="1.0" encoding="utf-8" ?>
<configuration>
  <system.web>
    <customErrors mode="On"
        defaultRedirect="ErrorPage.aspx" />
  </system.web>
</configuration>
```

In this example, the mode attribute is set to On while the `defaultRedirect` attribute contains the URL of the page where we want to display custom error information. Typically, such a page would inform the users that an error has occurred and that the system administrator has already been notified. Finally, it is useful to provide users with a link from this page that allows them to navigate back into the site—such as a link to the home page or a link back to the page that the users have just come from. Listing 9.4 shows a sample custom error page that tells users what happened.

> **Listing 9.4** A standard page can be used to display to users in place of the dreaded error page. This page can contain useful information and provide users with a way to continue their browsing experience.

```
<html>
  <body>
    <p>
        We are sorry for the inconvenience but an error has occurred.  A
detailed error
        message has been sent to the system administrator.  Please
```

```
      click <a href="javascript: window.history.go(-1);">here</a> to
return to the page
      that you were just at, or click <a href="Default.aspx">here</a> to
go our Home Page.
   </p>
  </body>
</html>
```

When critical errors occur on our website, users will no longer be subjected to the confusing and highly technical standard ASP.NET error page. Instead, users are shown a page with which they are more familiar, and which helps them to recover and continue using our application. In the case of the page shown in listing 9.4, we have explained that an error has occurred and we are providing users with links which will allow continued use of the site. However, even though we've provided users with a more friendly error page, we still need a way to log the failure and notify an administrator that it has occurred so that we take steps to fix the problem behind the failure.

9.3.2   Logging the failure

The simplest place to put notification code is in the Global Application class. To add a Global Application class to our application, we simply right-click on the Visual Studio solution tree from within our web application and use the Add New Item menu option to add a new Global Application file to our application. This adds a file named `Global.asax` to our project. In the Global Application class, we can write code that will run when certain application level events occur within the application. For example, whenever a new page is requested within the application, the `Begin-Request` event is fired and we can write code in the Global Application class to handle that event. Likewise, the Global Application class allows us to handle the Application's Error event, so we can handle this event and write code that runs when an unhandled error occurs. Listing 9.5 is an example of how to handle the Application's Error event from within the `Global.asax` file and use it to send an email to an administrator notifying them of the error.

Listing 9.5   By logging unhandled errors from within the Applicaion_Error event handler we can get notifications when unexpected failures occur.

```
void Application_Error(object sender, EventArgs e) {

    Exception ex = Server.GetLastError();

    if (ex != null) {
        string body =
          "The following error has occurred: " + ex.ToString() ;
        string subject = "Application Error.";
        string from = "ErrorHandler@AdventureWorks.com";
        string to = "Adminstrator@AdventureWorks.com";
```

```
    SmtpClient mailClient = new SmtpClient("http://localhost");
    mailClient.Send(from, to, subject, body);
  }
}
```

The code in listing 9.5 uses the GetLastError method of the Server object to access an instance of the actual error that occurred. Having the underlying exception object at our disposal provides access to a great deal of information about the error, such as the message of the exception and also a full stack trace of what was happening at the time the error occurred. We can use this information to diagnose what might have caused it.

> **NOTE** There's an excellent article on MSDN which discusses an extensible strategy for logging and reporting on errors that can be found at the following URL: http://msdn.microsoft.com/asp.net/default.aspx?pull=/library/en-us/dnaspp/html/elmah.asp

Now that our application has logging code, Health Monitoring code, and a custom error page, you might think that the application will be resilient in all kinds of disasters and that we have little to worry about. But if you're taking off your shoes to put your feet up on the desk, take heed of the following scenario.

9.4   WHEN ALL ELSE FAILS

A major selling point of web portals is that they facilitate the creation of modular user interfaces where we can deploy new web parts any time without having to re-publish an entire website. We saw this in chapter 8 with the custom dialog catalog, which allows us to add new web parts to our portal by simply dropping an assembly in the bin folder and then adding an entry to an XML file. Along with this ease of deployment comes the danger of deploying web parts that are not fully tested and contain errors. Think about what it would mean to deploy a web part which included a critical error and which threw an exception the instant it was added to the page. Once users added this web part to their pages, they would no longer be able to visit that page because the error page would be displayed instead. And because the users could not access their pages, they could not remove the web part. What to do?

We've seen in chapters 5 and 6 that the WebPartPersonalization class has a method which allows us to reset the entire set of personalization data for a user for a single page by using its ResetPersonalizationState method like so:

```
wpm.Personalization.ResetPersonalizationState()
```

So when a user has broken his page, we can fix it by finding a way to load the broken pages into the current context and then calling ResetPersonalizationState on the page. There are two issues with this. First, how can we load the page into the current context given that it won't load? Second, users will not be happy losing all their settings for a page that is heavily personalized, so ideally we need to provide a way that allows page resets to occur at a more granular level. We'll now investigate how to provide the users a self-management facility that allows them to go in and fix their own broken pages when this type of scenario occurs.

9.4.1 Self-maintenance of web parts

In a presentation at the PDC conference in Los Angles in late 2005, Mike Harder, who is a Software Design Engineer on the ASP.NET team for the web parts feature, showed us how to provide user self-management. We'll now implement Mike's solution into our Adventure Works portal. First, let's summarize the steps a user performs so that we can see where we are headed.

The user

- Adds a broken web part to his page
- Is instantly taken to a self-help administration page to fix the problem
- Removes the broken web part from the page
- Is returned to the original page and the error web part is no longer present

To implement this solution we will create an administration page that allows users to fix pages themselves. The page we'll create will display a list of web parts for a given page, and will allow the user to delete one or more web parts from that page. Figure 9.5

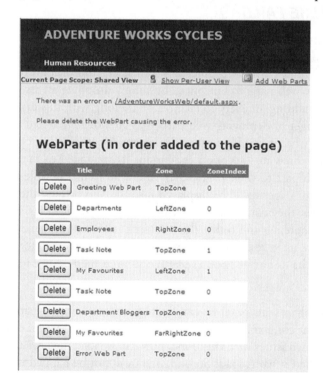

Figure 9.5
This grid displays all web parts for a given page and provides the user with a way to remove web parts which have caused the underlying page to stop working.

shows the administration page that users will use to remove troublesome web parts from their pages.

To get things started, add a new page to our portal named `WebPartAdminis-tration.aspx` and set it as the custom error page for the application by making the following `customErrors` entry in the web configuration file:

```
<?xml version="1.0" encoding="utf-8" ?>
<configuration>
  <system.web>
    <customErrors mode="On"
        defaultRedirect="WebPartAdministration.aspx" />
  </system.web>
</configuration>
```

As we see in figure 9.5, our administration page shows all web parts for a given page and allows them to be deleted from that page. In order to execute personalization operations on another page instance, we will be creating a helper class which can silently and invisibly instantiate a page in the background. Once we have that instance, we can access the web part manager on the instance to perform personalization operations. This helper class will also expose properties that allow us to view the web parts on the invisible instance. Figure 9.6 illustrates the relationship between the `WebPartAdministration.aspx` page and the helper class.

The helper class we create will be called `WebPartsAdministrator`, and as we see from figure 9.6 it can create an invisible instance of the web page that caused the user to arrive at the error handling page. The `WebPartsAdministrator` helper class also provides a method named `GetWebParts` that we can access from the administration page and use to return a listing of the web parts contained on the page with the errors. The web parts returned by the `GetWebParts` method will be bound to a list and displayed to the user—as shown in figure 9.5.

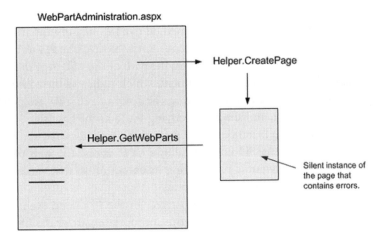

WebPartAdministration.aspx

Helper.CreatePage

Helper.GetWebParts

Silent instance of the page that contains errors.

Figure 9.6   The relationship between our error handling page and the helper class used to communicate with the page that has errors.

Silently running a web page

The most technically challenging part of this solution lies in creating the logic within the helper class to silently instantiate the underlying page that contains the errors. Luckily the ASP.NET framework provides us with many useful methods and classes, making the task quite simple. The first bit of help from ASP.NET arrives when we call the GetWebParts method of the WebPartsAdministrator class. When GetWebParts method is called, our helper class creates an instance of a page based on a virtual path we provide and returns the web parts for that page; this can be seen in listing 9.6.

Listing 9.6 The GetWebParts method executes a target page and uses a callback to read web parts off of its web part manager instance.

```
public static WebPartCollection GetWebParts(
        string path, HttpContext context) {

    Page page =
     (Page)BuildManager.CreateInstanceFromVirtualPath(
        path,
        typeof(Page)
        );

    WebPartCollection webParts = null;
    page.PreLoad += delegate {
        webParts = WebPartManager.
            GetCurrentWebPartManager(page).WebParts;
    };

    ExecutePage(page, path, context);

    return webParts;
}
```

Listing 9.6 shows that the GetWebParts method dynamically instantiates the underlying page instance by using the CreateInstanceFromVirtualPath method of the BuildManager class. This method takes the path of the ASP page that we wish to create an instance of, and also a type argument, which indicates the base type for the page class. In our case we are passing the aspxerrorpath that we are passed by the ASP.NET error redirection, and simply specifying Page as the base class.

Once we have the page instance returned from the BuildManager, we hook the PreLoad event for the page. Doing this allows us to access the web part manager instance attached to the dynamic page during its execution so that we can access the web parts and personalization services from it.

Now that we have an event handler registered for the PreLoad event, we execute the page and our handler will be called at the appropriate part of the lifecycle of the dynamic page. In addition, our code will run just as it would when we write event handlers in the code behind normal pages. The code that executes the page is contained within a private helper named ExecutePage, which is shown in listing 9.7.

```
private static void ExecutePage(Page page, string path,
                                HttpContext context) {
    string originalPath = context.Request.Path;
    context.RewritePath(path);

    try {
        context.Server.Execute(page, TextWriter.Null, false);
    } catch {}

    context.RewritePath(originalPath);
}
```

Notice—the first thing that we do in the ExecutePage method is to rewrite the path of the request by using the Context.RewritePath method. This ensures that code within the dynamic page will see the request URL as if the page really was the page requested by the user. This helps to ensure that the dynamic page runs exactly as it would for a normal request. After rewriting the path we use Server.Execute to execute the dynamic page, which processes the target page within the context of the current page. Notice in our code we are passing in a null TextWriter, so that even though the dynamic page is executed, it doesn't display anywhere. We also trap and gobble up any exceptions so they do not affect our administration page.

At the time the page is executed, it will run through its lifecycle in just the same way it would if it were being called directly from a browser request. So our event handler will receive a notification when the page is in its pre-loading phase. At that time we can access all the personalization and web part data directly from the web part manager in our PreLoad event handler and return them to our administration page where they will be displayed.

The last thing we do in the ExecutePage method is to rewrite the path of the request back to the original path, so that the remainder of the requested page will process in the right context.

The code for deleting a page is very similar to the code we used when we listed web parts. The only difference is that in our PreLoad event handler we write code that deletes a selected web part. Listing 9.8 shows the code for the DeleteWebPart method of our WebPartsAdministrator class.

```
public static void DeleteWebPart(string path, string ID,
                                 HttpContext context) {
    Page page = (Page)BuildManager.CreateInstanceFromVirtualPath(
        path, typeof(Page));
```

```
        page.PreLoad += delegate {
            WebPartManager webPartManager =
                WebPartManager.GetCurrentWebPartManager(page);
            WebPart webPart = webPartManager.WebParts[ID];
            webPartManager.DeleteWebPart(webPart);
        };

        ExecutePage(page, path, context);
    }
```

Notice that we again use an inline code block as our event handling code for the PreLoad event by using the delegate keyword in C# and assigning a chunk of code within curly braces. This form of attaching inline code blocks as event handlers is called anonymous methods and is an elegant way to attach event handling code without having to write separate methods for handling events. Writing our event handling code as an anonymous method also allows us to refer to the ID argument passed in to the DeleteWebPart method directly, which is something that we could not do if the event handling code was in a separate method.

Databinding in the administration page

Now that we've finished the WebPartsAdministrator helper class, we can get to work on the visual elements in the WebPartAdministration.aspx page we created earlier. This page will list the web parts for a given page and allow the user to delete individual web part items; listing 9.9 shows the mark-up code that we'll use to do this.

> **Listing 9.9** The methods for obtaining a web part list and deleting web parts are encapsulated within an ObjectDataSource which can then be bound directly to a GridView, providing the user with a way of working with the data.

```
<p>
    There was an error on <asp:HyperLink ID="TargetPage" runat="server" />.
</p>

<asp:ObjectDataSource EnableViewState="False"      ObjectDataSource
  ID="WebPartsDataSource" runat="server"       ⟵─ supports data binding
  TypeName="AW.Portal.Web.WebPartsAdministrator"    with business object
  SelectMethod="GetWebParts"
  DeleteMethod="DeleteWebPart">
                                        Parameters map to
        <DeleteParameters>        ⟵─── method arguments
            <asp:QueryStringParameter
                DefaultValue="&quot;&quot;"
                Name="path"
```

```
                    QueryStringField="aspxerrorpath"
                    Type="String" />
            <asp:ControlParameter
                    ControlID="WebPartsGridView"
                    Name="ID"
                    PropertyName="SelectedValue"
                    Type="String" />
            <portal:HttpContextParameter
                    Name="context" />
        </DeleteParameters>

        <SelectParameters>
            <asp:QueryStringParameter
                DefaultValue="&quot;&quot;"
                Name="path"
                QueryStringField="aspxerrorpath"
                Type="String" />
            <portal:HttpContextParameter
                    Name="context" />
        </SelectParameters>
    </asp:ObjectDataSource>
```

```
<asp:GridView ID="WebPartsGridView" runat="server"     | Display web parts using
    AutoGenerateColumns="False"                    <──────| a GridView control
    DataSourceID="WebPartsDataSource" DataKeyNames="ID">
    <Columns>
        <asp:CommandField ButtonType="Button" ShowDeleteButton="True" />
        <asp:BoundField DataField="Title"
          HeaderText="Title" SortExpression="Title" />
          <asp:TemplateField HeaderText="Zone">
            <ItemTemplate>
              <asp:Label ID="Label1"
              Text='<%# Eval("Zone.DisplayTitle") %>'
              runat="server" />
            </ItemTemplate>
          </asp:TemplateField>
        <asp:BoundField DataField="ZoneIndex" HeaderText="ZoneIndex"
            SortExpression="ZoneIndex" />
    </Columns>
</asp:GridView>
```

Three controls on our administration page are being used to fetch data and present it to the user. The first of these controls is a hyperlink control with an ID of Target-Page that is going to display a link back to the page which caused the error. Users can click on this link when they have removed the errant web part to return to the previous page. This provides a seamless browsing experience for users as they can fix their problem and return to their work without having to manually track an administration page or make a phone call to resolve their issue.

A GridView control is used to display a grid of all web parts for the target page to the user and is presented in such a way that the user can see the Name of the web part, the Zone that contains the web part, its index within that zone, and a delete button for each web part.

ObectDataSource and command parameter controls

The final control on the page is an ObjectDataSource. This control is bound to the custom WebPartsAdministration business class that we built, and is configured to use the GetWebParts method as its SelectCommand and the DeleteWebPart method as its DeleteCommand. Command parameters are used to tell these methods where to go for their argument data. The ObjectDataSource control is a specific type of the new DataSource control and is used to perform two-way data binding between data sources and data-bound controls. There are also specific DataSource controls for performing data binding to SQL Server data sources and XML data sources; however, binding directly to business objects is convenient as it allows us to ensure that certain business rules can be enforced when dealing with application data.

In the following code segment, notice that the GetWebParts method expects two arguments and the DeleteWebPart method expects three. Also note how these are all passed in through command parameters configured within the ObjectData-Source. In the same code segment, note the flexibility we have with command parameters for binding to many different targets. Specifically, using these command parameter objects, we can bind method arguments directly to Querystring values, Form values, Cookies, Session items, and even Controls on the web page. An example is where we bind the ID method argument of the DeleteWebPart method directly to the SelectedValue property of the GridView control.

In fact, to highlight just how flexible the command parameters are, you may notice that the HttpContextParameter is a custom parameter class because it has a control prefix of "portal:" instead of the standard "asp:" control prefix used for the in-built ASP.NET controls. The following fragment shows the entire code for the custom HttpContextParameter class:

```
public class HttpContextParameter : Parameter {
    protected override object Evaluate(
        HttpContext context, Control control) {
        return context;
    }
}
```

This class simply overrides the Evaluate method of the Parameter class and returns the HttpContext that it is passed as its output.

The only task remaining in our page is to set the Text and the NavigateUrl properties of the TargetPage hyperlink, so that users can navigate back to where they came from, as shown in listing 9.10.

```
protected override void OnLoad(EventArgs e) {
    base.OnLoad(e);

    TargetPage.Text = Request.Params["aspxerrorpath"];
    TargetPage.NavigateUrl = Request.Params["aspxerrorpath"]; ;

}
```

In this code we simply read the value of the aspxerrorpath that is passed to our page by ASP.NET and set it as the redirect path.

You've just seen how to manage personalization data at the level of individual web parts. It's now time to take a quick look at the PersonalizationAdministration class to see how we can work with personalization data at a wider level.

9.4.2   Managing personalization data

The PersonalizationAdministration class contains static members that provide us with the ability to perform queries over personalization data. Using this class, we could run queries to determine which users have not used the system recently and then use that information to decide how to reset their personalization data. This kind of functionality may be useful for large and active sites that do not wish to retain too much personalization data for inactive members.

Here's an example of a query that is used to return all personalization data older than 200 days:

```
DateTime inactiveSince = DateTime.Now.AddDays(-200) ;

PersonalizationStateInfoCollection inactiveUserResult =
    PersonalizationAdministration.GetAllInactiveUserState(inactiveSince) ;
```

A site administrator could run such a query and then use the results to decide which users should have personalization information deleted. To assist with such a task the administrator could write another query which allowed her to view all personalization data for a specific user before she deleted the data for that user. Figure 9.7 shows us how these queries might look when presented as a couple of administration web parts.

In the first web part, the user can enter the username for a specific user and have a collection of all his personalization data returned. In the second web part, an inactivity period can be entered and all personalization data for individual users and paths older than that date would be displayed in the grid. Notice how the data in the results grid displays the user's name and the path of the personalization data, and it also displays the size of the personalization data for that personalization instance. An administrator

Management Web Parts

Personalization Data for: ManagementFeatures

Specific User		
Username: admin1 Submit		
Count of User State: 1		
LastUpdatedDate	**Size**	**Path**
12/03/2006 9:17:15 PM	104	~/default.aspx

Inactive Users					
Inactive For Last 5 Minutes ▾ Submit					
Count of Inactive Users: 2					
LastUpdatedDate	**Size**	**LastActivityDate**		**Path**	**Username**
12/03/2006 8:51:33 PM	102	12/03/2006 8:51:38 PM		~/default.aspx	admin
12/03/2006 9:17:15 PM	104	12/03/2006 9:18:22 PM		~/default.aspx	admin1

Figure 9.7 Using the PersonalizationAdministration class allows us to run queries over personalization data and provides a way to perform administrative queries such as checking on the amount of stale personalization data in the system.

might use web parts such as these to locate inactive users for a given path and then query all personalization data for that user to see whether she has some current personalization data instances before deleting that data.

The code for finding the personalization data for a specific user looks like this:

```
PersonalizationStateInfoCollection userResult =
  PersonalizationAdministration.FindUserState(
    null, UserNameTextBox.Text
    );
```

When the administrator has decided to delete the personalization data for a specific user, he can simply call the ResetUserState method of the Personalization-Administration class like so:

```
PersonalizationAdministration.ResetUserState(null, UserNameTextBox.Text);
```

The PersonalizationStateInfoCollection class that is returned from the PersonalizationAdministration queries is a collection of Personaliza-tionStateInfo instances. The PersonalizationStateInfo class is an abstract class, and so each of the items will actually be an instance of either the UserPersonalizationStateInfo class or the SharedPersonalization-StateInfo class. The PersonalizationStateInfo class itself contains only three properties useful to us: LastUpdatedDate, Path, and Size. When looping through a collection of personalization data from a query such as GetAllInac-tiveUserState, we must therefore cast each item to a UserPersonalization-StateInfo object before we can get at the Username of the user associated with the personalization data. The following code snippet shows an example of how to get at the `UserPersonalizationStateInfo` specific properties from a specific `PersonalizationStateInfo` instance:

```
((UserPersonalizationStateInfo) userResult[0]).Username;
((UserPersonalizationStateInfo) userResult[0]).LastActivityDate;
```

It's these properties that are displayed to the administrator in the bottom grid in figure 9.7.

9.5   SUMMARY

At the beginning of this chapter we asked this question: how can we support and manage our web application when it is deployed and no longer directly under our control? By the end of the chapter, you have the answer. You can choose from a number of methods to keep an eye on the health of your code. Code instrumentation and health monitoring are two methods, and creating personalization queries and housing them within management web parts is another.

Often, instrumenting code and adding management features are unglamorous tasks. They are seldom found outside of commercial enterprise applications. For this reason, I wanted to take the time to discuss these practices here and show that with just a little foresight, a great deal of management capability can be injected into your applications—even if they are small and being written by a hobbyist!

CHAPTER 10

Into the future

10.1   INTRODUCTION

Working through this book, we've seen an idea spring into reality as we added one feature after another to the portal. At this point we've built something quite special—and possibly something not even possible to envision way back on page 1. Our work with the portal is finished for now and, as is customary when a milestone such as this is reached, it's time to both reflect and look forward. By looking back we can see the scope of our learning and remind ourselves of the usefulness of each skill and concept. By looking forward we can glimpse the latest round of technologies that are generating a great excitement in the world of portal development and fuelling major advancements in the community's experiences with portals. Witnessing these new technologies and learning how to implement them, you can build on what you've learned in this book as you dive into the future. The process of looking back as well as forward will help you understand how future technology meshes with what you've learned and provide a clear picture of where you currently stand within the overall landscape of portals and web parts.

10.2   REFLECTING ON THE PORTAL

In creating the Adventure Works portal we were able to lean on the features of the ASP.NET portal framework to do most of the heavy lifting. We also saw that when customizations to the portal were required, the portal framework facilitated those customizations by being extremely extensible through a wide array of base classes and interfaces. The next section provides a high-level look at the tasks we accomplished to bring the Adventure Works portal up and running, and which of these tasks were provided by the ASP.NET framework.

With the portal framework it's actually quite easy to build a web portal that uses nothing but out-of-the-box controls and components, and create an application that will generate a great deal of interest. In reality, when we create web portals, we are bound to customer expectations and requirements, so in practice we will nearly always need to apply the kinds of customizations have learned throughout this book.

Let's look back at some examples using the portal framework without customizations and then take a look at some of the areas that required changes.

We leveraged the portal framework by

- using and creating web part verbs
- using and creating connection transformers
- performing authorization checks
- creating custom catalogs
- customizing the loading and storing of personalization data

We extended the framework by

- adding custom editor parts to the `EditorZone`
- working with complex personalization data types
- customizing `WebPartChrome` to provide a custom look and feel for web parts
- enabling single-click operations to assist with usability
- creating an approval process for editing personalization data
- performing client-side interactions such as the pop-up catalog dialog

We have now a web portal that provides us with an excellent structure for hosting web parts. This is actually advantageous because it's through the use of new custom web parts that most new features will be added. By building custom web parts that provide specific functionality, we can add new features quickly, at low cost, requiring minimal testing, and which have low impact on the rest of the code base.

We've completed our web portal and can easily extend it through the use of web parts into the future. Does that mean that we have nothing more to do on our portal code base? Are we finished? In software the answer to that question is almost always a resounding "No." New technologies and trends continue to spring up at an alarming rate and so we can probably always plan for a next version (V-Next).

For the remainder of this chapter we'll spend time looking at the global portals that exist on the Internet and within businesses as intranet software. Looking at these global portals and taking note of the kinds of features they provide to their users, it will become clear that many of these features are the same as those we've added to our own portal throughout the course of this book. Seeing our features in the context of other portals can provide added awareness of how certain features are used by users. For example, in each of the portals we'll be seeing, users are able to select web parts from a catalog for addition to their pages. Each portal, however, displays its catalog in a slightly different manner. Some portals present the user with a catalog that displays as a dialog window, whereas others have the catalog embedded within the page itself. Some portals choose to display a very minimal amount of information about the web parts in the catalog, whereas others display icons and descriptive text. In the case of the Live.com portal, users can even preview the web part prior to adding it to their page.

When looking at each of these portals notice the features that we implemented and then compare our implementation to the way these more "worldly" portals present them. Understanding these subtle differences broadens our understanding of the feature itself and may even lead us to an epiphany in which we discover a whole new way to present a feature. Bingo.

10.3 *A WORLD OF WEB PORTALS*

Over the past few years a number of very large portals have sprung up across the globe. These large portals cater to an ever-growing consumer base using portals on a daily basis to reduce the complexity of finding information on the web and to provide an area for aggregating a common set of services. These portals range from internal sites used by employees to find and organize information within the enterprise to external sites used by customers.

To cater to internal portals (intranets) Microsoft has created a product called SharePoint. Businesses can install SharePoint on an internal server and use it to provide portal services to their employees. Outside of the enterprise, there has been a trend by large vendors such as Microsoft, Google, Yahoo, and others to create large public-facing portals. Typically, these public portals combine web parts and personalization in an attempt to provide a single view of a user's favorite links, her news, and her email, which can be accessed from a single portal view.

In just a moment we'll take a closer look at some of these large public-facing portals, but first I want to briefly discuss SharePoint and explain how some of the features we've created in this book were inspired by features found in SharePoint.

10.3.1 **SharePoint**

If you stop to think about how you use and consume data at your workplace, you will realize that much of the information you use is centered on the projects your team is working on. This project-centered information includes Office documents, email conversations, project schedules, and other collaborative material. SharePoint is designed to cater to all these types of information by providing a portal that closely models the project-centric nature of how we work. SharePoint is designed on the principle that users are members of teams and that the main task of teams is to collaborate over documents. Therefore, SharePoint makes it easy to create a team-based portal and add documents and users to it. A SharePoint portal enables users to collaborate over business documents by having tight integration with Microsoft's Office document suite of tools.

When users add a document to a SharePoint portal, they can invite other team members to collaborate on the document by making changes and tracking those changes over time. While working on documents, users can employ their portal site to add relevant information that other users can see and that will provide contextual help when needed. In addition to document collaboration facilities, SharePoint also provides other useful built-in services that you would expect from an enterprise solution such as search, notifications, content management, workflow, and reporting. These services are combined with personalization to create portals rich in collaboration.

As with all portals, SharePoint offers extensibility through the use of web parts. These web parts can be developed within an enterprise and then deployed alongside the portal, so that they are made available to all of the company's users. In keeping with the business nature of intranet portals, many of the web parts typically developed for intranet portals are used to expose different views of business data via a reporting interface, or to perform specific business functions via a forms-based interface. For example, intranet portals often have a wide array of business reporting web parts that present information about daily operations as KPI metrics. By having this data available from their main intranet page, users are instantly able to view important KPI metrics such as resource utilization, days lost to work injuries, actual sales versus budgeted sales data, and so forth. Having this information at their fingertips makes it easy for business users to gain access to the information they need in decision-making.

When using SharePoint 2007, users will notice the many new features and usability enhancements over the previous versions. Some of the features found in SharePoint 2007 inspired the ones that we added to our portal. For example, the Common Tasks menu bar we added to the Adventure Works portal is similar to the menu bar that has been added to SharePoint for launching common tasks. Likewise, in Version 3 of SharePoint a pop-up dialog catalog has been included to allow users to quickly add web parts to a specific zone without interrupting their current work. Finally, in Version 3 users can have different versions of personalization data for web pages that have been changed. The ability to have multiple versions of personalization data is part of a push for SharePoint to include more and more Content Management features, so that it will become a viable store for all of a company's documents, and not merely the project-centric information.

That's a quick overview of SharePoint and, as we can see, this is a real business portal with an emphasis on heavy-duty features for performing document collaboration. As I mentioned before, another class of portals exists beyond the company intranet. This class of portals is available to the general public and accessible via the public Internet. While these Internet portals are similar to their intranet cousins because they offer web parts and personalization, they differ in subtle ways because of the way they can handle a far greater diversity of requirements.

10.3.2 Internet portals

As it stands today, the public portal landscape is dominated by Internet giants Microsoft, Google, and Yahoo! But in recent times we see the emergence of new players making their mark by offering innovative new ways for users to interact with the portal. Table 10.1 lists the major portals on the Internet today.

Table 10.1 Major portals and who runs them

URL	Run By
http://my.Msn.com	Microsoft
http://Google.com/ig	Google
http://my.Yahoo.com	Yahoo!
http://Live.com	Microsoft
http://www.PageFlakes.com	Web 2.0 start-up

The first three portals listed in table 10.1 are based upon extremely large and successful search engines—MSN Search, Google, and Yahoo! One of the reasons that linking portals with search engines is such a successful formula is because people most often open a browser to perform a search. These large search companies know that by tempting us with personalization and other portal features such as a wide array of web parts, they can entice us to set their portal page as our home page and therefore boost the usage of their search engines. At this level of portals it's like a game of follow-the-leader, because no sooner does one player offer a new feature than it appears in each of the others. Over the past couple of years, this race to have the coolest features has provided fertile ground from which to grow the current, standard set of portal features. This standard set of portal features covers the features that were included as standard items in the ASP.NET portal framework including personalization, zones, connections and, of course, web parts.

The remaining two portals on the list—http://Live.com and http://www.Google.com/ig—are portals that offer us a glimpse into the next generation of portals because of the new types of features they provide. The most outstanding of these features—and the ones we'll focus on for the remainder of the chapter—are developer extensibility and client-side Ajax behavior.

10.3.3 Developer extensibility

In this brave new world of modern portals, developers can create custom web parts in their own development environments and upload them into the site galleries, so that they can be seen and used by other portal members. Although the developer-created web parts are known by various names such as Gadgets in http://Live.com, Flakes in the case of http://www.Google.com/ig, and Modules in the Google portal, they are web parts nonetheless. By providing specific APIs that developers must adhere to when creating these web parts, a developer can create a web part in the morning and have it displayed to users from around the planet on the Google home page that very afternoon.

As you might well imagine, providing the global base of developers with the ability to create unique, dynamic web parts means that the portal hosting these web parts literally explodes with content offerings simultaneously giving birth to interesting new communities. Suddenly the world of portals will be awash in a sea of web parts that reveal themselves to us as Clocks, Daily Comics, Quote of the Day, Travel Organizer, To Do Lists, News, Weather, Sport, Web-based email, puzzles, games—and the list goes on.

Having just learned a little bit about how portals are enabling developer extensibility, we'll soon get to take a tour of the Live.com website and see exactly how this developer extensibility works. But first let's learn more about the other major feature that is being offered by portals—Ajax behavior.

10.4 AJAX BEHAVIOR

In chapter 2 we learned that Ajax stands for Asynchronous JavaScript and XML and that a developer can use this technology to minimize the size of the packets of data that are sent to XML web services without requiring a complete page postback. But what exactly does this mean and how would we take advantage of it in our applications? Take a look at the web page shown in figure 10.1 and then we'll discuss where Ajax fits in the world of dynamic web applications.

Figure 10.1 shows the main milestone page from the collaboration site that was used when writing this book. This page displays quite a bit of information such as the navigation tabs, the mini-calendars, the main milestone calendar, and a list of upcoming milestones. When this page is requested, the browser sends a request to the server and the server dynamically generates the HTML required to display the page and sends it back to the browser. This roundtrip takes from 2 to 5 seconds to complete, depending on the speed of the underlying Internet connection.

From this page we can also see that the user may interact with the application by performing certain actions such as editing a milestone, marking a milestone as completed, or creating a new milestone. When the user clicks on a link to invoke one of these actions, the browser must send another request to the server so that the correct user interface elements are displayed to perform that task. When the user clicks a

Figure 10.1 A page like this that contains a good deal of information and allows user interactions such as marking milestones is an ideal candidate for a bit of Ajax magic.

checkbox to mark a milestone as "complete," it would be expected that the milestone is removed from the list.

In a non-Ajax application, clicking on the "complete" milestone checkbox will force a complete page postback, and the server will re-create the entire page and transmit the HTML for the entire page across the wire—a process we've already identified as taking anywhere from 2 to 5 seconds. If a user were visiting the page to perform a dozen activities, he would spend nearly a minute just waiting for pages to load and re-load.

In an Ajax application however, a developer can create the page in a way that requires only small, discrete parts of the page to postback. Using the "complete" milestone checkbox again as an example, when the user clicks on a checkbox, the only part of the page that is required to be re-drawn is the item that has been affected. Obviously, reducing the portion of the page that is redrawn dramatically reduces the processing time. On top of that, while a portion of the page is being redrawn, the user can perform other actions on that page. Ajax eliminates the dead time the user spent waiting for pages to load, so the user can continue working without getting disgruntled, and accomplish more in a much shorter period.

Ajax technology works like this—when a user performs an action on a web page, a region of the page is updated with new content fetched from the server without the whole page being fetched. This is accomplished by marking out a region of a page with a client-side DOM object and then replacing its contents with data from the server that was fetched by the JavaScript API, using an HTTP request to the originating server.

Ajax technology has been around for a few years, but its popularity exploded recently due to the success of web applications such as Google's GMail, Microsoft's Outlook Web Access Email, and a raft of junior company offerings such as the collaboration applications offered by the 37signals (http://www.37signals.com) company. Other popular Ajax implementations have included client-side mapping applications such as http://local.live.com/ which allow a user to navigate through a city map without requiring a page postback.

Microsoft realized the need to simplify HTTP requests using JavaScript when they originally released ASP.NET 2.0 by including support for HTTP requests through a feature known as Client-side Callbacks. Client-side Callbacks allow a control to execute an HTTP request back to the server to obtain additional data, without posting the entire page.

10.4.1 Making Client-side Callbacks

In order to show how the Client-side Callbacks feature works, we will create a small test page that uses them. The page we are going to create is extremely simple, but will be perfect for highlighting the steps comprising an Ajax callback. Namely, our page will allow us to walk through the following Ajax interaction:

1 We create a web page displaying the original time that the page was created.

2 A button is provided allowing the user to invoke a server-side operation.

3 Server processes the operation and returns the result.

4 The client user interface is updated with the result of the server-side operation.

In our test page the user will be able to enter a number in a textbox and have that number of days added to the current date and the resulting date displayed on the page. Figure 10.2 shows the simple user interface that we'll create for the test.

When the page is created by the server, we are displaying the current time in a label. This is so that we can see how often the whole page is being returned. The following snippet of code shows the HTML for the label and the server-side code that is used to write the current time:

Figure 10.2 This page uses Ajax to update a result without requiring a full page postback.

```
<h2>
    Page created at:
    <asp:Label ID="lblServerTime" runat="server" />
</h2>
```

```
protected override void OnLoad(EventArgs e) {
    base.OnLoad(e);

    this.lblServerTime.Text = DateTime.Now.ToString();
}
```

The idea is that when our user clicks the Get Result button, the value in the Days to Add textbox will be sent through to the server and added to the current date and time to produce another date. Performing this date calculation on the client using pure JavaScript would be cumbersome because the JavaScript APIs do not have very sophisticated methods for working with dates in this manner. Using a server postback to perform the addition of days to the date allows us to use the DateTime object in the .NET Framework where adding days to a date is a snap. The code for the button that will invoke the server callback and the label that will display the results is shown in the following snippet of HTML code:

```
<input id="btnGetResult"
    type="button"
    value="Get Result"
    onclick="AddDays(txtDays.value);"
    />
```

```
<span id="resultLabel" />
```

Notice that the button calls a JavaScript method named AddDays when it is clicked and that it passes the value contained in the Days to Add textbox as an argument to that function. It is the AddDays JavaScript function that will perform the "magic" of communicating with the web server without causing a full-page postback. This is the part that the ASP.NET Framework abstracts for us, and therefore makes the creation of this complex logic a simple affair.

For the Ajax postback to occur, two things must happen. First, the control that will act as the handler for the asynchronous callback must implement the ICallback-EventHandler interface. The second is to generate JavaScript that can used to invoke our server-side method from within the client using an Ajax call. The ICallback-EventHandler interface is like an Ajax version of the IPostbackEventHandler interface we used in chapter 8 when we needed to invoke a full-page postback from our catalog dialog. The ICallbackEventHandler interface requires us to implement two methods named RaiseCallbackEvent and GetCallbackResult. The RaiseCallbackEvent method is the method invoked when the callback first occurs, and is where we process the results of the callback operation. The GetCall-backResult is used to return the values that were calculated in the RaiseCall-backEvent processing. The following code snippet shows our implementation of these two methods:

```
private string _callbackResult;

public string GetCallbackResult() {
    return _callbackResult;
}

public void RaiseCallbackEvent(string eventArgument) {

    double daysToAdd = double.Parse(eventArgument);
    _callbackResult = DateTime.Now.AddDays(daysToAdd).ToString();
}
```

The snippet shows that we are simply grabbing the value passed through to us from the textbox, casting it to a double type, and then using the AddDays method of the DateTime class to add that number of days to the current date. We assign this new date value to a private variable which we return from the GetCallbackResult method. The only piece of the puzzle that we haven't seen so far is the "magic" code for the AddDays JavaScript function.

In chapter 8, when we created the callback method for the IPostback-EventHandler, we used the GetPostBackEventReference method of the ClientScript class. This generated some JavaScript that we could then invoke to cause a postback to occur and have specific arguments passed along with the post-back. In much the same manner, the ClientScript class exposes a method named GetCallbackEventReference that can be used to generate the JavaScript required to invoke a partial-page postback. This code is shown in the following snippet of code:

```
string callBack = ClientScript.GetCallbackEventReference(
    this, "arg", "ClientCallbackHandler", "context",
    "ClientErrorHandler", false);

string clientFunction =  "function AddDays(arg, context)
    { " + callBack + "; }";

ClientScript.RegisterClientScriptBlock(
    this.GetType(), "AddDates", clientFunction, true);
```

The most significant part of this code is on the first line where we use the GetCall-backEventReference method to generate a string that can be executed to invoke a callback. The string generated by the call to the GetCallbackEventReference method is shown in the following snippet of code:

```
WebForm_DoCallback(
 '__Page', arg, ClientCallbackHandler,
 context, ClientErrorHandler, false)
```

This string equates to the JavaScript that is required to invoke a special ASP.NET Java-Script method named `WebForm_DoCallback`, which then manages the asynchronous callback to our page behind the scenes. As you can see, the values passed to that special method will be the same as the values we pass into our `AddDays` function. So there are some useful abstractions going on here making our lives much simpler. First, the `WebForm_DoCallback` abstracts away the difficulty of invoking the asynchronous JavaScript call; but secondly, the `ClientScript.GetCallbackEventReference` method abstracts the complexity of producing that string in the first place.

At this point we can run the test page and click the button a few times to see that the Result label is updated, even though the Date Created time shown at the top of the page does not change at all. Having achieved our desired outcome of refreshing only the part of the page that is changing, we've saved users from twiddling their thumbs during a full-page postback.

In the grand scheme of things, updating the value of a label based on some arbitrary page event such as a button click rates as pretty minor. When faced with real application problems, we often find that working with client-side JavaScript can become extremely complex because the tools for working with JavaScript are not as advanced as the tools we have for working with pure .NET code. For example, we don't get Intellisense help when working with objects in JavaScript, and the debugging experience is far short of the experience we have when debugging native .NET code such as C#.

So there's a problem here. We have growing demand for Ajax-style web pages but the cost of producing this sort of page is much higher because of the added complexity. Thankfully the ASP.NET team has again come to the fore with a new set of extensions to ASP.NET, codenamed "Atlas." It's these Atlas extensions to ASP.NET that will bring Ajax-style application development within reach of all developers.

10.4.2   Announcing Atlas

When Microsoft introduced Atlas to the world at the PDC conference in Los Angeles in November 2005, it was warmly received by the development community. Up until that time there had been several third-party and open-source solutions for simplifying the task of creating Ajax-style applications in ASP.NET, but no clear standards had emerged. The announcement of Atlas would mean that ASP.NET developers could develop Ajax applications on top of a standard platform that would evolve and grow with the ASP.NET product, and that it would also receive the same level of tooling support as other ASP.NET controls within the Visual Studio IDE. In March 2006 Microsoft released the first publicly available version of Atlas that comes with a Go-Live license—which means developers can use that version to create applications they plan to deploy. This version of Atlas comes as a standalone assembly file which has a version number of 2.0.50727 and was made available at the newly created Atlas developer center, http://atlas.asp.net.

So what kinds of problems does Atlas solve for us? Let's look at a typical Ajax scenario and then look at how we'd solve it using Atlas.

10.4.3   Using Atlas

In web applications, people often search for a particular item and then display further details about it. As an example, consider a product inventory application where a user would search for a product. In such an application the user might drill into the product information by first locating a category and then choosing the product from a list of products within that category. Figure 10.3 shows us a simple example of this type of behavior.

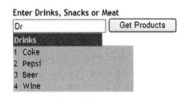

Figure 10.3   This sample uses Ajax to populate an auto-complete list from a web service based on text that a user has entered into the text box.

In figure 10.3 the user can type the name of a category into a textbox and then press the Get Products button to have the products for that category retrieved and displayed. Notice that beneath the textbox, Intellisense help is displayed to the user about the categories available based upon the characters that the user has already typed. This filtering behavior, known as *auto-completion* is a feature that clients ask for regularly when they want to present users with a large list of items and have them locate an item within that list. The term auto-completion comes from the way that the behavior automatically provides a list based on the characters that have been entered. This is a useful way to find words because a user can type his way through a list of words until there is only one word remaining.

Using Atlas we'll learn how to implement the auto-complete Intellisense items by calling a web service without needing to postback, and we'll do the same for the products that are displayed. We'll display those when the user clicks the Get Products button without requiring a postback either. Let's get started…

NOTE   To complete the examples shown in this chapter you will need version 2.0.50727 of the Atlas .dll. This can be obtained by running the ASPNET-Atlas.vsi file from the chapter 10 section of the resources website for this book. This version of Atlas may be superseded in the near future as it is still regarded as a beta release. Check the http://atlas.asp.net developer center for information about the current release version of Atlas.

From within Visual Studio 2005, create a new Atlas website by choosing the file menu and then click New, and WebSite. The New WebSite dialog box will appear. Select the ASP.NET 'Atlas' WebSite template item and choose a location for the files. Figure 10.4 shows the New WebSite dialog.

In order to run, our application will require data and according to our solution description this data will be coming from a web service. In the real world, this web

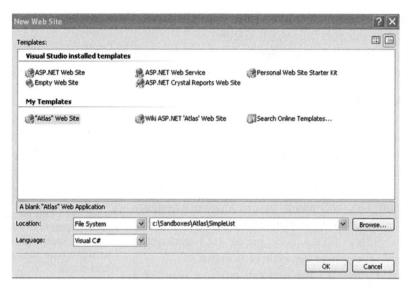

Figure 10.4   Once Atlas has been installed we can select from these Atlas templates to get started building web applications with Ajax-style behaviors.

service might not be a service that we've created, but could instead be exposed by our trading partners or simply by a third-party website.

Creating a web service

The web service that we create will expose two methods. The first method will be called `ListCategories` and will return a list of the product categories. The second method will be called `ListProductsByCategory` and this method will return a list of products for a given category. Start by adding a new web service named `ProductsWS.asmx` to the project and place it within the namespace of `AtlasSamples`. At this time the `ProductsWS` file should look like the code in the following snippet:

```
<%@ WebService Language="C#" Class="AtlasSamples.ProductsWS" %>

namespace AtlasSamples {

    public class ProductsWS : System.Web.Services.WebService {

    }
}
```

The first method we'll create will be called by the Atlas components whenever the user changes the value in the Category textbox. The following snippet shows the code for the `ListCategories` method that will return a list of available categories based on the text which the user has already entered.

```
[WebMethod]
public string[] ListCategories(string prefixText, int count) {
    string[] categories = GetAllCategories() ;

    List<string> suggestions = new List<string>();
    foreach (string category in categories) {
        if (category.StartsWith(prefixText)) {
            suggestions.Add(category);
        }
    }
    return suggestions.ToArray();

}
```

As the user types characters into that textbox, Atlas will call the `ListCategories` method passing in the characters already in the textbox as the `prefixText` argument. The `ListCategories` method then uses the `prefixText` value to return only category names beginning with that text. In just a moment we'll see how this method is called from the client.

The next method we need must take a category as its argument and return a listing of products for that category. This method will be called when the user clicks on the `GetProducts` button. The following snippet shows the code for the `List-ProductsByCategory` method.

```
[WebMethod]
public List<Product> ListProductsByCategory(string category) {

    List<Product> products = GetProducts( category ) ;
    return products;
}
```

The `ListProductsByCategory` web service method is a simple method which calls a database helper method, `GetProducts`, to retrieve all products for a given category from an inventory database and then return them to the calling application. That's all of the functionality we'll need from the web service and we can now get to work creating a client-side Atlas application to consume these two methods.

Creating an auto-complete textbox

Prior to the availability of Atlas, the task of creating an auto-complete list and having its values populated from a web service call would most likely have required several hundred lines of highly complex JavaScript code. The user would be obliged to write JavaScript that knew how to work with visual elements on the page, how to work with web service protocols, and how to work with the XML that was returned from the service. Getting this code to run in a single browser would be treacherous enough without the added complexity of writing code to work against the individual quirks of all browsers. In this next section we'll see how Atlas provides controls that abstract all of this complexity away from us. While the auto-completion example we are about to create is conceptually much more complex than our first simple Atlas example which added two date values to produce a result, this example still goes through the same set of logical actions to perform its behavior. Namely. in this example we will

1 Create the Atlas client-side controls that will support the auto-completion behavior

2 Wire-up calls from within the client and marshal them on to the appropriate server-side handler

3 Receive the results from the server and bind that data to the relevant Ajax client-side controls

To create an auto-completion list, Atlas provides us with the new `AutoComplete-Extender` control which we can bind to a textbox to show a list of auto-completion results that a user can select. The code for creating an `AutoCompleteExtender` control and associating it with a textbox is shown in the following snippet of code:

```
<asp:TextBox ID="TextBox1" runat="server" />

<atlas:AutoCompleteExtender runat="server"
    ID="Extender1"
    ServicePath="ProductsWS.asmx"
    ServiceMethod="ListCategories">

    <atlas:AutoCompleteProperties
        Enabled="True"
        MinimumPrefixLength="1"
        TargetControlID="TextBox1" />
</atlas:AutoCompleteExtender>
```

The `AutoCompleteExtender` requires very little information to perform its duties. We provide the `AutoCompleteExtender` with the `ServicePath` to our web service file, as well as the name of the method to call when the list needs updating. Finally we embed an `AutoCompleteProperties` element within the control that defines the target control. This will act as the input filter.

That's all! At this point we can run the page and enter values in out textbox to see that a dynamic auto-complete list is indeed displayed immediately underneath the target control—which in our case is a textbox with an ID of `TextBox1`. Selecting an item from the auto-complete list will populate that value into the target textbox.

Displaying results using declarative data binding

Once the user has arrived at the category he needs, he can click the Get Products button to procure the products for that category and have them displayed. When the button is clicked we need to call the `ListProductsByCategory` method on our web service and bind the resulting list of product entities to presentation elements on the page. In Atlas, this is done by creating placeholder HTML elements to perform the layout of data, and then defining templates that map the data to those HTML elements. The following snippet of code shows the HTML elements used to display our product items that are returned by a call to the web service method.

```
<div id="listview" class="listView"></div>

<div style="display: none;">
  <div id="listView_layoutTemplate">
    <div id="listView_itemTemplate">
      <span id="listView_ProductID"></span> 
      <span id="listView_ProductName"></span>
    </div>
  </div>
</div>
```

The first HTML DIV element with the ID of listview is the actual DOM node to which the data will be bound while the next set of elements is used as a template to hold the actual data. As we see, these elements define an outer DIV with the ID of listView_layoutTemplate which defines the template structure; then the inner DIV with the ID of listView_itemTemplate contains the nodes that will be bound to each row of data. Within the listView_itemTemplate we see two HTML SPAN elements are used to bind to the actual fields within the row—in this case we will be displaying a product ID followed by its name.

The HTML code shown in these templates merely defines layout but doesn't provide any information about how to map data from the bound objects to those nodes. To define data bindings we can use the new Atlas declarative mark-up components as shown in listing 10.1.

Listing 10.1 Atlas logic for binding a data list to a client-side element

```
<script type="text/xml-script">
  <page xmlns:script="http://schemas.microsoft.com/xml-script/2005">
    <components>

      <listView id="listview"
        itemTemplateParentElementId="listView_layoutTemplate"
        itemCssClass="item">
        <layoutTemplate>
          <template layoutElement="listView_layoutTemplate" />
        </layoutTemplate>
        <itemTemplate>
          <template layoutElement="listView_itemTemplate">      ◁────  Binding
            <label id="listView_ProductID">                            information
              <bindings>                                              to map data
                <binding dataPath="ID" property="text" />            to individual
              </bindings>                                            elements.
            </label>
            <label id="listView_ProductName">
              <bindings>
                <binding dataPath="Name" property="text" />
              </bindings>
```

```
            </label>
          </template>
        </itemTemplate>
      </listView>

    </components>
  </page>
</script>
```

First you want to notice that the Atlas mark-up component is contained within a special script section with a type of text/xml-script. This special script section is used by the Atlas code at runtime to determine the action to take when data is bound to HTML DOM nodes. As we look through the mark-up for the data bindings we can see that within the itemTemplate of the listView component that labels are declared, and their binding information is what tells Atlas how to map data to element IDs.

All that remains for us to do, now that we've described the layout and binding information, is to write the code that will run when the user clicks on the Get Products button. This will query the web service and pass the resulting data to the data-binding component. Listing 10.2 shows the pieces of JavaScript that handle the button click event and invoke a call against the web service we created earlier.

Listing 10.2 Using an Atlas generated proxy to invoke a web service call

```
<script language="javascript" type="text/javascript">

    function GetProducts() {
        var category = document.getElementById("TextBox1").value ;
        AtlasSamples.ProductsWS.ListProductsByCategory(
            category, OnComplete, OnTimeout);
    }

    function OnComplete(results) {
        var listview = document.getElementById("listview");
        listview.control.set_data(results);
    }

    function OnTimeout(result) {
        alert("A call to a Web Service timed out");
    }

</script>
```

The GetProducts function handles the actual click event of the Get Products button; it simply calls through to a proxy class that has been created by the Atlas framework to access the web service. Even though it seems trivial to call the web service, this code actually encapsulates hundreds of lines of complicated JavaScript code.

Aside from the category information passed to the web service proxy, we can see that there is also a reference to a function that will be used to handle the completion of the asynchronous web service call which is named `OnComplete`. All that this function has to do is to get a handle to the DOM node that the data will be bound to, and bind the data to it using the `set_data` method of the underlying Atlas object.

At this time we can run the sample to see that we are able to use both the auto-completion textbox and the Get Products button to perform complex data operations, all from within the client.

NOTE   The full source code for the SimpleList Atlas project can be found in the chapter 10 section of the resources website for this book.

Think of the power available to us here. Using this Atlas technology we can now consume and submit data to and from any page method or web service without forcing a complete page postback. This is very much how we can expect most web applications to function in the future. Already we see evidence of this on a daily basis with the release of nearly every modern website offering some level of support for Ajax behavior. With the added ease of the Atlas framework to spur on rapid development of these types of websites, we can expect to see this number grow at an increased pace into the future.

As mentioned earlier in the chapter, web portals with Ajax-style behaviors that also provide the ability for developers to create their own web parts and upload them have emerged as the de-facto standard for how portals should behave. Live.com is an example of this style of portal, and the good news for ASP.NET developers is that their portal is based on this very same Atlas framework for creating client-side behaviors.

Now that we have a proper appreciation for Ajax and have seen how Atlas simplifies the task of creating Ajax-style websites, it's time to visit the http://Live.com portal to see exactly how these features combine in this exciting breed of interactive portals.

10.5   INTRODUCING LIVE.COM— A MODERN MEGA-PORTAL

How many guided tours have you taken where you found yourself listening to a lecture while craning your neck and stuffing your hands into your pockets? This tour of the Live.com site is different; we'll explore the features by taking a hands-on approach and trying things out. First we'll create an account so that we can personalize the content to our liking and then see how to add Gadgets onto our portal page. Finally, we'll take a look at how to develop our own Gadgets and upload them to the Start.com portal so that we can customize it in our own unique way. Let's begin!

To start our tour, open a browser and point it at the http://Live.com website. When you arrive, you will be greeted by a plain web page containing several rows of fairly generic web parts—such as news, sport, weather, and health information web parts. Figure 10.5 shows an image of the default start page for the Live.com portal.

While the default Live.com page displays useful information such as the latest news and weather, it's hardly personalized. For personalization, we must first log in

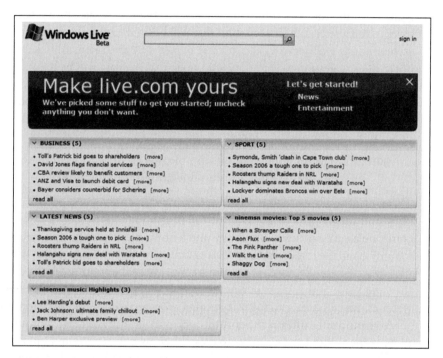

Figure 10.5 The home page of the Live.com portal displays a selection of "stock" news and information web parts prior to making any specific personalization customizations.

using a Microsoft Passport account. To begin the login process, click on the Sign In link at the top of the page, and if you already have a Passport account you can enter your credentials to log in; otherwise you'll have to create an account first.

10.5.1 Personalizing the Live.com portal

After logging in to the Live.com site we are presented with a directory of web parts—woops... I mean Gadgets—which we can add to our page. Conceptually, this is no different than the custom catalogs we created for our Adventure Works portal. The only difference is that what we called a Catalog is called a Directory on Live.com; and while our Catalog was full of web parts, the Live.com directory is full of gadgets. On the Live.com site, these Gadgets are grouped into categories such as Fun, News & Info, People & Sharing, Productivity, and so on. Figure 10.6 shows the user interface provided for browsing the directory and adding Gadgets.

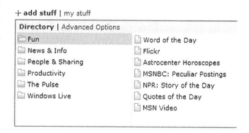

Figure 10.6 Within the Live.com portal we can choose to customize our page by selecting from a directory of Gadgets.

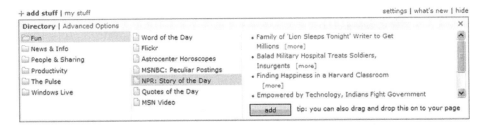

Figure 10.7   The Live.com directory provides us with a handy preview feature we can use to view the content of a Gadget prior to adding it to our page.

When we find a Gadget that we'd like to add, clicking on it will display a preview of the Gadget's content. Figure 10.7 illustrates what happens when we click on the "NPR: Story of the Day" Gadget.

After clicking on a Gadget and viewing its content, we can either drag that Gadget out onto our page or simply click on the Add button and have it added automatically. Once again, the semantics of adding web parts on Live.com is not terribly different from how we added web parts to our own portal; although in the actual implementation of the Live.com site, having a preview of the web part is a nice feature of their gallery.

In the same way that the web parts we added to the Adventure Works portal were remembered between browser sessions, any Gadgets added to the Live.com site will be persisted by their own personalization system. Another nice feature of the Live.com portal is that, in addition to offering a wide variety of Gadgets, they also allow the user to create "page" tabs which can contain groupings of Gadgets. Figure 10.8 shows a Live.com page configured with custom Gadgets and custom "page" tabs.

In figure 10.8, the main tab contains Gadgets that display random images, weather information from cities we're interested in, and also some random quotes to make the page more interesting. Other tabs on the page display other types of information. On this particular portal we can see that there is a News, Sport, and Weather tab to display news reports from the leading news providers, and a Blogs tab which aggregates the RSS feeds from our favorite bloggers. One of the strengths of the Live.com site is the wide variety of Gadgets offered; so this site already possesses an elevated level of appeal because, as a portal, it allows us to aggregate all the information we need in a single place.

10.5.2   MicrosoftGadgets.com—a repository of custom gadgets

Having said that the Live.com site provides us with a rich variety of Gadgets, it's still fair to assume that there will always be information we'd like to have that is not available via the standard set of Gadgets. This is where the real power of the Live.com site comes into play. Remember at the beginning of this chapter we discussed the new trends in portals, and how a major new trend is for portals to offer developers the

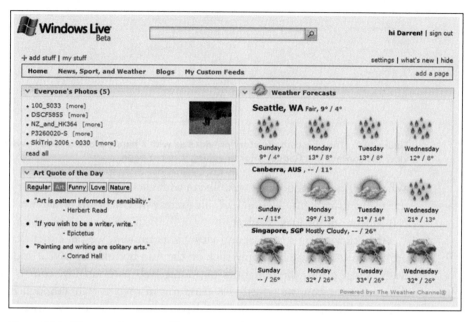

Figure 10.8   The portal pages on Live.com can also be expanded through the use of tabs to categorize content when we have more content than is practical to display on a single page.

ability to add their own web parts to them. Live.com provides a client-side API to which developers can conform to create custom Gadgets and then upload them. In this way, developers can use custom Gadgets privately or share them with all users of the portal. Figure 10.9 displays the main page of the MicrosoftGadgets.com website, which serves as the place where custom Gadgets can be uploaded or selected by users to be added into their own portal pages.

Figure 10.9 shows us some of the diversity that can be found on the MicrosoftGadgets site. On this site we can find hundreds of user-submitted Gadgets exposing information such as Google searches, e-Bay searches, games, movie critiques, and more. To the developer-centric user, the most interesting part of the MicrosoftGadgets site is certainly likely to be the fact that we can upload our own custom creations there.

10.5.3   Creating a custom Live.com gadget

OK, it's been a long journey and we're well in to the home stretch of learning about modern portals and, in particular, Live.com; but let's push forward because we're about to enter the most exciting part of the journey so far. In this next section we will use the Atlas framework to develop our very own custom Gadget and upload it to the Live.com site where we'll then be able to add it to our portal page. To do this we'll create a special kind of Atlas project which has been designed specifically for the purpose of creating Live.com Gadgets, and will then add in the Atlas code permitting us to communicate with the server using Ajax postbacks.

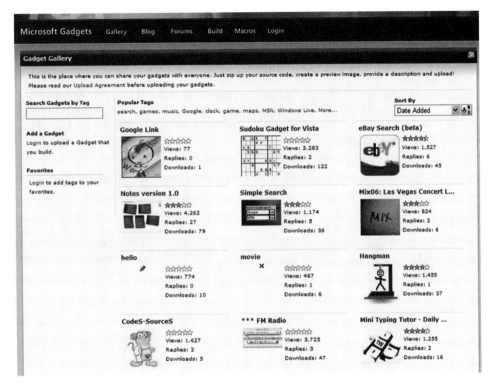

Figure 10.9 There is also a community site where we can view Gadgets added by other developers, that we can add to our own portal pages.

Suppose that there was some information you really wanted to see on the home page of your portal. That information might be the latest stock quotes from stocks contained within your portfolio or it might be the most recent image uploaded to the NASA image gallery. Generally we will find that, for readily available information such as this, there are already Gadgets which exist to display such information and all we need to do is locate the Gadget from within the directory and add it to our home page. However, it is sometimes useful to have information available for which no Gadget yet exists. This might happen when the information we require is exposed from an obscure web service, such as from one of our own websites. For occasions such as this we can create our very own custom Gadgets and upload them either directly into our own portal or, if we'd like to make the Gadget available to the general public, we can upload it into the MicrosoftGadgets directory.

Gadgets can be added to the Live.com gallery because there is a standard format for packaging all the elements of a Gadget—such as the user interface elements, the CSS style definitions, and the JavaScript behaviors. Documentation on the MicrosoftGadgets site describes the standard format for creating a Gadget and exposing it to the Live.com website. Luckily for us the Atlas framework actually includes a special type of control that we can use to simplify the task of creating Gadgets. This control is the `atlas:Gadget` control.

Defining a custom Gadget

In this section we will create our own Gadget and learn how to upload it to the Live.com website. For simplicity the Gadget we create will be somewhat lame in that it will merely display the current time on the screen. Our Gadget will use an Atlas Timer control to display an update of the time every second. To get things rolling, create a new Atlas WebSite named `SimpleClock` and add a new `WebForm` named `ClockGadget.aspx` to hold our simple clock. When complete our gadget will resemble the image shown in figure 10.10.

> **Time Gadget**
>
> The current time is: Mon Mar 27 17:09:57 UTC+1100 2006

Figure 10.10 The Gadget we are creating is a simple one that uses Atlas scripts to update the time on a page.

When creating an Atlas page, we must first add a `ScriptManager` control to the page. Add the following server control tag at the top of the HTML document:

```
<atlas:ScriptManager runat="server" ID="scriptManager" />
```

You can think of the Atlas `ScriptManager` as being similar to the `WebPartManager`. While it appears to do very little, it is highly significant to the operations of the page and its presence is required.

Next we must add an Atlas Gadget control to our page. This control will define the layout of our Gadgets and provide a template for which to bind data resulting from Atlas operations. The markup for our simple Gadget is shown in the following snippet of code:

```
<atlas:gadget runat="server" ID="clockGadget"
  Title="A Simple Clock" Description="Displays the time">
    <ContentTemplate>
        <div style="border:
          dashed 1px Navy; background-color: InfoBackground">
            <h1>Time Gadget</h1>
            The current time is:
            <label id="timerLabel"></label>
        </div>
    </ContentTemplate>
</atlas:gadget>
```

The attributes on the Gadget element will provide the definition shown to the users of our control while the `ContentTemplate` contains the layout elements which define the appearance of our Gadget. By looking at the elements contained within the `ContentTemplate` we can see that there is a label control with the ID of `timerLabel` which has been created to display the current time. It's this label to which we'll be binding the current time.

In order to update the display of the `timerLabel` control we will need to create an Atlas Timer control and handle its Tick event so that we know when to display a new time. The Timer control is an Atlas client component we use to raise events at a specified interval. In our case we'll set the interval of our timer to 1000 milliseconds and associate a JavaScript function with the tick event of the timer where we will put our logic for changing the display. All of this will give the effect of a clock which ticks over each second. Listing 10.3 contains the Atlas script element which defines our timer control, and also has the client-side `OnTimerTick` method that is used to handle the tick event of the timer control.

Listing 10.3   The tick event of this Atlas timer control is handled by a client-side JavaScript method.

```
<script type="text/xml-script">
  <page xmlns:script="http://schemas.microsoft.com/xml-script/2005"
    xmlns:atlas="http://schemas.microsoft.com/atlas/2005">
    <components>
      <timer id="timer1" interval="1000"
        enabled="true" tick="OnTimerTick" />
    </components>
  </page>
</script>


function OnTimerTick(sender, eventArgs) {

    var d = new Date();
    var label = document.getElementById('timerLabel');
    label.innerText = d ;
}
```

That's all there is to creating our Gadget. Our timer is contained within the declarative script block and has its interval set so that the tick event fires every 1000 milliseconds. Because we've enabled the timer it will begin firing its tick event as soon as the page loads, and therefore our `timerLabel` will begin updating from that time on. Run the page by pressing F5. Verify that the page runs and the `timerLabel` displays the time correctly.

Uploading our Gadget to Live.com

Now that we've built and tested our simple little Gadget we are ready to set it free by deploying it to the Live.com portal and there are a few simple steps required before we can achieve this. In a nutshell, the steps we are must take are

- Host our gadget on a web server
- Configure Internet Explorer to work with Gadgets
- Upload our Gadget to the Live.com portal

For a simple Gadget such as ours, hosting the Gadget is not very difficult if all we need to do is host it for ourselves and make it viewable from our single machine. However, if we want to share our Gadget with the entire Live.com community, or if we need to access our Gadget from more than one machine, then we'll need to deploy our Gadget to a site that is accessible from a central place. This would mean deploying a website that was permanently visible via the Internet and making that site host our Gadgets for us. But for the purposes of getting something up and running in this example, we will simply host our Gadget from the IIS web server on our own machine. This means the Gadget we upload will only be visible when browsing the Live.com portal from our own machine.

Configuring IIS to host our Gadget

The point of creating an IIS site to host the website containing our Gadget is to assure that whenever we browse the Live.com site that the web server will be running and our Gadget will therefore be available. Up until now this would not be the case, because we've merely been using the in-built ASP.NET development web server that comes as a part of the ASP.NET toolkit. An instance of this web server is spun up by Visual Studio and used to host our websites when we are in development, but that instance does not persist beyond the current development session. In other words, were we to restart our machine and browse back to a site which had previously been served up by an instance of the development web server, it would not be present until we manually ran the server again and configured it to listen on the right port. With IIS, however, our application will be available whenever we browse to Live.com because IIS automatically restarts whenever the machine is started.

The first step to hosting our site in IIS is to create a virtual directory and the best place to do this is via the IIS Manager tool. To access the tool we can either type inetmgr from the Run dialog box or we can browse directly to the tool using Windows. To browse to the IIS Manager tool from within Windows, click the Start button and then choose Control Panel. Once the control panel is open, click Administrative Tools. From there, choose Internet Information Services. At this point the IIS Manager tool should appear as shown in figure 10.11.

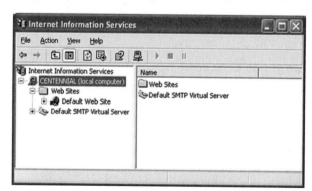

Figure 10.11
The IIS Manager allows us to create Virtual Directories and use them to host websites.

From within the IIS `Manager` tool, right-click on the Default WebSite folder, choose New from the context menu and click on Virtual Directory. Doing this will start the Virtual Directory Creation Wizard. In the first screen of the Virtual Directory wizard click Next. The second screen of the wizard will ask us for an Alias for our Virtual Directory, so type `SimpleClock` and click Next. In the third screen we need to set a path so IIS knows where the files for the `SimpleClock` web application are located. Browse to the physical directory we created for our `SimpleClock` project in Visual Studio, and once that folder has been selected, click on Next. Finally, select the check boxes for the access permissions needed to run the application. In our case simply keeping the default access permissions of Read and Run Scripts should be sufficient.

That's all there is to creating an IIS application to host our Gadget website. If everything went according to plan, we should now be able to browse to the IIS hosted application by typing the following URL into a browser: http://localhost/Simple-Clock/ClockGadget.aspx. The result will appear the same as the time we ran the application from within Visual Studio using the ASP.NET development web server, but now it is being hosted from within IIS and therefore the site will be available whenever IIS is running.

Configuring Security permissions

Now that we've hosted our application in IIS and tested it by browsing to it in Internet Explorer, we must configure the local security settings on the IIS machine that is hosting our web application to work with Gadgets.

To do this, click the Tools menu in Internet Explorer and open Internet Options and select the Security tab. Within the Security tab, select the Trusted Sites zone and click the Sites button. We are about to add the Live.com domain as a trusted site so that data can be exchanged between the Live.com site and our machine.

To enable the permissions required to work with Gadgets, enter the following domain information as a trusted Site:

```
*.Live.com
```

After entering that domain information, click Add followed by Close.

The last thing we must do to enable the right permissions for Gadgets to work from our machine is to allow for the exchange of data between our local host website and the Live.com website. To enable this interaction, select the Internet zone setting from the Security tab and click on the Custom level button. In the settings window, locate the setting titled Access data sources across domains. Select the Prompt option for this setting and then click OK twice to return to Internet Explorer.

Uploading our Gadget

Having configured the security on our machine to allow data to be exchanged with the Live.com site, everything is now in place for us to upload our Gadget and run it from the Live.com portal site. To upload our Gadget we must procure an XML version of it, because that is what Live.com is expecting to receive from us. Atlas makes obtaining this XML data a trivial task because all we need to do is browse to the URL of the Gadget and append the following text to the URL:

```
?gadget=true
```

Now press Enter to refresh the page, and see that our Gadget is now presented as some XML in the shape of an RSS feed within the browser—this is exactly the information that Live.com will use to obtain the metadata for our Gadget. Now we copy the URL from the address line of the browser and we can head off to the Live.com site to add our Gadget.

When we arrive at the Live.com site we can click the Add Stuff link in the upper right corner of the page and click on the Advanced Options link from there. Paste the URL we obtained for our Gadget into the text box next to the Subscribe button and press the button to upload the Gadget. At this time the name of our Gadget will appear in the page and we can click Install Gadget to complete the installation process. Dragging the installed Gadget onto our page will present the Gadget as a standard web part on the portal as shown in figure 10.12.

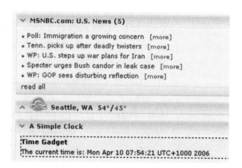

Figure 10.12   Our own custom Gadget is shown as it appears when uploaded to the Live.com website.

That's it—we're all done! We've now run through all of the steps required to build and publish our own custom Gadgets to the Live.com portal.

The area to focus on from here is to improve our knowledge of Atlas in order to build infinitely more exciting and dynamic Gadgets that access data from web services and present that information in smart and interesting ways. As our skills in this area grow we might even consider uploading some of our coolest Gadget creations to the MicrosoftGadgets.com Gadget directory, allowing others to use them.

Regardless of where we choose to go from here, it's easy to see how extensible this technology is and how easy it makes the job of presenting XML-based information on the web.

10.6   CALL TO ACTION

That's the end of chapter 10, and it's also the end of our trek through the world of building portals with the ASP.NET portal framework together. By this time I sincerely hope and expect that your head is full of ideas for implementing ASP.NET portal solutions.

However, as we've seen in this chapter, the excitement of creating web parts and portals extends way beyond building our own portals. Because of their componentized nature, web parts lend themselves very well to being included in other portals that support a common set of protocols. Currently, Live.com and SharePoint are two platforms that are compatible with ASP.NET, and so we should look beyond our own portal implementations when thinking of ways to provide a valuable user experience with web parts.

Moving forward, the very same Atlas-style web parts Gadgets supported by the Live.com website will be supported by the Windows operating system itself. In the next major release of Window, named Windows Vista, developers will be able to create a special type of Gadget—a Sidebar Gadget that users can add to their desktops to provide the same kind of web part experience we've seen throughout this book.

I thank you for taking the time to read this book. I'm sure that with all of the exciting new frontiers opening up for web part development, the things we've learned so far will ensure that our skills are relevant in the brave new world of portals.

Creating the Adventure Works project

A.1 INTRODUCTION

This walkthrough shows how to create an ASP.NET web project in Visual Studio 2005. This web project forms the basis for building the web portal that is referred to throughout the book. The tasks that are illustrated in this walkthrough include

- Creating a new web project
- Referencing an Assembly which contains data access logic
- Configuring the application
- Implementing a Master Page
- Creating a Theme

> **NOTE** All the files for the completed version of this project can be found in the chapter 2 section of the resources website at www.manning.com/neimke. Feel free to copy the source files from there to save yourself some typing.

A.2 STARTING THE PROJECT

Open Visual Studio 2005 and create a C# web project named `AdventureWorksWeb` and save it to a convenient location in your filesystem such as C:\Sandboxes\AdventureWorks. Once the project has been created, add a reference to the `AW.Web-Parts.Data` assembly that we created in chapter 1. To do this, right-click on the project folder and choose Add Reference; this will launch the Add Reference dialog as shown in figure A.1.

NOTE   If you didn't complete chapter 1, you can find the `AW.Portal.Data` assembly in the chapter 1 section of the resources website for this book.

Browse to the location of the `AW.Portal.Data` assembly file and add it as a reference. With the data layer now referenced by the web application, we are able to use the methods we created in that assembly to perform all our data access operations.

Recall that the data layer requires a connection string to be defined in the web configuration file, so our next step is to add a Web.config file to store this configuration entry. To add a Web.config file to the project, right-click on the project element in the Solution Explorer and choose the Add New Item menu option. After adding a Web.config file to our project, we can open it and add the connection string information. Make sure that the Web.config file now contains the configuration data shown in listing A.1:

Figure A.1   The Add Reference dialog window in Visual Studio 2005.

Listing A.1   In ASP.NET 2.0, the new connectionStrings element is used to store sensitive connection string information.

```xml
<?xml version="1.0"?>
<configuration
  <connectionStrings>
    <add name="AdventureWorksConnectionString"
      connectionString=
      "Data Source=.\skl2k5;Initial
      Catalog=AdventureWorks;
      Integrated Security=True"
      providerName="System.Data.SqlClient"
      />
  </connectionStrings>

  <system.web>
        <pages theme="Blue" />
      <compilation debug="false"/>
```

```
        <authentication mode="Windows"/>
      </system.web>
    </configuration>
```

A.3 ADDING A MASTER PAGE AND STYLES

Master pages are another of the new features in ASP.NET 2.0. In this section we will create a master page to define a standard look and feel for all of our pages. Our master page will provide a standard header and footer for our pages, as well as the global navigation elements we need. Once we've created a master page, individual pages become known as content pages as they just define the content unique to the page. At runtime the master page will be merged with these content pages into a single page, which is then displayed to the user. Right-click on the project element for the AdventureWorksWeb project in the Solution Explorer and add a new master file named Default.master to the project. Open the master file in source view and ensure that it contains the HTML code shown in listing A.2:

Listing A.2 All of the layout HTML that is standard across all pages is included in the Master page

```
<%@ Master Language="C#" AutoEventWireup="true"
  CodeFile="Default.master.cs" Inherits="_Default" %>
<!DOCTYPE html PUBLIC "-//W3C//DTD XHTML 1.1//EN"
  "http://www.w3.org/TR/xhtml11/DTD/xhtml11.dtd">
<html xmlns="http://www.w3.org/1999/xhtml">
<head runat="server">
  <title>Adventure Works Cycles - HR Portal</title>
  <link rel="Stylesheet" href="Styles/Default.css" />
  <meta http-equiv="content-type"
    content="text/html; charset=iso-8859-1" />
</head>
<body>
  <form id="form1" runat="server">
      <div id="container">
          <div id="header">
                  <h1>Adventure Works Cycles</h1>
                  <h2>Human Resources</h2>
              </div>
          <div id="content">
                  <asp:contentplaceholder id="Main"
                    runat="server" />
              </div>
          <div id="footer">
```

```
                            Copyright &copy; 2005 Adventure Works Cycles.
                    </div>
                </div>
            </form>
        </body>
    </html>
```

The HTML in the master page will define the standard layout for all pages in our portal application. As we can see, it provides a common header and footer as well as creates a standard title for the page and imports the stylesheet. Also notice that, in the
middle of the page, a ContentPlaceHolder server control is defined. This control
allows the content from an associated content page to be injected into the master page
at runtime. When we create the content page for our application we will see that this
control has an associated control in that page named a Content server control.

Having created the master page, we need to add a stylesheet to our application to
provide the layout information for the HTML. Add a folder named Styles to the
project and then add a stylesheet named Default.css to the folder. Open the
Default.css stylesheet and add the listing A.3 CSS layout code to it:

Listing A.3   The presentation and layout logic for our HTML is held in a Cascading Stylesheet.

```css
body {
    margin: 15px auto;
    padding: 0;
    font-family: "Lucida Grande";
    color: #333;
    background-color: #f0f0f0;
    text-align: center;
}


a {text-decoration: underline; padding: 1px; }
a:link { color: #03c; }
a:visited { color: #03c; }
a:hover {
    color: #fff; background-color: #30c; text-decoration: none;
}


#container {
    width: 760px;
    border: 1px solid #ccc;
}
```

```
#header {
    position: relative;
    background-color: #036;
    height: 81px;
    margin-left: auto;
    margin-right: auto;
}

#content {
    text-align: left;
}

#footer {
    width: 100% ;
    height: 55px;
    text-align: center;
    font-size: 10px;
}

#header h1 {
    position: absolute;
    left: 37px;
    color: #fc0;
    top: 12px;
    text-transform: uppercase;
    font-size: 18px;
}

#header h2 {
    position: absolute;
    left: 37px;
    top: 60px;
    color: #fff;
    font-size: 11px;
}

#rightcolumn {
    margin: 0px 0 0 0;
    padding: 5px;
    float: right;
```

```
    width: 240px;
    border-left: 1px solid #ccc;
}


#leftcolumn {
    margin: 0px 0 0 0;
    padding: 10px;
    float: left;
    width: 450px;
}
```

Now that we have all the necessary information for defining the structure and main layout of our pages, we can start creating content pages that will contain the content of our site.

A.4 CREATE THE DEFAULT WEB PAGE

If a Default.aspx page was not automatically added when we created the project, we should add one now by right-clicking on the project element for the AdventureWorksWeb project in the Solution Explorer and choosing Add Web Page. Open the Default.aspx page and add the listing A.4 HTML layout code:

Listing A.4 Content pages render the unique content area for each page and rely on a Master page for rendering the outer area.

```
<%@ Page Language="C#" MasterPageFile="~/Default.master"
  CodeFile="Default.aspx.cs" Inherits="_Default" %>


<asp:Content ContentPlaceHolderID="Main" ID="Content1" runat="server">


<div id="leftcolumn">
    Left
</div>


<div id="rightcolumn">
  <div class="sidebar">Right</div>
</div>


</asp:Content>
```

By now we've added a good deal of code, so this is a dandy time to open our site in a browser and see what's happened so far. Right-click on the Default.aspx file and choose View in Browser. At this point our page should appear as shown in the figure A.2.

Figure A.2   When rendered, our page displays outer areas from the Master page file and the left and right columns which are defined in our content page.

While viewing the page in the browser, we can see that what was seemingly a large mess of CSS and HTML has become the basis for our portal. Notice also that the base layout logic which we put into the master page has merged seamlessly with the content we put into the content page. The left panel in the content section of the page is where the web parts will live, whereas the right panel will contain the editor zone for managing the properties of web parts and the catalog zone, so that users can choose which parts to add or remove from their page. Of course, before we go ahead and add those elements to the page, we must add the `WebPartManager` control to the page and ensure that it is the first web part control in the control hierarchy.

After adding the `WebPartManager` to the content page, we can go ahead and add two `WebPartZones`, an `EditorZone` and a `CatalogZone`. After adding those controls, the page should now look similar to figure A.3 when it is displayed in design mode within the Visual Studio Editor.

Figure A.3 shows the Default.aspx page with some added text and some static links into the right side panel to give a more complete effect.

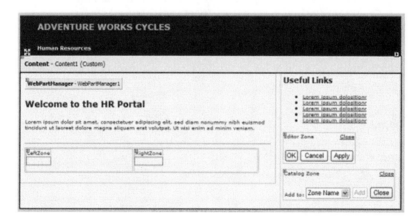

Figure A.3   The Visual Studio designer faithfully renders our page as it will appear when displayed in a browser.

A.5 ADD A THEME

In our project, all of the style information for HTML elements is contained in our stylesheet, but the style information for our server controls will be held within a .skin file within a Theme. To add a Theme to the project, right-click on the project folder and choose Add Folder, then select Theme Folder as the folder type. Name the folder Blue. To add a .skin file to our new Blue theme, right-click on the Blue theme folder and choose Add Item. Add a new skin file to the theme folder and name it Blue.skin.

Finally, ensure that the .skin file contains the skin definition for web parts shown in listing A.5:

Figure A.4   The App_Themes folder is a special ASP.NET folder containing files that describe the visual themes for our web application.

Listing A.5   Skin files contain the style information for server controls. When combined with CSS files and images they form a theme.

```
<asp:WebPartZone runat="server" BorderColor="#CCCCCC"
  Font-Names="Verdana" Padding="6">
  <PartChromeStyle BackColor="#EFF3FB" BorderColor="#D1DDF1"
    Font-Names="Verdana" ForeColor="#333333" />
  <MenuLabelHoverStyle ForeColor="#D1DDF1" />
  <EmptyZoneTextStyle Font-Size="1.0em" />
  <MenuLabelStyle ForeColor="White" />
  <MenuVerbHoverStyle BackColor="#EFF3FB" BorderColor="#CCCCCC"
    BorderStyle="Solid" BorderWidth="1px" ForeColor="#333333" />
  <HeaderStyle Font-Size="0.8em" ForeColor="#CCCCCC"
    HorizontalAlign="Center" />
  <MenuVerbStyle BorderColor="#507CD1" BorderStyle="Solid"
    BorderWidth="1px" ForeColor="White" />
  <PartStyle Font-Size="1.0em" ForeColor="#333333" />
  <TitleBarVerbStyle Font-Size="0.8em" Font-Underline="False"
    ForeColor="White" />
  <MenuPopupStyle BackColor="#507CD1" BorderColor="#CCCCCC"
    BorderWidth="1px" Font-Names="Verdana"

Font-Size="0.8em" />
  <PartTitleStyle BackColor="#507CD1" Font-Bold="True"
    Font-Size="0.8em" ForeColor="White" />

</asp:WebPartZone>
```

Good job. You've stuck to it and worked hard to build the application. As you work through this book, you'll see that this hard work has been worthwhile. After all, you've created a good base for the portal application.

index

GridView 23, 60, 278
GUI 177

H

hacker 269
handling exceptions 261
HasHeader 249
HeaderStyle 131
HeaderText property 11
Health monitoring 262
   categories 264
   configuring 265
   custom logging provider 264
   events 265
   usage of 263
Help Mode property 145
HTML 10
HTML DOM 298
HtmlTextWriter 40, 135, 222
HtmlTextWriterTag 222
HTTP 289
HttpContext 216, 224, 278
HyperLink 189, 203

I

IBusinessEntity 30
ICallbackEventHandler
   interface 290
IComparer interface 213
IDictionary 186
IIS 306
Image 189
import/export
   scenarios 108
   simple example 110
   XML definition 116
ImportCatalogPart 108, 149
ImportWebPart 115, 153
InitComplete 100, 170
InitialScope 168
InstructionTextStyle 132, 137
instrumenting 259
intellisense 293
Internet 284

Internet Explorer 232, 307
Intranet 284
InvalidOperationException 101
IPersonalizable interface 183,
   192
IPostBackDataHandler
   interface 139
IPostBackEventHandler 254,
   291
   interface 226
IsAuthenticated 216
IsAuthorized 105–106
IsClosed property 36
IsDirty 183, 196
IsEnabled property 103
IsSensitive 185
IsShared 106
ItemDataBound 252
ItemTemplate 251
ITrackingPersonalizable
   interface 186
   members 186
ITransformerConfigurationCon-
   trol interface 89
IVersioningPersonalizable
   interface 185
IWebActionable interface 48
IWebEditable interface 52
IWebPart interface 46, 155
IWebPartParameters 84
IWebPartRow 84–85, 90

J

Javascript 223, 250, 254, 290
   handling verbs client-side 51

K

key performance indicator
   (KPI) 65

L

Label 11
LastUpdatedDate 280

LayoutEditorPart 13, 146, 219
LinkButton control 163, 251
List 212
ListDepartments 26
ListEmployeesByDepartment
   26
listeners 260
ListJobCandidates 26
Live.com 244, 286
   custom gadgets 304
   overview 299
   uploading to 305
Load 183, 186, 192
LoadPersonalizationBlobs
   172, 175, 236–237
logging 259
LoginName control 162
LoginStatus control 163
loosely-coupled 203

M

Master Pages 60
   defining 119
MasterPageFile 119
metaData section 118
Microsoft Office 285
Microsoft Word 232
MicrosoftGadgets 302
Mike Harder 272
Modules 287
MSDN 18
my.msn.com 243
MyBase 176

N

NavigateUrl 278
.NET 2.0
   Generics 30
notifications 264

O

ObjectDataSource 60, 278
   using 278

S

Save 183, 192
SavePersonalizationBlob 172, 175, 239
Schema property 85
Scope 168, 185
ScriptManager 304
SDLC. *See* Software Development Lifecycle
SelectedCatalogPartID 138
SelectedPartChromeStyle 218
SelectedValue property 278
SelectedWebPart 217, 246
serializable 184
Server Explorer 44
Session 160
SetConsumerSchema 86
SetPersonalizationDirty 187, 238
    method 181
shared scope mode 187
SharedPersonalizationStateInfo 280
Sharepoint 6, 133, 174, 197
    expand/collapse editor 219
    intranet portal 284
    overview 284
    pop-up catalog 248
Sharepoint 2007 285
ShowHiddenWebParts 103
SimpleMailWebEventProvider 263
SmtpClient 271
Software Development Lifecycle 257
SQL Server 18, 171, 264
    XML data type 27
SQL Server Setup Tool 176
SqlCommand 28
SqlDataReader 27
SqlPersonalizationProvider 173
    configuring 242
SqlWebEventProvider 263

T

Start.com 32, 197
static connections 120
Stopwatch class 267
Stored Procedures 179
StringsToNumbersTransformer 83
strongly typed Dataset 23
Subtitle property 46
Succeeded event 89
SupportedDisplayModes 101
SyncChanges 209, 227
System.Configuration 25
System.IO.File class 153
System.Security.Cryptography namespace 193
System.Web.UI.Web-Controls.Style 133

T

Tables 179
tag prefix 42
tagname 63
tagprefix 63
Task Zone 246
testing 258
TextBox 192
Themes 55, 317
    App_Themes 57
    Skin Files 57
    Visual Studio support 55
tightly coupled 203
Timer control 305
Title 155
Title property 36, 46
TitleIconImageUrl property 46
TitleUrl 130
TitleUrl property 46
ToggleScope 164, 167
ToolZone 128
Trace class 259
TraceWebEventProvider 263
TracksChanges 186
Transform method 82

transformers 79
    introducing 66
    pre-defined transformers 83
TripleDESCryptoServiceProvider class 194
Trusted Sites 307
try block 261
TypeConverters 206
    using 207
TypeDescriptor 91

U

UploadHelpText 150
UserControl 38, 42
UserPersonalizationStateInfo 280

V

Value 185
verbs 48
Verbs property 48, 215
Views 179
ViewState 39, 160
Visual Studio
    design time experience 207
    design-time experience of user controls 42
Visual Studio 2005 9
Visual Studio Properties window 11

W

Warn method 260
web part
    overview 6
web part description files
    format of 118
Web Parts
    Visual Studio Toolbox 11
web service 294
web.config 59
    connectionStrings 22
    customErrors 269